# THE CHURCH AND SOCIAL REFORM

# THE CHURCH AND SOCIAL REFORM

## The Policies of the Patriarch Athanasios of Constantinople

*by*
John L. Boojamra

Fordham University Press
New York
1993

LC 93-26603
ISBN 0-8232-1334-X (*cloth*)
ISBN 0-8232-1335-8 (*paper*)

Library of Congress Cataloging-in-Publication Data

Boojamra, John Lawrence
The Church and social reform : the policies of Patriarch Athanasios of Constantinople / John L. Boojamra
p. cm.
Includes bibliographical references and index.
ISBN 0-8232-1334-X
ISBN 0-8232-1335-8 (pbk.)
1. Sociology, Christian (Orthodox Eastern)—History of doctrines—Middle Ages, 600–1500. 2. Church and social problems—Byzantine Empire. 3. Athanasios I, Patriarch of Constantinople, ca. 1230–ca.1323—Political and social views. 4. Byzantine Empire—Church history. 5. Byzantine Empire—History—Andronicus II Paleologus, 1282–1328. I. Title.
BX337.B66 1993 93-26603
281.9'561'09022—dc20 CIP

Printed in the United States of America

Third Printing 2002

# CONTENTS

# ACKNOWLEDGMENTS

It is with appreciation that the author wishes to acknowledge the assistance of many friends and colleagues in the preparation of this history. This is an ideal opportunity to mention the friends and family who permitted the time to put together a manuscript whose final form never represents the actual time, labor, and research that went into it. My family enabled me as well as inspired me to delve more deeply into the person of the Patriarch Athanasios and, more especially, his social reform—which reform speaks so loudly to us today. My late wife, Stellie, had always been my greatest inspiration, fan, and motivator. My sister-in-law Pamela has always made my life easier and freed me to do the research and writing I love so much. My children, Dean and Niki, on the other hand, each a scholar in his/her own way, merely tolerated anything that did not occur in a test tube or appear on the evening news.

Special appreciation goes to both a friend and benefactor without whose moral and material support this manuscript would not have made it through the many dark nights that only a researcher can know. Mr. Albert Joseph and the Albert and Rosemary Joseph Foundation have been consistently encouraging of my work and conscious of the need of the Orthodox Church for more scholarly research on practical aspects of Church history. Special thanks to Albert Joseph.

Finally, my thanks to my colleagues at St. Vladimir's who would willingly check the smallest of details, my fellow sufferers at Brooklyn Tech who tolerated my all-too-easy distraction from the work at hand to check this or that footnote, and the staff of Fordham University Press, particularly Dr. Mary Beatrice Schulte, whose long-suffering patience brought the reforms of Athanasios, Greek and all, to these published pages.

# ABBREVIATIONS

| | |
|---|---|
| *B* | *Byzantion* |
| *BZ* | *Byzantinische Zeitschrift* |
| *DOP* | *Dumbarton Oaks Papers* |
| *EO* | *Echos d'Orient* |
| KVA | Joseph Kalothetos, "Βίος καὶ πολιτεία τοῦ ἐν ἁγίοις πατρὸς ἡμῶν ἀρχιεπισκόπου Κωνσταντινουπόλεως Ἀθανασίου" |
| Gregoras | Nikephoros Gregoras, *Byzantina Historia* I |
| Miklosich and Müller | *Acta et diplomata graeca medii aevi sacra et profana* I–II, edd. F. Miklosich and J. Müller |
| Pachymeres | George Pachymeres, *De Andronico Palaeologo* |
| PG | *Patrologiae cursus completus*, Series graeca |
| *REB* | *Revue des Études byzantines* |
| *Regestes* | *Les Regestes des actes du patriarcat de Constantinople* |
| Rhalles and Potles | Σύνταγμα τῶν Θείων καὶ Ἱερῶν Κανόνων, edd. G. A. Rhalles and M. Potles |

| | |
|---|---|
| Talbot | Alice-Mary Talbot, *The Correspondence of Athanasius I* |
| TVA | Theoktistos the Studite, "Vita Athanasii" |
| V | Codex Vaticanus graecus 2219 |
| Zepos and Zepos | *Jus graeco-romanum* II |

For complete information regarding these Abbreviations, see the Bibliography.

# 1

# Introduction

In 1261, under the vigorous leadership of Emperor Michael VIII Palaiologos, the Byzantine empire regained its capital, Constantinople, after fifty-seven years of Latin occupation. The city retained only a hint of its former glory and prominence, however, the effective reach of the empire having been reduced to western Anatolia, some islands in the Aegean Sea, Macedonia, the Morea, and Thrace. Even this remnant was subject to regular assaults by marauding Turks and pillaging mercenaries and to mercantile exploitation by the great Italian sea powers.[1] With the empire struggling on a variety of fronts merely to maintain the status quo (Byzantine political and military policy was essentially a holding operation), many Byzantines were convinced that only a moral regeneration would save it from total subjugation to an alien religion and an alien people.

In contrast to the widespread and continuing disagreement about the reign of Emperor Andronikos II (1282–1328)[2] and the nature of the political, social, and religious events and trends which characterized it, there is little controversy about Athanasios—the man who twice occupied the patriarchate of Constantinople (1289–1293 and 1303–1309) during Andronikos' reign.[3]

The Byzantine Orthodox Church, although perhaps the strongest institution in the empire after the *reconquesta*, was also in a state of turmoil, racked by the persisting schism of the Arsenites and by moral and disciplinary decay, the aftereffects of the hated Union of Lyons (1274). In spite of what has been characterized as the "disastrous reign" of Andronikos,[4] the Orthodox Church managed to produce the most aggressively reform-minded patriarch of its history—Athanasios.[5] Inasmuch as I have dealt with the ecclesiastical reforms of Athanasios in another work,[6] this study will be devoted to the nature and extent of his social reforms and his political involvement during his two tenures on the patriarchal throne of Constantinople. The traditional influence, power, and authority that resided in the patriarchate of Constantinople made the involvement of an aggressive patriarch in the social affairs of the empire virtually inevitable.

It cannot be denied that Athanasios sought social and political reforms, and although his letters do not use classic reform terminology, both the idea and the practice of reform are strongly evident. What the two meant to Athanasios will be seen in terms of the relationship between the Church and the empire (Chapter 2), the role of the Church in his reforms (Chapter 3), the ideological foundations of his reforms (Chapter 4), the specific measures by which he sought to meet immediate social and political needs (Chapter 5), and the expansion of the patriarchate into new areas as state services declined (Chapter 6).

What constitutes reform thinking at any one time can be determined only by studying the reforms and their context. One thing is clear: for Athanasios the idea of reform was part of the renewal of the centralized institutions of the empire, and it was rooted in the commitment to Christian baptism, cenobitic mutualism, and the metaphor of Israel's covenant with Yahweh. There was nothing simple about Athanasios' reform; and his thinking was far from systematic. This is the challenge of working with Athanasios: to avoid the ever-present danger of historical distortion in the attempt to systematize what is inchoate.

## Nature of Reform

Significant for this study of Athanasios' reform is the criterion of reform established by Gerhart Ladner: namely, that the idea of reform must imply the conscious pursuit of an end. "Whether reform be predominantly contemplative or active, its starting point is the element of intention rather than of spontaneity, urge, or response."[7] Although the intention is absolutely essential, it must be one with an outside, autonomous reference point and be occasioned by a specific situation or pattern of social or political behavior. All too often, these elements are ignored, and reactionary traditionalism or atavism is referred to as reform. This was not the case with Athanasios' thinking or his policies.

But Athanasios was not a millenarian renewalist, seeking total perfection. There was no mystique of a return to a "golden age" in his letters, no revolutionary call for poverty so characteristic of radical Christian movements in the contemporaneous Latin West. Nor did he make any allusions to the *vita apostolica* or the *ecclesia primitiva* as reference points for reform. He was radically rooted in the immediacy of the human situation. His was a centripetal effort to reform the Byzantine empire and to restore the traditional application of statist controls to reduce the suffering of the people. Nowhere in his epistolary corpus is there a call for an end time or an apocalyptic perfection; his was an ameliorative approach. His reform thinking and measures returned to past patterns only where those patterns were statist and centralized, thus allowing not only for control but for good order in the *oikoumene*. The intention was to build a system that was the mirror of the heavenly kingdom. Nothing is clearer in Athanasios' letters than that the basis of his reform is the theological notion that the world is fallen, irradicably imperfect but capable of relative perfection.[8] He was rooted in Greek patristic notions congenial to the idea of eternal progress (as opposed to Augustinian "rest" in the Divinity); this sense of progress and the semi-Pelagian tendencies endemic to Byzantine *synergeia* allowed for the possibility of human improvement, while avoiding the trap of utopianism so common among contemporaneous Western spiritual maximalists.[9]

Although reform has roots in pre-Christian Greek thought, it is essentially a biblical and patristic notion. Christianity is a religion of reform, primarily in the sense of personal and spiritual growth, albeit with political and social implications. Although Athanasios nowhere undertook the exposition of any speculative theology, this parallel and transfer of values are clearly present and will be highlighted. Christian reform is rooted in the Pauline notion of the "new creation" (2 Cor. 5:17), the Christian teaching on baptism, and the patristic, especially Alexandrian, distinction between "image" and "likeness."[10] Because the first step in this process is baptismal regeneration, it is no accident that Athanasios placed so much emphasis on it, writing to his bishops that their first duty is to teach the meaning of baptism to the priests and the people.[11] His was a dynamic notion of a baptism coming to fruition as a process throughout life. This emphasis on baptism and relative "perfectibility" was his contact with the very essence of patristic thought as applied to reform, but he developed the baptismal element of his thought in the context of cenobitic mutualism and a prophetic sense of righteousness.

The two objects of Athanasios' reform efforts were the two components of the Byzantine polity; the Church and the secular community, each with its own demands and needs. Athanasios was no frustrated sentimentalist or do-gooder. His policies were a call to social justice and action based on evangelical purity, mutuality, and prophetic righteousness. The church needed freedom, and the secular community needed right order. Above all, his reforms were a call to action and a continual reminder that "word and work" (λόγος καὶ ἔργον) were inseparable aspects of Christian life and true repentance;[12] the salvation of the empire lay in works, not in belief.[13] In fact, after quoting the famous passage of St. James (2:26), he goes on to threaten that it is to the peril of Christians to believe that faith is *not* from works, but from confession alone (ἀλλ' ἐν μόνῃ ὁμολογίᾳ ἐπιζημίως βρενθύεσθαι).[14] This monastic view of the faith as action and confession and of the empire as *imperium* and *sacerdotium* led him to interpret his pastoral ministry as necessarily involving both the spiritual and the secular aspects of Byzantine life.

## Athanasios' Personality

Fortunately for our knowledge of Athanasios and the period, he was a prolific writer and left a voluminous correspondence. What is perhaps most outstanding about its content is the role it portrays him as playing in the life of the empire, a role that can be described as, at times, nothing short of determinative. Bănescu has commented that the letters "le présentent incontestablement comme une des grandes figures de l'Église orientale et confirment pleinement les données de l'histoire au sujet de règne sans relief et sans grandeur d'Andronic II."[15] Two contemporaneous historians, George Pachymeres and Nikephoros Gregoras, confirm the salient features of Athanasios' letters.[16]

From the very beginning of his patriarchate Athanasios' efforts to rebuild Byzantine social and political structures were obvious and earned him many enemies. Both Gregoras and Pachymeres affirm the harsh and extremely ascetic nature of his personality both as a political and as a social reformer. Bănescu, in referring to

Athanasios' letters, comments that his personality was "dur et impitoyable," without making any reference to the depth of compassion the letters manifest for the needs of the people and the safety of the empire.[17] Although Gregoras is more generous in his treatment, both he and Pachymeres cite Athanasios' monastic background as the source of his harsh personality and the rigorous administration of the Byzantine Church.

## The Political and Social Context

More interesting for the study of Byzantine state theory is the relationship the letters describe between the emperor as the personification of the *regnum* and the patriarch as the personification of the *sacerdotium.* The letters portray a watershed in Byzantine political ecclesiology, approaching what may be referred to as Byzantine papalism on the part of Athanasios. This centralizing tendency, which began with him, expressed itself in such forms as the fourteenth-century codification of the liturgy and the Palamite summary of Greek patristic thought. A strong, centralized church was a necessary condition for promoting monastic discipline as well as social reform. Meyendorff infers this centripetal tendency beyond the limited political hegemony of the empire at the turn of the fourteenth century and describes Constantinople, and specifically the patriarchate, as the center of religious and political life in the Slavic world, with an unending flow of diplomats, pilgrims, and merchants.[18]

It is characteristic of this period, and particularly of the reign of Andronikos, that one part of the symbiotic partnership of *regnum* and *sacerdotium*—the ecclesiastical—stands out as the more dynamic and innovative, though it was often ineffectual. It is indeed one of the tragedies of this period that we meet Athanasios as a prophetic-monastic type in the tradition of Jeremiah, but, unhappily for his genuine efforts at reform, without the support of a Josiah (2 Chron. 33:33, 35:25–26) in the secular office.

Athanasios' correspondence is invaluable not only for understanding his motivation, but also in portraying the social turmoil of the late thirteenth and early fourteenth centuries, and in showing the need for reform in a period of social decay and political corruption. The Palaiologan period, especially during the early fourteenth century, was one of the most significant and most complicated periods of Byzantine history. A period of transition on several levels, it was filled with social and political turbulence, confusion, and human tragedy.

Athanasios' letters show his influence on many of Andronikos' political and social policies, his personal reactions to the social collapse of the period, and his attempts to reverse the decline of the empire.[19] It was a period, not unusual in Byzantine history, that brought out the strengths and weaknesses of the Byzantine bureaucratic, statist system and of the individuals involved in leadership. In both the life of the church and the political life of the empire there was evident great stress that demanded action. Athanasios, as his letters demonstrate, was precisely that—a man of action in the tradition of the prophets of the Old Testament and the great monastic ascetic reformers of earlier Christian centuries, such as Sts. John Chrysostom, Basil the Great, and Theodore the Studite.

During the first half of Andronikos' reign, the Church, though divided by the Arsenite schism and the bitter aftereffects of the union effort, proved to be the dominating influence in the internal affairs of the empire. This was partly the result of a reaction to the blatant caesaropapism of Michael VIII and his attempt to coerce the Union of Lyons (1274). With the rejection of the Lyonese union, the Byzantine Church emerged stronger; it was now the guardian of Byzantine "nationalism."[20] Perhaps had Andronikos been a stronger personality or been even less pious and less anxious about the legitimacy of his house, he might have taken a firmer stand against the church and prevented its concerns from dominating his time and generating disturbances. In the endless and quiet tension between the *imperium* and *sacerdotium*, Andronikos' piety as well as the nature of events inclined him to side with the church. The twofold problem of the union and the Arsenite schism, "étant essentiellement religieux, explique les incessantes interventions de l'authorité ecclésiastique."[21]

Sources of the period give the distinct impression that Athanasios, more than Andronikos, grasped what had to be done to reestablish the social and political life of the empire. It is, however, difficult to say that any contemporary Byzantine genuinely understood the nature of the multi-faceted dilemma. Many modern historians have suggested Andronikos' incompetence as the reason for the decline of the empire, but whatever the reasons, they were far more deep-seated than any one man's incompetence. Clearly, though Andronikos was in no way an outstanding leader, he scarcely deserves the hostility that has recently been directed against him.[22]

There were also general patterns of social and ecclesiastical development that apparently transcended the individuals and their developing influences. Peculiar to this period was the domination of ecclesiastical life, and therefore much of political life, by what may loosely be described as an ascetic–monastic party. From the eighth century on, a great number of monks and ascetics, often with no formal education, served the church in an administrative and spiritual capacity as patriarch of Constantinople. This was largely the result of the iconodule victories of 787 and 843 over the Isaurian ecclesiastical policy, which had been at the same time both iconoclastic and anti-monastic. What is important for this study is the fact that after the victory and with a few significant exceptions—notably Patriarchs Tarasios, Photius, and Gregory II (of Cyprus)—monastics dominated the ecclesiastical administration of the church.[23] This tendency was accelerated in the thirteenth century when the Palaiologan house failed to win the allegiance of the people after the usurpation of the Lascarid throne by Michael VIII (1261) and the violence of the effort to enforce the hated Union of Lyons, especially on the conservative monastic element. It was natural, even inevitable, that the church, as the only credible institution, should move into a position of leadership. The church, in fact, was struggling to redefine its relationship with the state in more autonomous terms. This tendency, which began with Athanasios, was to reach its apogee in hesychasm.[24]

In the mid-fourteenth century, after the triumph of hesychasm, the monastic element began to dominate the life of the church. The tendency was clear, and Athanasios (having been trained on Mt. Athos after traveling about early in his career) fell well within this so-called monastic tradition. We see the conflict formalize when the secular clergy of St. Sophia complained about Patriarch Athanasios and his refusal to allow them advancement because they were not monastics. The complaint that the so-called secular clergy was being eliminated from the episcopal and patriarchal offices was common in the period after the victory over iconoclasm (843).[25] The manner in which Athanasios dealt with the clergy, on the one hand, and its complaints against him, on the other, provide a significant episode in his ecclesiastical reform policy, which drew heavily on monastic categories.

Paralleling this growth in the strength and influence of a monastic element was a more general growth in the power, authority, and prestige of the Byzantine Church as the empire faced a relentless degeneration. The growth of the monastic element, which under Andronikos' pious and Athanasios' aggressive personalities received great impetus, was a particularly strong aspect of this ecclesiastical aggrandizement.[26]

Athanasios' two patriarchates were models of the new power and authority acquired by the church, as well as signs of the growing predominance of monks and "monastic" theology within the church. Later, in the mid-fourteenth century, the hesychast Patriarchs Kallistos and Philotheos further accelerated the growth of monastic power, often enabling the church to pursue policies at odds with those of the emperor.[27] Athanasios was the fountainhead of the new authority and the spiritual regeneration of the Byzantine Orthodox Church in the hesychast period. In fact, by the mid-fourteenth century—the height of hesychasm, identified with the canonization of Gregory Palamas in 1368—Emperor John V Palaiologos could submit himself to the papacy as a purely personal matter and raise no response from the church. It was presumably *his* business; he had gone *his* own way.[28] Athanasios demonstrated the same independence vis-à-vis the state, which belies the oft-repeated claims that Byzantine ecclesiastical institutions were state bureaus. An adjustment, an adaptation, was taking place in the relationship between the *hierosyne* and the *basileia*, and Athanasios was at the watershed of the new power then moving into the hands of the patriarchate of Constantinople.

## Athanasios as Reformer

We reap from Athanasios' letters not only a picture of contemporaneous Byzantine society, but also, even more significantly, a picture of the manner in which one ecclesiastic interpreted the meaning and importance of the apparently cataclysmic events going on around him. These descriptions by Athanasios can be interpreted only in the context of his monastic vocation, his paradigmatic application of Israel as a model for what was happening to the Byzantines, and his emphasis on baptism. Athanasios believed himself to be the spiritual father and moral guardian of the Byzantine body politic, a not unreasonable conclusion given the fundamentally spiritual and religious aspect of Byzantine culture.

There is in Athanasios' thought no dualist rejection of the world and its mundane affairs. For him such a rejection was not an option. The Christian option, the monastic option, was always to throw oneself into the battle against evil. For the prophet-monk Athanasios, the battle was to have a system conform to the monastic ideals and maximalism of a cenobitic community—namely, social mutuality, justice, and a more equitable sharing of the wealth of the empire. This threefold theme of monastic mutuality, Byzantium as the New Israel, and the baptismal imperative will be seen to be the underpinning of Athanasios' political theory and social reform. (See Chapter 4.)

The writings of George Pachymeres and Nikephoros Gregoras, along with Athanasios' letters, affirm the harsh and extremely ascetic nature of Athanasios' personality as well as his focus on reforms of social and political life. Although Gregoras is more generous than Pachymeres, both present Athanasios' monastic nature as the source of his ascerbic, reforming zeal. According to Gregoras, from the very beginning, Athanasios, who was filled with divine ardor and severity, threw a somber light on the life of the people in the city.[29] Athanasios was unique as an ecclesiastic inasmuch as the post-patristic Byzantine Church gave little attention to ethical or social thinking; theological affirmations and elaborations prevailed, with no real effort made to relate them creatively to the *Lebenswelt* of Orthodox believers. Hans-Georg Beck claims that ethical thinkers were largely foreign to this period, with the specific exceptions of Isidore Glabas of Thessalonica and Theoleptos of Philadelphia. They were not, however, entirely absent from Byzantium. Using the example of John Chrysostom as a Byzantine reference point, Beck writes:

> Christian instruction, sermon, and catechism were embedded in dogma without making dogma fertile. Moreover, [it] was stifled with classical rhetoric and ancient reminiscences. A homily containing a strong ethical impulse, as one would expect from John Chrysostom, is distant from this epoch; it is—with the exception of a few barely investigated exceptions—simply foreign to it.[30]

Unfortunately, Beck compounds his inadequate understanding of the period by caricaturing the monastic mentality and its prevalence as the reasons for the lack of ethical consciousness. He makes the point that the church, now in the hands of the monks, could not produce an aggressive ethical leadership: by its nature the goal of monastic ethos, contemplation (ϑεωρία), did not encourage practical action.[31]

As Gerhard Ladner has shown,[32] the idea of reform is not something extraneous to Christian thinking. In fact, he produced an entire study that subsumes a variety of disconnected topics under a broadly defined "reform." Demetrios Constantelos exhaustively demonstrates the presence of active philanthropy in the Byzantine empire up to the eleventh century, but offers no real foundational theological reflection on Byzantine social and political life.[33] The radical nature of ethical thinking was evident in the Fathers of the first centuries, particularly Clement, John Chrysostom, and Basil the Great.[34] For the Greek Fathers, especially those of the fourth century, reform was rooted in the image–likeness tension and distinction of the Septuagint (Gen. 1:26). In our period the centrality of the same tension is evident in hesychast emphasis on the collaborative (συνεργεία) nature of human attainment to God's likeness. Ladner refers to the rendering of the Hebrew *d*$^{e}$*muth* (Gen. 1:26) in the Septuagint Greek by κατ' εἰκόνα καὶ καϑ' ὁμοίωσιν, which connotes a distinct element of action.[35] Alexandrian Christian thought early developed the distinction, even antithesis, between εἰκών and ὁμοίωσις. The latter implied a process of permanent progress, which begins with baptism, ends in the kingdom, and is directed by the person as creative agent, capable of new beginnings or "reforms" both social and personal.

Ladner also roots reform in the development of Christian monasticism, which is actually an early expression of a Christian reform mentality. Indeed, it may be noted here that social and ecclesiastical reform in both East and West, sprang from among monastics, in the Byzantine Christian Church the most "conservative" element. Reform is built into the foundational monastic notions of growth and renewal. In a real sense the history of the church is a history of new beginnings—and Athanasios is one of those new beginnings that culminated in the reform movements of mid-fourteenth century hesychasm.[36]

But Byzantine writers did not give formal attention to the question of reform and social thinking. The empire was an eternal given, a *typos* of the archetypical heavenly monarchy; alternatives were not even considered, except in the most catastrophic of times.[37] The uniqueness of Athanasios' letters rests in their social and political exhortations and programs. It is rare indeed to find a late Byzantine writer dealing with social unrest and political corruption. Yet fourteenth-century Byzantine writers were not totally silent on social issues, and many were sensitive to the tensions of society and the plight of the poor. Ecclesiastics such as Philotheos Kokkinos and Joseph Bryennios dealt with these subjects in their moralizing sermons, which advised the lower classes to endure suffering patiently; poverty was potentially valuable as a teacher.

Although social injustice and political corruption were blamed for the decay of the empire,[38] treatment of the subject by such contemporaneous writers as Nicholas Kabasilas, Nikephoros Choumnos, and Thomas Magister amounted to aristocratic observations, necessarily distant, on the needs of the lower classes and on injustice; they offered no real programs for action. In the case of Nicholas Kabasilas, for instance, his information is often vague and even hostile to the lower classes.[39] Out of such thinking, we do not expect to find social revolution or even ameliorative measures. The closest any writer in the fourteenth century comes to Athanasios' sentiments is Alexios Makrembolites, with his "Dialogue Between the Rich and the Poor," which condemns exploitation of the poor as the source of the collapse of imperial power and urges a return to Christian principles as the solution.[40] Athanasios was therefore unique, in that he offered a sympathetic and practical treatment of the subject, as well as a program of action.

At the same time as Constantinople was socially distressed, Thessalonica was on the verge of revolution. Charles Diehl, in his introduction to Tafrali's *Thessalonique au quatorzième siècle*, points out that the situation in Thessalonica was analogous to that in Constantinople, but more serious. In Thessalonica, for the first time in Byzantine history, a social-revolutionary movement, led by so-called Zealots, came into existence.[41] Early in the fourteenth century, Choumnos, after returning from a stay in Thessalonica with the Empress Irene, wrote a "Discourse for Those Engaged in the Practice of Justice,"[42] a guide for state officials at a time when injustice was rampant and resources and the empire were shrinking. Choumnos, for whom justice was the basis of all human society, described a terrible state of judicial corruption and exploitation of the poor by the rich.

Thomas Magister composed a "Discourse to the Thessalonians on Concord,"[43] and although it is not clear what events he was referring to, they were no doubt the same type of events that led to the mid-century Zealot revolution. Theodore Metochites, another scholar of the time, spoke of the same things in some of his writings.[44] Like Magister, Metochites blamed Andronikos' financial policies and heavy taxes, which fell more severely on those least able to pay.[45] The Thessalonian revolt of the Zealots in 1342 indicates that the conditions complained about had not been corrected. We might safely conclude, in fact, that Athanasios may have prevented Constantinople from degenerating to the degree that Thessalonica had. Donald Nicol notes that there is evidence during this very period "for thinking that some leaders of the Church had a better understanding of the social inequalities and injustices that might lead to revolution."[46] Athanasios, as well as Palamas in the mid-fourteenth century, is an example of such a churchman.

But Athanasios was not a systematic thinker and certainly no revolutionary. He served as mediator between the emperor and the people, and was the first resort in the search for political reform and social justice.[47] Both social justice and political well-being were the responsibility of all, but especially of the emperor and the patriarch, the absence of which was as deadly to the soul as the Ottoman troops threatening the Byzantine borders and people. In Athanasios' mind the loss of soul was not unrelated to the loss of empire.

## NOTES

1. Averkios T. Papadopulos, *Versuch einer Genealogie der Palaiologen (1259–1453)* (Amsterdam: Hakkert, 1962), No. 58. Andronikos had been designated co-emperor since 1272.

2. George Ostrogorsky, *History of the Byzantine State*, trans. Joan Hussey (New Brunswick, N.J.: Rutgers University Press, 1969), pp. 466–98; Ostrogorsky, "The Palaeologi," in *The Cambridge Medieval History*, IV.1, ed. Joan Hussey (Cambridge: Cambridge University Press, 1966), pp. 331–32. See also D. A. Zakythinos, *Crise monétaire et crise économique à Byzance du XIIIe au XVe siècles* (Athens: L'Hellénisme contemporain, 1948), p. 145, who refers to this period as "ce pathétique phénomène de la mort de Byzance"; and Louis Bréhier, "Andronic II," *Dictionnaire d'histoire et de géographie ecclésiastique* I (Paris: Letouzey et Ané, 1914), col. 1786.

3. Two vitae of Athanasios are extant: (*a*) Joseph Kalothetos' "Βίος καὶ πολιτεία τοῦ ἐν ἁγίοις πατρὸς ἡμῶν ἀρχιεπισκόπου Κωνσταντι-

νουπόλεως 'Αθανασίου," ed. Demetrois G. Tsames, in *'Ιωσήφ Καλοθέτου Συγγράμματα* (Thessalonica: Center for Byzantine Studies, 1908), pp. 453–502 (KVA); and (*b*) Theoktistos the Studite's "Vita Athanasii," in *Zapiski-istoriko-filologiceskago fakul'teta Imperatorskaga S. Peterburgskago Universiteta*, 76 (1905), 1–51 (TVA).

4. W. Heyd, *Historie du commerce du Levant au moyen-âge* I (Leipzig: Harrassowitz, 1959), pp. 444, 483–84. Ostrogorsky, *History*, p. 479; Donald M. Nicol, *The Last Centuries of Byzantium, 1261–1453* (New York: St. Martin's, 1972), pp. 99, 114. See also André Andréadès, "Les Juifs et le fisc dans l'empire byzantin," in *Mêlanges Charles Diehl* I (Paris; Leroux, 1930), p. 9*n*12, who notes that Andronikos II gave panegyrists a difficult time. They praised him in two ways: either they attributed the political successes of Michael VIII to him or they praised his erudition. Andronikos' reign has been reappraised in Angeliki Laiou's *Constantinople and the Latins: The Foreign Policy of Andronicus II* (Cambridge: Harvard University Press, 1972).

5. For details of the chronology of Athanasios' two patriarchates, see Vitalien Laurent's "La Chronologie des patriarches de Constantinople au XIIIe siècle (1208–1309)," *REB*, 7 (1950), 147, and his "Notes de chronologie et d'histoire byzantine de la fin du XIIIe siècle," *REB*, 27 (1969), 209–34. See also Joseph Gill, "Emperor Andronicus II and the Patriarch Athanasius I," *Byzantina*, 2 (1970), 16, who cites the incorrect dates of 1304 and 1310.

6. John L. Boojamra, *Church Reform in the Late Byzantine Empire* (Thessalonica: Patristic Institute, 1982).

7. *The Idea of Reform* (Cambridge: Harvard University Press, 1959), p. 26. Ladner has expanded on his notion of reform in a more recent work, categorizing it as (1) renovation, in the sense of "imperial" renovation as in the Carolingian period; (2) reform as a continuation of spiritual regeneration of baptism, as in Gregorian renewal; (3) rebellion, as in the revolutionary trends in the Western High and Late Middle Ages; and (4) renaissance, as in the renewal of mutual life and reaction to cosmological reintegration. See his "Terms and Ideas of Renewal," in *Renaissance and Renewal in the Twelfth Century*, edd. Robert L. Benson and Giles Constable (Cambridge: Harvard University Press, 1982), pp. 1–33, at pp. 1, 2. Ladner defines "reform" in such broad categories as to render it an unworkable term.

8. Ladner, *Reform*, pp. 31–32. He expands on this: "The idea of reform and ever perfectible, multiple, prolonged and ever repeatable efforts by men to reassert and augment values pre-existed in the spiritual–material compound of the world." See ibid., pp. 35–48, for discussion of the terminology and related ideas. See also Giles Constable, "Renewal and Reform in Religious Life," in *Renaissance and Renewal in the Twelfth Cen-*

*tury*, edd. Robert L. Benson and Giles Constable (Cambridge: Harvard University Press, 1982), p. 48, where he develops the theme of reform as reintegration into a primordial event. In developing this he necessarily makes use of the brilliant work of Mircea Eliade, *Images and Symbols in Religious Symbolism* (New York: Sheed & Ward, 1961), p. 221.

9. Ladner, *Reform*, pp. 161–62.

10. Ibid., p. 2. See Gen. 1:26.

11. See Boojamra, *Church Reform*, pp. 137–38, on the role of baptism in Athanasios' thinking. Constable, "Renewal," p. 37, notes that the earliest expression of reform in the early church was associated with baptism and the consequent demand for penance.

12. All references to Athanasios' letters are from the Cod. Vat. Gr. 2219 (= V). Where the letters have been edited, with a parallel translation, by Alice-Mary Talbot, *The Correspondence of Athanasius I, Patriarch of Constantinople* (Washington, D.C.: Dumbarton Oaks Press, 1975), they will carry the Talbot designation as well as the numbering used in the *Les Regestes des actes du patriarcat de Constantinople* I.4, ed. Vitalien Laurent (Paris: Institut français dÉtudes byzantines, 1971). Approximately two-thirds of V remains unedited and is a promising area for investigation. References to this portion of the manuscript will carry the folio number and the Laurent designation.

13. Talbot 82, line 55 (*Regestes*, 1717).

14. Talbot 82, line 57 (*Regestes*, 1717).

15. See Nicholas Bănescu, "Le Patriarche Athanase I et Andronic II Paléologue: État religieux, politique, et social de l'empire," *Académie Roumaine, Bulletin de la Section Historique*, 23 (1942), 56. See also Rodolphe Guilland, "La Correspondance inédite d'Athanase, patriarche de Constantinople (1289–1293, 1304–1310)," in *Mélanges Charles Diehl* I (Paris: Presses Universitaires de France, 1930), pp. 121–40.

16. George Pachymeres, *De Andronico Palaeologo*, ed. Immanuel Bekker (Bonn: Corpus Scriptorum Historiae Byzantinae, 1835). Nikephoros Gregoras, *Byzantina Historia* I, ed. L. Schopen (Bonn: Corpus Scriptorum Historiae Byzantinae, 1829).

17. Bănescu, "Athanase," 28. This aspect of his personality has largely been overlooked by most modern historians.

18. John Meyendorff, *Byzantium and the Rise of Russia* (Cambridge: Cambridge University Press, 1981), pp. 124, 131.

19. Ibid.

20. Donald M. Nicol, *Church and Society in the Last Centuries of Byzantium* (Cambridge: Cambridge University Press, 1979), p. 19.

21. *Regestes*, vi.

22. Laiou, *Constantinople*, pp. 2–3.

23. A. A. Vasiliev, *History of the Byzantine Empire* II (Madison: University of Wisconsin Press, 1958), p. 659. Vasiliev writes that beginning

in the twelfth century two irreconcilably opposed parties struggled for influence and control of ecclesiastical administration. He includes the Arsenite faction of the mid-thirteenth and early fourteenth centuries as part of this traditional Byzantine party system divided between *politikoi* and *zelotai*. Inasmuch as traditionally those termed *zelotai* were opposed to secular control of church affairs, he labels the Arsenites *zelotai*. As will be seen, the Arsenites had little concern for the independence of the ecclesiastical hierarchy as such and are wrongly labeled zealots. In fact, Athanasios himself, devoted to the freedom of the Church, labels them "so-called zealots."

24. Klaus-Peter Matschke, "Politik und Kirche im spätbyzantinischen Reich: Athanasios I, Patriarch von Konstantinopel (1289–1293, 1303–1309)," *Wissenschaftliche Zeitscrift der Karl-Marx-Universität Leipzig, Gesellschafts- und Sprachwissenschaftliche Reihe*, 15 (1966) 485.

25. Pachymeres, 648. See Louis Bréhier, *Le Monde byzantin*. II. *Les Institutions de l'empire byzantin* (Paris: Michel, 1970), p. 385, who notes that in the years between 379 and 705, 25 clergy of Constantinople (18 from St. Sophia Cathedral), 2 laymen, and only 3 monks acceded to the patriarchate of Constantinople. Between 705 and 1204, however, the selection fell to 15 clergy from Constantinople, 6 or 7 laymen, and 45 monks. Bréhier ascribes this shift in influence to the monastic role in defeating iconoclasm and the rise of animosity between the so-called secular clergy and the monastics. See ibid., p. 387, where he writes, "Depuis la réforme des Studites, le gouvernement de l'Église était disputé par les deux clergés séculier et régulier." After 1320, the patriarchate fell exclusively into the hands of monastics. After 1289, no priest of St. Sophia became patriarch.

26. For instance, in 1312 Andronikos transferred the jurisdiction of all monasteries on Mt. Athos from imperial control to that of the patriarchate of Constantinople. See P. Meyer, *Die Haupturkunden für die Geschichte der Athosklöster* (Amsterdam: Hakkert, 1965), pp. 190–94. The full significance of this monastic domination was realized in the monastic victory in the Palamite controversy in 1347; see John Meyendorff, "Society and Culture in the Fourteenth Century Religious Problems," in *Actes du XIVe Congrès International des Études byzantines* (Bucharest: Académie de la République Socialiste Roumaine, 1971), p. 51.

27. John Meyendorff, "Spiritual Trends in Byzantium in the Late Thirteenth and Early Fourteenth Centuries," *Art et société à Byzance sous les Paléologues* (Venice: Institut hellénique d'Etudes byzantines et post-byzantines de Venise, 1971), p. 60. Bréhier, *Institutions*, p. 388, writes that after the hesychast victory there was a divorce between the concerns of the emperor for the salvation of the empire and of the monks for the defense of the faith.

28. Oscar Halecki, *Un Empereur de Byzance à Rome* (London: Variorum, 1972), pp. 199–212, and Nicol, *Last Centuries*, pp. 281–83. See below, chap. 2, on the significance of John V's conversion.

29. Gregoras, I:180.

30. Hans-Georg Beck, *Kirche und theologische Literatur im byzantinischen Reich* (Munich: Beck, 1959), p. 39. Beck refers to such ethical thinking as *einfach fremd* in this period. On Isidore Glabas, see A. Ehrhard, *Lexikon für Theologie und Kirche* (Freiburg: Herder, 1930–1938), p. 625. On Theoleptos of Philadelphia, see S. Salaville's "Deux Documents inédits sur les dissensions religieuses byzantines entre 1275 et 1310," *REB*, 5 (1947), 116–36; "La vie monastique greque au début du XIVe siècle," *REB*, 2 (1944), 119–25; and "Une Lettre et un discours inédits de Théolepte de Philadelphia," *REB*, 5 (1947), 101–15. See also Demetrios J. Constantelos, "Mysticism and Social Involvement in the Later Byzantine Church: Theoleptos of Philadelphia, A Case Study," *Byzantine Studies/Études byzantines*, 6 (1979), 83–94.

31. Beck, *Kirche*, p. 40.

32. Ladner, *Reform*, p. vii. Ladner touches only briefly on social and political issues; he deals primarily with spiritual development.

33. *Byzantine Philanthropy and Social Welfare* (New Brunswick, N.J.: Rutgers University Press, 1968), pp. 88–110; see also his "Life and Social Welfare Activity of Patriarch Athanasios I of Constantinople," *Theologia*, 41 (July–September 1975), 611–25.

34. Charles Avila, *Ownership: Early Christian Teaching* (Maryknoll, N.Y.: Orbis, 1983).

35. Ladner, *Reform*, p. 83. He traces its use to pre-Christian Platonism (*Republic* 10.12, 613A) where it was tied with the conception of the "assimilation of man to God." See Gregory of Nyssa, *De Spiritu Sancto* 9.23 (PG 32:109C).

36. Boojamra, *Church Reform*, pp. 160–63. John Meyendorff, *A Study of Gregory Palamas* (London: Faith, 1964), pp. 20–22.

37. Nicol, *Church and Society*, pp. 113–17.

38. Matschke, "Politik und Kirche," 482*n*56.

39. Among the upper classes there was a scant tradition of social analysis. Good style often demanded the use of generalities, allowing no pinpointing of issues, personalities, or groups. Such seems to be the problem with the so-called zealot movement of Thessalonica and was specifically the object of Nicholas Cabasilas' anti-zealot discourse. On the difficulty of identifying the zealots, see Ihor Ševčenko, "Nicolas Cabasilas' 'Anti-Zealot' Discourse: A Reinterpretation," *DOP*, 11 (1957), 79–171; Ševčenko sees dishonest public officials as the object of Cabasilas' anger. There is a considerable body of literature on the nature of the movement and its virtues; see, for instance, V. Parisot, *Cantacuzène, Homme d'état et his-*

*torien* (Paris, 1845), p. 191, where they are described as rabble and demagogues; see also C. N. Sathas, Μνημεῖα ἑλληνικῆς ἱστορίας, in *Documents inédits relatifs à l'histoire de la Grèce* IV (Paris, 1882), pp. xv–xvi, xxvi–xxix. A positive view is presented by O. Tafrali, *Thessalonique au quatorzième siècle* (Paris: Geuthner, 1913), pp. 225–75, esp. p. 271, where they are described as an articulate movement with a social program worthy of a twentieth-century liberal. Ševčenko, "Cabasilas," 148, notes that the zealots in Thessalonica had social programs similar to the "time-honored social ethics of the Church." Peter Charanis sees them as a movement of political reformers who believed in the need for economic reorganization of the empire; see his "Internal Strife in Byzantium During the Fourteenth Century," *B*, 15 (1940–1941), 225–28.

40. Ihor Ševčenko, "Alexios Makrembolites and his 'Dialogue Between the Rich and the Poor,'" *Zbornik Radova Vizantološkog Instituta*, 6 (1960), 202.

41. Charanis, "Internal Strife," 208–209, notes that a series of popular revolts broke out in "virtually every city of the empire"; this fact demonstrated the potential political force of the urban masses in Byzantium. Tafrali, *Thessalonique*, p. 97, observes that Thessalonica was a classic example of class conflict, with landed wealth held by the aristocracy, the church, and the monasteries, all of which were active in commerce and manufacturing. See pp. 99–101, for a list of the monasteries in Thessalonica and their holdings. He concludes, that "Il est cependent vrai que les moines jouissaient de la sympathie du peuple. Leurs établissements charitables étaient ouverts à tout venant; les pauvres et les malades y trouvraient la consolation et l'allègement de leurs maux" (p. 102).

42. Nikephoros Choumnos, "Θεσσαλονικεῦσι συμβουλευτικὸς περὶ δικαιοσύνης," in *Anecdota Graeca* II, ed. J. F. Boissonade (Hildesheim: Olms, 1962), pp. 137–87; for a discussion of Choumnos, see Zakythinos, *Crise*, pp. 45, 116–17. See also Tafrali, *Thessalonique*, p. 99.

43. Thomas Magister, "Λόγος τοῖς Θεσσαλονικεῦσι περὶ ὁμονοίας," in Cod. Par. Gr. 2629, fol. 127ᵛ, quoted in Zakythinos, *Crise*, pp. 118–25.

44. For instance, Theodore Metochites, "Ὑπομνηματισμοὶ καὶ Σημειώσεις Γνωμικαί," in *Miscellanea Philosophica et Historica*, ed. C. Muller (Leipzig, 1823), pp. 538–94. See also Ernest Barker, *Social and Political Thought in Byzantium* (Oxford: Clarendon, 1961), pp. 161–62.

45. Metochites, "Ὑπομνηματισμοί."

46. Nicol, *Church and Society*, p. 25. See also Tafrali, *Thessalonique*, p. 282: "Le gouvernement, composé des nobles et des riches, était incapable de comprendre la gravité de la situation intérieure de l'empire."

47. From a reference in Pachymeres, 583, it seems that Andronikos had given Athanasios an office that might be termed "chief justice" of Constantinople.

# 2

# Athanasios and Political Ecclesiology

ATHANASIOS' POLITICAL REFORMS and his involvement in Byzantine affairs may be considered from the perspective of (*a*) traditional Byzantine political ecclesiology, (*b*) the peculiar phenomena of the empire in the thirteenth and fourteenth centuries, (*c*) the philanthropic definition of imperial power, and (*d*) the increasing power, authority, and prestige of the church,[1] and of its monastic element in particular. In general, reforms were possible because of Athanasios' personality. The traditionally intimate association between empire and church favored reform and precluded revolutionary violence.

When a nation is most vulnerable, it may also be most able to gather its energies to foster a revival of its essentially healthy elements, and to work out new forms and relationships within the chaos of a changing social structure. In the case of fourteenth-century Byzantium this revival was most pronounced in secular learning and monastic spirituality, the former being seen in Theodore Metochites and the latter in men such as Athanasios and Gregory Palamas.[2]

In the context of church–state relationships, Athanasios represented both a traditional example of the Byzantine political and ecclesiological pattern and a watershed for the new moral and spiritual power of the ecclesiastical sphere in Byzantine history. He was the spokesman for a new and growing ecclesiastical self-consciousness rooted in an autonomous relationship with a weakened empire, and it is in this context that we must interpret his social and political reforms regardless of the question of their permanence.

Athanasios' thought and programs reflected a larger movement that was to live well beyond his specific reforms. His patriarchate represented deeper forces at work behind specific reform measures and political philosophy—namely, the drive for Christian purity, spiritual maximalism, and social mutuality. These were tied together by his monastic asceticism and the Christian conviction that the military and economic catastrophes besetting the empire were spiritual problems arising from a failure of moral, social, and theological purity. These were immediate issues: Byzantines were obsessed with theology and mysticism. Byzantium was a thoroughgoing theological society, and only the identification of the *basileia* and the *hierosyne* could make reform a feasible option for a patriarch to pursue. This identification would come to fruition in the Palamite hesychast movement.

As the empire faced more numerous and increasingly more serious crises, relationships among church, nation, and politics shifted. The church, replete with a theoretical rationale explicated by Athanasios, moved explicitly into the political life of the empire, and as the empire declined, the influence of the patriarchate of Constantinople actually expanded among the Orthodox in the Slavic world. Paradoxically, this trend reached its greatest extent with the collapse of the empire in 1453, when the patriarch of Constantinople became the head of the *millet*, and universally responsible for the political and religious life of all the Orthodox under the *Turkokratia*.

Athanasios' relations with Andronikos followed the fundamental patterns established over the centuries, the significant exception being the shift in the balance of prestige and authority into the hands of the church. Athanasios greatly accelerated this process and in this sense altered the traditional pattern. The great hesychast patriarchs of the second half of the fourteenth century—Isidore (1347–1349), Kallistos (1350–1354, 1355–1363), and Philotheos (1354–1355, 1364–1376)—continued the process until ultimately the church could pursue a policy independent of that of the emperor.[3] Athanasios' connection with hesychasm has been well established, and recent research on his canonization has associated it with the official ecclesiastical endorsement of Palamism.[4] As noted in Chapter 1, Palamism specifically, and hesychasm in general, were rooted in the very monastic teachings that were at the same time the foundations of Athanasios' reforms.

The fundamental theme dominating Athanasios' reform thinking, and in which he was consistent with the past, was the essential unity of the Byzantine polity or commonwealth, a unity distorted by such formal terms as "church and state"[5] and more appropriately represented by the terms *hierosyne* and *basileia.* For Athanasios the empire was not interpreted as a state having a parallel ecclesiastical partner, but as a Christian commonwealth for which the "Old Israel" of the prophets was the only paradigm. The church was not a separate corporation, and his frequent use of τὰ τῶν Χριστιανῶν cannot be rendered appropriately as "Christianity," but as the Christian people, the commonwealth of church and empire. The basic assumption was that the *imperium* (the *basileia*) was a divine gift, as was the *sacerdotium* (the *hierosyne*), and that ideally both were to cooperate.

Practically, however, throughout the Byzantine experience the two "spheres" came to be distinguished through a long series of conflicts in which their respective functions were hammered out and each achieved freedom in its proper sphere. With such a close and intimate association and the simultaneous claim for independence in certain spheres, conflict was inevitable. This lack of clear constitutional delimitation of responsibilities is mirrored in Athanasios' letters. The Byzantine political and social situation was largely fluid, which is one reason the empire enjoyed such a long life. Both ecclesiastical and civil officials functioned within broad parameters of constitutional permissibility. Personalities largely determined the manner in which the game would be played. Athanasios believed that, as a corollary of the partnership of church and state, spiritual authority, by its very nature, was more pervasive than secular, for all situations had spiritual analogies. This assumption both marked him as a reformer and made reform possible. Athanasios never tired of reminding Andronikos of this belief, which was relatively unique in Byzantine political ecclesiology.

In no way can we interpret the existing harmony, which was the principle of Byzantine church–state relationships, as the capitulation of the church to the needs of the empire. There were indeed parties who played this role and were loosely defined as *politikoi*, those who, by *economia*, were ready to oblige the will of the emperor. But the freedom of the church was a constant theme in Byzantine ecclesiastical life from the time of Constantine and the Council of Arles and had been jealously guarded by such men as Patriarch Germanos (715–730), with his opposition to iconoclasm, Patriarch Nicholas Mystikos (901–907 and 911–925), who opposed the *tetragamia*, and Theodore the Studite (759–826). Athanasios carried this guardianship of ecclesiastical freedom to impressive heights when he demanded and received significant concessions from Andronikos by which the emperor recognized the protection of the rights and freedoms of the church as his premier duty.[6] Although he exercised great power over the church, the emperor was never the ruler of the church, and submitted in principle to the demands of its internal canonical and theological freedom. The label of "caesaropapism" distorts the reality of the Byzantine situation.[7] In fact, in this period of imperial decline, exactly the opposite was true.

In the fourteenth century, the church had matured into a classic example of Piagetian moral autonomy as evidenced in the so-called *Promissory Letter* of Andronikos.[8] Gerhart Ladner points out with regard to Gregorian reforms that the thrust for priestly superiority was accompanied by the impulse toward social reform rooted in ecclesiastical control of the church and the reform of the church. There were significant caesaropapistic episodes, and no claim to the contrary can make light of them. Although the word "caesaropapism" should be used with caution, it is in fact always a danger when nations so intimately intertwine things political and things spiritual, as Byzantines were wont to do. The claim that there was no caesaropapism in Byzantine history because there was no pope begs the question.[9] Similarly, the claim that there was no caesaropapism because there was no distinct reality of church and state, of sacred and profane, is to make a play on words.[10] The term should be used with caution, precisely because there was no pattern, constitutional or customary, by which to define the relationship. But the apparent carte blanche the emperor enjoyed was never the norm for the internal life of the Byzantine Church, and the doubtful usefulness of this term among modern historians is witness to the equivocal nature of the reality.[11]

The Christian polity (πολιτεία), the *Epanogoge* proclaims, has several members, the emperor and the patriarch being the most significant. The peace and concord of the people of God depend on the unanimity of the imperial and patriarchal authorities. Although the emperor is the supreme ruler, he can never act arbitrarily, and must always display the virtue of beneficence (εὐεργεσία).[12] At the same time as Byzantine political ecclesiology elevated the role of the emperor, it demanded the highest virtues and dogmatic orthodoxy from him; he was to embody what was expected of every Christian. He could lose his right to rule and the support of the church by becoming a tyrant. But this did not alter the fact that in the normal exercise of his functions the Christian king and emperor, in the East even more than in the West, was ipso facto considered a minister of God on earth, and that he saw himself and his actions in this light.[13] The emperor, more often in the East, attempted to reform the church; Emperors Justinian (527–565), Leo VI (886–912), Nikephoros Phokas (963–969), and Alexios Komnenos (1081–1118) were well known for their keen concern with ecclesiastical abuses. The definition of imperial virtues as essentially moral and spiritual went a long way toward placing the emperor under the judgment of the church. The Byzantine emperor may well have been absolute, but he could never be arbitrary; this significant distinction constituted the "freedom" of the Byzantines. A strong patriarch was always able to recall a wayward emperor to *philanthropia* and *eusebia*, the two Christomimetic virtues.[14]

Athanasios appears in his letters as a papist, making claims worthy of a Hildebrand but not quite an Innocent III. In fact, the overall trend in the Byzantine East from the period of iconoclasm (726–843) to the fourteenth century favored an ecclesiastical and, more specifically, a monastic predominance. The position of the emperor was unique and, as has been noted, normally not even the patriarch could rival his power. The only enduring locus of opposition was monastic, which began to crystallize in the early ninth century with the controversy over iconoclasm around such figures as St. Theodore the Studite. Father Georges Florovsky has perceptively referred to Byzantine monasticism as a "permanent resistance movement" within the empire.[15] However, nothing until the Council of Lyons could shake the Eusebian predominance of the emperor.[16] After the fiasco of Lyons (1274) everything was in flux politically, so thoroughly had the imperial authority been compromised by Michael VIII's abuses.

## Historical Roots

Eusebios of Caesarea, Constantine's panegyrist, biographer, and historian, laid the foundation for reform categories by identifying the kingdom of God with the Roman empire, and thus establishing an intimate link, even identity, between them.[17] Eusebios and his successors in imperial panegyrics extolled the terrestrial *basileia* of Constantine and his successors as the actual, unique representation of the celestial kingdom[18]—a parallel that throughout Byzantine history was to constitute good order, ὀρθὸς λόγος.

For the Byzantines, the βασιλεία, the terrestrial kingdom, was a foundational aspect of social and ecclesiastical life; the intimacy of the Roman empire with the celestial kingdom was ingrained. With Eusebios and Constantine there is a clear affirmation of the emperor as the reformer and the restorer of humanity.[19] For Eusebios the emperor rules for the *Logos* as the *Logos* rules for the Father. Eusebian Christomimesis was the basis of Byzantine political ecclesiology. This sense of mission was heightened all the more when in 457 Leo I was crowned by the patriarch. Though never legally defined, the act of coronation by the patriarch became a constituent element in imperial legitimacy.[20]

Indicative of the mimetic basis of Athanasian reform and of the survival of at least the terminology of Eusebios was the unclear distinction between the Christian empire and the church. Thus we hear Athanasios not only calling on Andronikos to imitate God's mercy (θεομιμήτως), but informing him that his reign is not accidental but foreordained by God (προώρισε καὶ προέγνω).[21] The traditional policy of close, even inseparable, ecclesiastico-secular cooperation had been established by Constantine and Eusebios, with the mixed blessings of the Pax Ecclesiae.[22]

The introduction to Justinian's sixth Novel, dated March 16, 535, is a classic development of Eusebian theories. It defines more clearly the relationship between *imperium* and *sacerdotium*:

> There are two major gifts which God has given unto men of his supernatural clemency, the priesthood and the imperial authority [*hierosyne* and *basileia*]. Of these, the former is concerned with things divine; the latter presides over human affairs and takes care of them. Proceeding from the same source, both adorn human life. Nothing is of greater concern for the emperors than the dignity of the priesthood, so that the priests may in their turn pray to God for them. Now, if one is in every respect blameless and filled with confidence toward God, and the other does rightly and properly maintain in order the commonwealth entrusted to it, there will be a certain fair harmony established [συμφωνία], which will furnish whatsoever may be needful for mankind. We therefore are highly concerned for the true doctrine inspired by God and for the dignity of the priests. We

> are convinced that, if they maintain their dignity, great benefit will be bestowed by God on us, and we shall firmly hold whatever we now possess, and in addition shall acquire those things which are not yet secured.[23]

With some significant exceptions, the basic pattern of Byzantine political ecclesiology was firmly established in the sixth century and would not be successfully challenged until the fourteenth. *Symphonia* was the basis of the ongoing life of the two spheres of the single polity. Yet Justinian, like Constantine, defined the proper sphere for the *hierosyne* as the "supplication" of God. This was hardly the dynamism of Athanasios' policies through which he sought to permeate every aspect of Byzantine life. Justinian's was a tight system (as indeed was the empire he tried to rebuild) in which the imperial authority predominated and the priesthood was guaranteed respect in exchange for its prayers for the increase, especially geographical, of an empire waning before barbarian onslaught—an essentially passive role! Nonetheless, the essential element remains: both spheres serve the ends that God has established for the increase and well-being of humankind, which is identified with the empire. In return for the support of an honorable priesthood, the empire would use its coercive power to support the defined dogmas of the Christian faith. Theoretically, if the emperor fought against that faith, then the priesthood was liberated from its duties to the *imperium*. It is a fundamentally Constantinian theme, with classic Roman and Hebrew parallels, that God's good will toward the empire depended on the fulfillment of certain prescriptions, a *quid pro quo*. Hence, the well-being of the church and the purity of its priests became, by definition, a political issue of concern to every emperor. Interestingly enough for our period, Justinian specifically referred to the geographical increase of the empire and its expansions into northern Africa and Spain. Athanasios would make the same promises to Andronikos concerning the loss of Asia Minor.[24] God would restore the empire to the Romans, who had become a joke to their neighbors, if Andronikos would meet certain conditions set by Athanasios.[25] The covenantal relationship is fundamental to understanding Athanasios' political theory.

That ecclesiastical authority moved from the passivity of Justinian's schema to the more parallel postulation of the ninth-century *Epanagoge*[26] no doubt resulted from the strong ecclesiastical reaction to the iconoclastic fiasco of the Isaurian emperors in the eighth century. The *Epanagoge*, a legal compendium probably drawn up by the famous Patriarch Photios and left unpublished, defined the roles of the emperor and the patriarch as parallel. Although the document proclaimed equality, thus allowing the church a more dynamic participation in the life of the empire, reality often limited this participation.[27] The *Epanagoge* defined the parallelism of the patriarch in ecclesiastical and the emperor in secular affairs. "Caesaropapism," as a descriptive term, is inadequate to the fluidity of the Byzantine experience. The most adequate terms to describe the relationship between the *hierosyne* and *basileia* are parity, parallelism, and symphony, all implied in the *Epanagoge*. It is significant that the *Epanagoge* was never officially published. Sections, however, later found their way into legal collections and the writings of several hesychast patriarchs of the fourteenth century.

In the *Epanagoge*, the role of the patriarch, unlike that described in Justinian's sixth Novel, was less passive. He is defined as "a living and animate image of Christ, by deeds and words typifying the truth."[28] The statement continues: "The attitudes of the patriarch are that he should be a teacher; that he should behave equally and indifferently to all men, both high and low; that he should be merciful in justice, but a reprover of unbelievers; and that he should lift up his voice on behalf of the truth and the vindication of the doctrines before the emperor and not be ashamed."[29]

Harmony is still the ideal, for the empire is an essential unity, but the patriarch must, when needed, defend the faith to the emperor, who presumably could be corrected. The patriarch is no longer exclusively a cultic functionary. The boundaries between the two powers are already being blurred, and the image of Christ, contrary to Eusebios, is now referred to as the "living image of Christ" (εἰκὼν ζῶσα Χριστοῦ).[30]

During the ninth and tenth centuries the power and influence of the patriarchate, the church, and the monasteries steadily increased, passing through what has been described as the "Byzantine Canossa," the confrontation between Patriarch Polyeuktos (956–970) and Emperor John Tzimisces (969–976).[31] In the twelfth century, however, Balsamon defined patriarchal and imperial powers in fifth-century terms: "The service of the emperors includes the enlightening and strengthening both of body and soul: the dignity of the patriarch is limited to the benefit of souls, and only that, for they have little concern for bodily well-being."[32] Balsamon's view represents not only an eccentric aside in the larger development of Byzantine ecclesiastical life, but also the thinking of a period when imperial power was on the increase. It points up the persistent ambiguity of Byzantine political and ecclesiastical life, because it was all but impossible to find any constitutional delimitation of the respective powers of the emperor and the patriarch. The Byzantines faced the problem of how far the emperor could act in ecclesiastical affairs. Inasmuch as the empire had no written constitution, the issue remained flexible and dependent upon personality.[33] As late as the thirteenth century, the canonist Demetrios Chomatianos could write that "the emperor has all the prerogatives of a priest except the right of administering the sacrament."[34] Athanasios, however, comes down clearly on the side of mutuality and affirms to Andronikos, "Will not each of us have to render an accounting to the Creator of the world for that which has been entrusted to us?"[35]

The mid-fourteenth century treatise of the *curopalates* George Kodinos describes the growth of the ecclesiastical nature of the Byzantine court.[36] It illustrates the heavily liturgical nature of imperial court life and the growth of the influence of the church, and offers us a picture of the emperor almost totally submerged in liturgical practices. Imperial ceremonies had become appendices to the offices of the church.[37] In addition, during the thirteenth century the emperor was not only consecrated by the patriarch, a practice that had begun in the fifth century,[38] but also anointed with chrism by the patriarch at the time of his crowning,[39] increasing at least popularly the appearance of imperial dependence on the church.

The anointed emperor came in fact to bear a great burden that was largely defined by the church; the patriarch, especially one with the strong and determined nature of Athanasios, was always ready to call the emperor to the virtues of good rulership. Hence, although Athanasios was firmly rooted in the tradition of a unitive political ecclesiology, he represented at the same time a radical turning point in the actual power of the church, resulting from Andronikos' weak leadership, a declining empire, and the compromised imperial power after the enforced Union of Lyons.

The absolutism of the Byzantine emperor had been declining in practice if not in theory at least since the failure of the Isaurian iconoclastic enterprise, with further corrections resulting from the realities of everyday life. Although no sweeping pattern of development can be discerned (as was often the case with the growth of papal power in the West), battles between the emperor and the patriarch were among the most dramatic events in Byzantine history.[40] The church, the patriarchs, and particularly the countless numbers of monks were always able to force a situation to their own ends, destablize a political situation, or wait out an emperor's determined efforts, as in the case of Union of Lyons.[41] Church opposition was always issue-specific; the church was part of an empire and as such never opposed it in principle. Although churchmen may have promoted reform on occasion, revolution was never one of their options. Political turmoil was regarded as a spiritual threat to God's people, who required and, indeed, had a right to social stability, "healthful seasons, abundance of the fruits of the earth, and peaceful times," as the Byzantine liturgy proclaimed.

In addition, Byzantium as the earthly analogue of the heavenly paradigm was an "eternal" given. Nicol refers to the so-called zealot revolution of Thessalonica (1342–1349) as the "worst affront ever offered to the political ideology of Byzantium."[42] There was no antistatism in Byzantine ecclesiastical opposition. Opposition among Byzantine ecclesiastics was always, with the exception of the imperialist claims of Michael Kerolarios, ad hoc, not based on theoretical foundations.[43]

The traditional policy of churchmen, like Athanasios, was one of vigilance in deference to the freedom of the church to function according to its own rules when it was in conflict with the state. This was no easy matter, given the intertwining of secular and ecclesiastical legislation, in such matters as marriage and in nomocanonical literature in general.[44] Churchmen believed that they had a right to raise their voice in behalf of the canons, the faith, and good order (εὐταξία) in church and society. They were ready to oppose anyone who violated these principles, whether emperor or bishop. In fact, Athanasios was, if anything, a strong statist who saw the stability of the statist tradition as the only way to protect the citizens of the empire from being exploited by the civil and ecclesiastical bureaucracy and the merchants, especially foreign, who seemed to offend and anger him more than the operation of foreign missionaries.[45]

## Development of Patriarchal Authority

By the fourteenth century, Byzantine caesaropapism was an anachronism. There was a growing tendency in Byzantine ecclesiastical thought and practice which accorded the church a pre-eminent place. It was, however, the very identification of the βασιλεία and ἱερωσύνη that made reform a possibility in the Byzantine empire. In periods of great turmoil, and particularly in times of weak emperors, the intrusion of the patriarch into the affairs of the empire and society in secular matters could be "flagrant." Although a theocratic patriarchate was never achieved, there was a tendency toward it, as Athanasios' letters bear witness. Meyendorff has made this centripetal tendency clear, noting that the hesychast Patriarch Philotheos, writing to Russian princes in 1370, referred to himself as "the common father, established by the most high God, of all the Christians found everywhere on earth."[46]

In fact, we find in Athanasios' letters the stirrings of a new political ecclesiology that affirmed the traditional pattern and laid the foundation for a new relationship. In a synodal letter Athanasios affirms the inviolability of the state and defines the church as the unifying element of society. According to the letter, God has crowned the church with (*a*) the priesthood and (*b*) the kingship; when both support the church, it can bring forth fruit. This is an apparent reversal in church–state relationships, with the church as the superior body, the matrix of the commonwealth. It is the church, he notes in another letter, that has given the gift of priesthood to humankind,[47] a reversal of Justinian's political ecclesiology. On the other hand, Athanasios' synod is described in the same letter as taking the relatively unprecedented step of both deposing and excommunicating the priest-conspirator John Drimys for his anti-Palaiologan acts. Claiming to be both a priest and a descendant of the Lascarid house of Nicaea, he attempted to overthrow Andronikos II. He was apprehended with his conspirators before the event and condemned by the holy synod. Apart from Athanasios' horror at Drimys' betrayal of his priestly ministry, it is important to ask whether the synod of bishops, the *synodos endemousa*, was acting as an ecclesiastical or civil court. Such double punishment was quite uncommon and actually against canon law.[48] Both the double punishment and the synodal use of ecclesiastical censure for a civil crime are unique. The synod under Athanasios went further and declared, "And also from now on whoever is found guilty of such a crime of madness and Godlessness and treason we bind with this excommunication."[49] The synodal letter does not stop here; the priest, unlike Drimys, is to be a perfect example to the people, especially "to urge the people to be well disposed toward the emperor."[50]

Athanasios represents the transfer of power to the church when he claims, for instance, "For what other reason, I ask, did God adorn the church with an empire, if not for the [exercise of] protection?"[51] In the same place he reminds the emperor, as he does in only one other place in his collected letters, that he is the *epistemonarches* of the church.[52] Athanasios used the term to describe the almost exclusive role of the emperor in regard to the church as unique. The emperor is the protector of the faith, the regulator of ecclesiastical life. Although Athanasios seems to grant the emperor a great deal of power over the church, the context of the letter is subtly the opposite—that is, the emperor is established by God for a purpose: to be a new David and to support the *hierosyne*. The patriarch defined the purpose for which the imperial authority was created. On the other hand, he wrote that the church had "wondrously reared and rightly justified" Andronikos to rule and reign[53]—a significant claim in light of the manner in which Andronikos' father came to the throne, and in that it actually constitutes Athanasios' political confirmation of the Palaiologan house, still questioned by a large party of dissident pro-Lascarid Arsenites.

In another letter, written on the occasion of the emperor's efforts in 1309 to secularize ecclesiastical property for military reasons or on the eve of Athanasios' deposition, Athanasios reminds Andronikos:

> Since you have been reborn in holy baptism and brought to this peak of greatness by the church of Christ, I mean, by Jesus Christ, . . . Who foreordained and chose and decided that your divine majesty should rule the Christian people, your divine majesty has a just obligation to Him to set nothing in this world before the protection and honor of the churches, and to strive vigilantly on their behalf.[54]

The emperor, for quite understandable reasons, had a vested interest in the selection of the patriarch for the see of Constantinople. It was a concern no less central than that of the English kings for the diocese of Durham. The state of the church was in fact the state of the empire, and peace in the church was essential to peace in the empire. The emperor could not allow the election of a patriarch who would not work cooperatively.[55] His potential for political involvement led to the unique nature of the bishopric of

Constantinople, a uniqueness that went beyond normal canonical legislation.

In the time of Athanasios, the patriarch was not merely an ecclesiastical official as in a pluralistic society, but rather one whose regular functions were at once ecclesiastical and secular. Such had been the case with the quasi-judicial functions of the bishops since the earliest days of the Christian empire. This judicial tendency was accentuated during and following Athanasios' patriarchate. Moreover, the patriarch, depending on his personality, could function as a focal point of opposition (such may indeed have been the case had an Arsenite patriarch, hostile to the Palaiologan House, been elected instead of Athanasios).[56]

The regulations for electing a patriarch, like those for a bishop, were quite clear. In the case of the see of Constantinople, these regulations were usually ignored, as they were in Athanasios' second accession to the throne; the role of the patriarch of Constantinople was too important to rely on regular canonical procedures for elections. As Gasquet puts it, "A Constantinople, nous avons montré que les prescriptions canoniques furent, sinon violées, du moins habilement tournées par des césars."[57] The emperor was accustomed to designate and depose the patriarch with or without the canonically required participation of the synod. From 1258 to 1354 the emperors had designated the patriarchs of their choice. If the arrangement did not work out, the emperor could provoke a resignation and seek a more cooperative candidate. Moreover, the popularity of a particular patriarch among the people greatly influenced the ease with which the emperor could proceed. In the case of Athanasios' removal in 1293, not much caution was required. He had acquired many enemies among the powerful of the empire.

Athanasios' career in general outline fits the traditional Byzantine pattern, especially in his first accession (1289) to the throne. His second accession (1303) was largely irregular, accomplished by imperial fiat and without the agreement of the synod, in the expectation of episcopal opposition. In both cases, his position, as he well recognized, was maintained by personal imperial favor. In spite of the weakness of his position, and in the tradition of the Studites, Nicholas Mystikos, and other outstanding spokesmen for ecclesiastical freedom, Athanasios refused to be used by the emperor; instead, he did his best to have the emperor endorse and enforce his own policies of social and political as well as ecclesiastical reform. It was with Athanasios that the church reached its apogee of influence within the empire. After Athanasios, we can detect dualist political tendencies—two organs often pursuing different and contradictory policies. In this regard Athanasios was at the watershed of the new bi-directionalism that Meyendorff has noted as a common feature of the mid-fourteenth-century patriarchate. The church was emotionally liberated from the state by the obviously political nature of the enforced Union of Lyons (1274).[58] The *basileia* and the *hierosyne* each would go its own way, a prefiguration of the break so violently foisted upon the church by the Ottoman conquest of the city on May 29, 1453.

The first incident indicative of this sense of emotional independence—even more significant given the prominence of hesychasm—involved Gregory Palamas, who was captured in March 1354 by the Ottoman Turks. He used the occasion to discuss theology with Jews and Muslims. The Osmanli occupation was to Gregory's mind permanent—an idea that in itself represents a break with the Byzantine myth of the eternal *imperium.* He recognized the freedom of religion, which the Turks permitted Christian residents, as a challenge to a church in need of purification to survive and even to convert its Muslim overlords.[59]

The second occasion of this independence involved the personal conversion of Emperor John V Palaiologos to the Roman Church. John obtained nothing in return but a private altar for the celebration of Mass[60] and a promise of military assistance. The private altar is symbolic of the private nature of the act, which possessed no ecclesiastical significance. The Orthodox Church apparently took little note of John's conversion and went about its business.

By the end of the century, it was difficult to maintain the myth of the essential unity of empire and church as more and more of the Orthodox faithful were living under Slavic and Turkish control and fell beyond the pale of imperial authority. Finally, the church was freed of imperial control and itself became the universal arbiter, albeit by Muslim *berat*, for all Orthodox within the Ottoman empire.

It was becoming common to believe that the empire was not necessarily eternal, and Athanasios could affirm without any contradiction that one must obey the emperor in all things that do not violate God's law.[61] This was not only traditional, but, more especially, the result of the fiasco of the political union of 1274. It followed from the logic of the essential solidarity of the commonwealth that only Christians, and more specifically Orthodox, could be citizens. The same logic, incipient in Constantine, was already explicit in the identification by Theodosios (378–395) of citizenship with Nicene orthodoxy. This sense of social and political unity and mutuality was behind Athanasios' drive to rid the capital of all Roman Catholics, Muslims, Jews, and Armenians.[62] Citizens by definition were obliged to be Orthodox, because the empire by definition was Orthodox.

## Piety and Philanthropy

As already said, the church and Byzantine tradition had generally defined the duties of the emperor. At the time of his coronation he swore to defend the Orthodox Church. Furthermore, throughout Byzantine history patriarchs and saints would recall wayward emperors to *philanthropia* and *eusebia* (beneficence and piety), two essentially charitable qualities that Demetrios Constantelos has traced as a legacy of Greek philosophy from the Hellenistic tradition. To this legacy Christianity then added a revolutionary dimension.[63]

These qualities (and this is necessary for understanding Athanasios as more than a "do-gooder") enable a person to imitate God. They covenanted God to the empire. "Philanthropia had become a revolutionary ideal in medieval Greek Christianity and even political philosophy and it had influenced church, state, and individuals."[64] In the words of St. Gregory of Nazianzus (330–390), "Nothing other than deeds of philanthropy make a person resemble God."[65] This, written in the fourth century, apparently became a touchstone of the Byzantine religious and social ethic in the medieval period. Numerous manuals on kingship, including the *Epanagoge*, refer to philanthropy and righteousness.

Athanasios addressed the same exhortations to Andronikos, but, eschewing the abstraction of political and theological treatises, he couched them in the practical and concrete terms of actual situations that confronted him in the everyday reality of urban Constantinople. Sad to say for Athanasios' sense of charity and justice, occasions for such exhortations were abundantly available in the countryside and in other cities of the empire.

In Athanasios' letters we meet the clear affirmation that the very basis of the empire and its continued survival are the qualities of philanthropy and righteousness. Only the prevalence of these two virtues, actively cultivated among the people, could save the empire from a collapse that the convenantal relationship with God would demand. In one letter to Andronikos, Athanasios wrote, "The God of all Who entrusted the empire of the Orthodox Christians to your majesty has decided and wishes that it be administered not like pagan kingdoms, but in accordance with conscience, so that when He becomes aware of your good administration of it, He may also grant you the heavenly kingdom as a victorious crown of sorts."[66]

Athanasios was no doubt familiar with the example of John III Vatatzes (1222–1254) who was honored as a saint in the Orthodox Church after his death. Here was the perfect model of the philanthropic emperor. He was known as the "eleemosynary king" for his sense of justice and social welfare. Almost one hundred years after John III's death, Gregoras wrote that he had attempted to purify the Roman state on the basis of justice.[67] The author of John's vita refers to his qualities of *dikaiosyne* and *philanthropia*, righteousness and love of neighbor, as the foundation of his social and political reforms.[68] Neither John III nor Athanasios was a mere sentimentalist or a do-gooder; both went beyond the mere charitable level and based their programs, as any reform effort must, on objective external principles. For Athanasios this reference point was to serve Christ by serving the suffering people of the empire.

Athanasios clearly affirmed the traditional Byzantine myth of imperial rule. He spoke of the *hierosyne* and the *basileia* as two aspects of one reality, whose respective lines of responsibility were never clearly delimited. He continually referred to the typology of Old Testament incidents and used the terminology to urge the emperor to act appropriately. The interpenetration of the two powers was so thorough that it was difficult for Byzantines to believe that the church could ever exist without the empire[69]—hence, the significance of the often-quoted exchange between Patriarch Anthony and the Russian Prince Vasily.[70] The empire was conceived of as a single polity composed of church and state. The perpetuation of this myth was not, however, inevitable. The church was beginning to believe it could exist without the empire, and Athanasios was the beginning of a tradition that could only enhance the objectivity required for reform.

## NOTES

1. Ostrogorsky, *History*, pp. 486–87.

2. Deno J. Geanakopolos, *Interaction of the "Sibling" Byzantine and Western Cultures in the Middle Ages and Italian Renaissance* (New Haven: Yale University Press, 1976), p. 51.

3. Meyendorff, "Spiritual Trends," passim.

4. Ruth Macrides, "Saints and Sainthood in the Early Palaiologan Period," in *The Byzantine Saint*, ed. Sergei Hackel (London: Fellowship of St. Alban and St. Sergius, 1982), pp. 84–86. See also Alice-Mary Talbot, *Faith Healing in Late Byzantium* (Brookline, Mass.: Hellenic College Press, 1983), pp. 28–30; and chap. 6, below.

5. Georges Florovsky, "Faith and Culture," *Christianity and Culture* (Belmont, Mass.: Nordland, 1974), p. 29. See also the brilliant analysis in G. Tellenbach, *Church, State, and Christian Society*, trans. R. F. Bennett (Oxford: Blackwell, 1966); Tellenbach makes the valuable distinction between the use of the terms "church and state" and "*imperium* and *sacerdotium.*"

6. See Vitalien Laurent, "Le Serment de l'empereur Andronic IIème Paléologue au Patriarche Athanase Ier, lors de sa seconde accession au trône oecuménique (Septembre 1303)," *REB*, 23 (1965), 135–37. See also John Boojamra, "The Eastern Schism of 907 and the Affair of the Tetragamia," *Journal of Ecclesiastical History*, 25 (April 1974), 113–33, esp. 132–33.

7. See Geanakopolos, *Interaction*, p. 27, for a description of the traditional, semi-sacerdotal character of the emperor and his relationship to the Church. On caesaropapism, see Geanakopolos' *Byzantine East and Latin West: The Two Worlds of Christendom in Middle Ages and Renaissance* (Oxford: Blackwell, 1966), pp. 55–83; John Erickson, "The Orthodox Canonical Tradition," *St. Vladimir's Theological Quarterly*, 27 (1983), 155–68; and Bréhier, *Institutions*, p. 355, who notes that the Byzantine system does not deserve the name caesaropapism. If anything, it could be referred to as a theocracy in which the emperor held the predominant, albeit not exclusive, place.

8. John L. Boojamra, "Constantine and Justinian: A Study in Heteronomous Development," in *Orthodox Synthesis*, ed. J. Allen (Crestwood, N.Y.: St. Vladimir's Seminary Press, 1981), pp. 189–90.

9. John Meyendorff, *Byzantine Theology* (New York: Fordham University Press, 1974), pp. 5–6.

10. Erickson, "Canonical Tradition," 164.

11. Anton Michel, *Die Kaisermacht in der Ostkirche (843–1204)* (Darmstadt: Gentner, 1959), pp. 2, 83, 127. Raymond Janin, "L'Empereur

dans l'église byzantine," *Nouvelle Revue de Théologie*, 77 (1955), 49–51, considers the term "theocracy" preferable to "caesaropapism."

12. *Epanagoge*, in Zepos and Zepos, pp. 240–43.

13. Ladner, *Reform*, p. 119.

14. Constantelos, *Byzantine Philanthropy*, 60.

15. "Antinomies of Christian History: Empire and Desert," *Christianity and Culture* (Belmont, Mass.: Nordland, 1974), p. 88.

16. Steven Runciman, *The Byzantine Theocracy* (New York: Cambridge University Press, 1977).

17. Ladner, *Reform*, p. 20. It was this unity that Augustine wanted to sunder in his *City of God*.

18. Eusebios of Caesarea, "Oration on the Tricennalia," in *Nicene and Post-Nicene Fathers* I, ed. E. C. Richardson (Grand Rapids: Eerdmans, 1952), p. 483.

19. Eusebios of Caesarea, "Ecclesiastical History" 10.4.60, in ibid., p. 377. On the role allotted to the church in Eusebios, see F. E. Cranz, "Kingdom and Polity in Eusebius of Caesarea," *Harvard Theological Review*, 45 (1952), 47–50; Norman H. Baynes, "Eusebius and the Christian Empire," *Mélanges Bidez* II (Brussels: Institut de Philologie et d'Histoire orientales, 1934), pp. 13–18.

20. Ostrogorsky, *History*, p. 61.

21. Ladner, *Reform*, p. 121. Talbot, 8, line 12 (*Regestes*, 1647) and Talbot, 1, line 10 (*Régestes*, Appendix 3). The only significant exception in the Eastern Christian development of church–state ideology is St. John Chrysostom, for whom the monk was the true king; the dignity of the priesthood is extolled over all merely terrestrial kingships. See *De sacerdotio*, 3.1–4, in PG 48:641; John Chrysostom lost his life because of his opposition to the emperor.

22. Norman H. Baynes, "The Byzantine State," *Byzantine Studies and Other Essays* (London: Athlone, 1955), p. 50. For a general introduction to political life in Byzantium to the time of Justinian, see Francis Dvornik, *Early Christian and Byzantine Political Philosophy*, 2 vols. (Washington, D.C.: Dumbarton Oaks Press, 1966). See also John Meyendorff, *The Byzantine Legacy in the Orthodox Church* (Crestwood, N.Y.: St. Vladimir's Seminary Press, 1982), pp. 43–66; Boojamra, "Constantine and Justinian," pp. 189–209.

23. *Corpus iuris civilis*. III. *Novellae*, edd. Rudolph Schoell and Wilhelm Kroll (Berlin: Verlagsbuchhandlung, 1963), Novel 6, pp. 35–36.

24. Ibid. Certainly this was a major concern to Justinian in his efforts to rebuild the Roman empire and re-establish it in its "lost" territories. Justinian's efforts to rebuild the empire were also evident in the legal responsibility he placed on the bishops to fulfill social welfare functions; see John Boojamra, "Christian *Philanthropia:* Justinian's Welfare Policy and the Church," *Byzantina*, 7 (1975), 345–74.

25. For an example of his belief that the empire could be restored, see Athanasios' general Διδασκαλία to the people of Asia Minor on his second accession to the throne (V, 230r–232r; *Regestes*, 1589).

26. *Epanagoge* 2.3, in Zepos and Zepos, p. 241. For a discussion of this, see Karl Zachariae von Lingenthal, *Geschichte des griechisch-römanischen Rechts* IV (Berlin: Weidmann, 1892), pp. 22–23.

27. Ostrogorsky, *History*, pp. 240–41.

28. *Epanagoge* 2.1, in Zepos and Zepos, p. 242.

29. Ibid. 2.4, in Zepos and Zepos, p. 242.

30. Ibid., 2, in Zepos and Zepos, p. 182. Using the language of the *Epanagoge*, the hesychast Patriarch Anthony in 1393 referred to himself as τὸν τόπον ἔχει Χριστῷ ("Vicar of Christ"); see Miklosich and Müller, II:189.

31. Ostrogorsky, *History*, p. 293.

32. Theodore Balsamon, *Meditata*, in PG 138:1017. For the English text, see Barker, *Social and Political Thought*, p. 106.

33. Nicol, *Church and Society*, p. 8, writes that the empire could have used a constitution and the church an army of canon lawyers, neither of which became a fact. Circa 1380, the church agreed to a document of John V that clarified and defined the constitutional rights of the emperor in ecclesiastical affairs. See Vitalien Laurent, "Les Droits de l'empereur en matière ecclésiastique: L'accord de 1380–1382" *REB*, 13 (1955), 5–20; Runciman, *Theocracy*, pp. 158–59.

34. "Letter to Constantine Kabasilas," in *Analecta Sacra et Classica Spicilegio Solesmensi parata* VI, ed. J. B. Pitra (Rome, 1891), cols. 631–32.

35. Talbot, 49, line 94 (*Regestes*, 1615): οὐ λόγον ὑφέξομεν ἕκαστος ("both will have to answer"). See *Epanagoge* 1, in Zepos and Zepos, p. 181.

36. (Pseudo-)George Kodinos, *Traité des offices*, ed. and trans. Jean Verpeaux (Paris: Centre National de la Recherche Scientifique, 1966).

37. André Grabar, "Pseudo-Codinus et les cérémonies de la cour byzantine au XIVe siècle," in *Art et société à Byzance sous les Paléologues* (Venice: Institut hellénique d'Etudes byzantines et post-byzantines, 1971), p. 200.

38. Ostrogorsky, *History*, p. 61.

39. Donald M. Nicol, "Kaisersalbung: The Unction of Emperors in Late Byzantine Coronation Ritual," *Byzantine and Modern Greek Studies*, 2 (1976), 37–52.

40. Ernest Stein, "Introduction à l'histoire et aux institutions byzantines," *Traditio*, 7 (1949–1951), 95–168, at 136. Stein makes a fundamental error common to many historians when he writes; "L'Eglise byzantine ne conteste guère à l'empereur, et moins que jamais après la querelle des

images, le droit de légiférer en matière de constitution et de discipline ecclésiastique." See also Andrew Sharf, *Byzantine Jewry from Justinian to the Fourth Crusade* (London: Routledge & Kegan Paul, 1971), p. 12: "it was rarely claimed that the emperor had no right to make [doctrine]."

41. The reaction to the Union of Lyons is succinctly treated in Geanakopolos, *Interaction*, pp. 156–70. See also Aristeides Papadakis, "Ecumenism in the Thirteenth Century: The Byzantine Case," *St. Vladimir's Theological Quarterly*, 27 (1983), 207–18.

42. *Church and Society*, p. 20. The maintenance of social stability was a sacred obligation inasmuch as it imitated the divine stability of the kingdom of God; see Hélène Ahrweiler, *L'Idéologie politique de l'empire byzantin* (Paris: Presses Universitaires de France, 1975), pp. 129–47.

43. See Mahlon H. Smith, *And Taking Bread . . .* (Paris: Beauchesne, 1978), passim, on Kerolarios.

44. Boojamra, "Tetragamia," 130–31. The mutual interpenetration of the legislation of the two "powers" is described by Erickson, "Canonical Tradition," and this "interpenetration" is most evident in the so-called nomocanonical collections of both ecclesiastical (κανόνες) and civil laws (νόμοι), compiled according to topic.

45. John L. Boojamra, "Athanasios of Constantinople: A Study of Byzantine Reaction to Latin Religious Infiltration," *Church History*, 48 (March 1979), 27–48, esp. 45–46. Much of Athanasios' activity was directed at maintaining state services. See Ostrogorsky, *History*, pp. 939–41.

46. Miklosich and Müller, I:516. In another letter, Philotheos writes that all Christians in the world "depend on me" (ibid., 521); quoted by John Meyendorff, "The Council of 381 and the Primacy of Constantinople," in *Catholicity and the Church* (Crestwood, N.Y.: St. Vladimir's Seminary Press, 1983), p. 137.

47. Talbot, 81, line 2 (*Regestes*, 1636): ὅτι τὴν ἐκκλησίαν ἱερωσύνῃ καὶ βασιλείᾳ ἁρμοζόντως κατέστεψεν.

48. Talbot, 81, lines 135, 140–42 (*Regestes*, 1636). Pachymeres, 592–93. On the rejection of double punishment and the dual standard for clergy and laity, see Canon 16 of I Nicaea (Rhalles and Potles, II:149–50) and Balsamon's commentary on the meaning of clerical excommunication, which he defined as deposition or suspension from his office. See also Canon 15 of Apostolic Canons (Rhalles and Potles, II:20), Canon 4 of the Council in Trullo (Rhalles and Potles, II:339), and Canon 25 of Apostolic Canons (Rhalles and Potles, II:32).

49. Talbot, 81, lines 144–46 (*Regestes*, 1636).

50. Talbot, 81, lines 14–15 (*Regestes*, 1636).

51. Talbot, 61, lines 44–45 (*Regestes*, 1704); see also the *Epanagoge*, 2.1, in Zepos and Zepos, p. 240, and Talbot, 49, lines 37–39 (*Regestes*,

1695), where Athanasios reminds Andronikos that he is obliged as a "son of the Church" to chastise the people.

52. Talbot, 61, line 48 (*Regestes*, 1704); see also Talbot, 95, line 21 (*Regestes*, 1725). On the definition of the ἐπιστημονάρχης, see Michel, *Kaisermacht*, pp. 140–42. See other uses of the term in C. du Frense DuCange, *Glossarium ad scriptores mediae et infimae graecitatis* I–II (Graz: Akademische Druck- und Verlagsantalt, 1892), p. 427.

53. Talbot, 1, lines 9–10 (*Regestes*, Appendix 3).

54. Talbot, 104, lines 1–8 (*Regestes*, 1730).

55. A. Gasquet, *De l'Authorité impériale en matière religieuse à Byzance* (Paris: Thorin, 1879), p. 187: "Toutes les élections étaient controlées par l'empereur ou par ses déléguées, et soumises à sa confirmation." See Nicol, *Church and Society*, p. 29, who notes that of the twenty-six patriarchs between 1261 and 1453, twelve resigned for "political" reasons. Emperors, it seems, still preferred their patriarchs to be submissive and obedient.

56. Gasquet, *Authorité*, p. 85.

57. Ibid., p. 183; (pseudo-)Kodinus, *Traité*, p. 280, describes the imperial appointment of the patriarch, which is done in the name of the Holy Trinity, who gave him his royalty; the patriarch received his staff from the emperor. The *Traité* also offers a description of the patriarchs of Alexandria, Antioch, and Jerusalem who resided in Constantinople for safety, their sees being in hostile foreign hands.

58. Aristeides Papadakis, *Crisis in Byzantium* (New York: Fordham University Press, 1983), pp. 15–18. Papadakis places the effects of the council in a Byzantine context. He repeats their unique approach to the so-called union council in "Ecumenism," pp. 155–68.

59. Meyendorff, *Gregory Palamas*, pp. 103–107; idem, "Grecs, Turcs, et Juifs en Asie Mineure au XIVe siècle," *Byzantinische Forschungen*, 1 (1966), 211–17.

60. Halecki, *Un Empereur*, pp. 199–212 and Nicol, *Last Centuries*, pp. 281–83.

61. V, 234[v] (*Regestes*, 1779).

62. See, for instance, his complaints in V, 151[r]–152[r]; Talbot, 41, lines 8, 16–17 (*Régestes*, 1622). See also Boojamra, *Church Reform*, chap. 4.

63. Constantelos, *Byzantine Philanthropy*, pp. 3–17.

64. Ibid., p. 102.

65. Gregory of Nazianzos, *Oration 14*, in PG 35:892c–893A.

66. Talbot, 57, lines 1–6 (*Regestes*, 1701).

67. Gregoras, 42–45; see also Pachymeres, 38–39.

68. Demetrios Constantelos, "Emperor John Vatatzes' Social Concern: Basis for Canonization," *Kleronomia*, 4 (1972), 92–104. John came to be

venerated in Magnesia and Nymphaion after his death, but his vita was not composed until late in the fourteenth century and he was not officially recognized as a saint by the Orthodox Church until the seventeenth century. See also Talbot, *Healing*, p. 23.

69. Bréhier, *Institutions*, p. 346.

70. Nicol, *Church and Society*, pp. 4–5.

# 3

# The Freedom of the Church

THE RELATIONSHIP BETWEEN ECCLESIASTICAL AND POLITICAL AUTHORITY in Byzantium has been seen from the perspective both of traditional political ecclesiology and of the changes characteristic of the thirteenth and fourteenth centuries. From this viewpoint Athanasios is the ardent reformer, harvest of the past and fountainhead of the future. This role forced him to extend the sphere of patriarchal power and influence into the political and social life of the empire. Part of this reform effort was grounded in the need to establish the freedom of the church as a necessary condition for "right order" in Christian society. The prosperity of the empire and victory over its adversaries were closely tied to the political freedom of the church *as an institution.*

In the last chapter we saw that Athanasios gave the church precedence over the empire both chronologically and qualitatively, in letters averring that the church not only had existed before the empire but was also superior to it, and was the matrix of Byzantine life. His claims would make sense from the pen of a medieval pope, but they were hard words from a Byzantine patriarch, traditionally reared in dependency on the secular administration of the *imperium.* Athanasios claimed, for instance, that after the establishment of the church on a "rock" (Matt. 16:18), God "crowned Her with the supreme imperial power, so that she might be served in all matters pleasing to God and be supported by [the imperial power]."[1] Historically quite the contrary was true; the empire predated the church. But Athanasios assumed that the conversion of Constantine and his empire to a specifically Christian form was the "Golden Age," the beginning of Christian society.

In principle Athanasios carried political and ecclesiastical developments to their logical conclusion. His reforms sought to establish the "freedom of the church." And this freedom meant to him that the church must function in accordance with its canons and traditions. Athanasios set his political and social reforms in this very "freedom," expressing this imperative for reform primarily in terms of struggle against social and political injustice and of good order in church and society.[2] He sought to bring this about not only by preaching, but also by the force of the state. He demanded that the church be unencumbered in its internal life and free of any external pressure or exploitation, whether from emperor, tax collector, or corrupt bishop who sought to impose their will for political or monetary reasons.

The process of affirming freedom was strengthened by the failure of secular leadership (in the person of Andronikos) to restrain the civil bureaucracy or maintain control over it. In claiming the superiority of the *hierosyne* Athanasios had both the theoretical tools and the practical occasions to justify his moving into the political and social vacuum created by Andronikos' weak leadership and the general social, moral, and religious decay around him. What tools he did not possess he created by interpreting the events around him in cataclysmic terms.

## Promissory Letter

When Athanasios resumed the patriarchate in June 1303, he was far from universally supported by his episcopal confreres because of the notorious reputation for harshness and the rigorous application of church canons to church life he had gained during his first patriarchate (1289–1293). Among the aristocrats and bureaucrats in Constantinople he was equally unpopular. In light of the weakness of his position and the coercion necessary to re-establish communion with a significant number of bishops and clergy, Athanasios demanded and received from Andronikos the so-called *Promissory Letter* (Γράμμα Ὑποσχετικόν). Unknown until it was discovered among the letters of Athanasios in Vaticanus graecus 2219 and commented on by Laurent,[3] this *Promissory Letter* is primarily concerned with the freedom of the church to operate in keeping with its own canonical legislation and with the prohibition of any civil interference not already permitted by ecclesiastical canons.

In the *Letter*, which Athanasios apparently had extracted from Andronikos as a sine qua non for his return to the patriarchate, and which, to judge from the style and content, was certainly written by Athanasios himself, Andronikos promised to submit to the church in every matter that was legal and in conformity with the will of God. What is even more significant, Andronikos promised personal support to the patriarch in his efforts at social, political, and ecclesiastical reforms, and committed himself in particular to sending bishops back to their proper dioceses.[4] No doubt Athanasios wisely demanded such an oath from Andronikos before he would take up patriarchal responsibilities for a second time. There was, in fact, no one else on whom he could rely for support in the reform work he had undertaken. In addition, he had a right to expect this support from the man who had pressed for his return to the patriarchate after a ten-year hiatus. In this situation, it is not unreasonable to assume that he felt he had the right, indeed the leverage, to dictate terms and exact a number of guarantees.

The first paragraph of the *Promissory Letter* is a rambling statement of political ecclesiology, beginning with an affirmation of the *pronoia* (care, plan) of God, who established the emperor and granted him great blessings. Embodying Athanasios' covenantal theme, Andronikos wrote that in return for all these gifts, visible and spiritual, "I promise not only to wish to keep the church entirely free, but to have toward it the obedience of a slave and to submit myself to it in all that is legal and conforms to the will of God, to have nothing more precious and to prefer nothing so much as its progress, security, and advancement."[5] In even more specific terms, Andronikos refers to Athanasios:

> Concerning the one who [i.e., Athanasios] holds his function . . . of the good will of the Divinity by means of a legal election and without passion, just as of a sincere prayer made to God by the body of the church, I will attach more of a value to support him in all that I consider as conforming to the commandments of God and the canons.[6]

At the price of an untruth, the emperor declared that Athanasios' second accession to the patriarchate was accomplished legally, by an election. This contradicts Pachymeres' account, which portrays Andronikos as simply declaring, with some bishops, Athanasios reestablished.

Andronikos goes further, emphasizing the freedom of both the church and of Athanasios to reform the church:

> And if he [Athanasios] desires to reinvigorate certain laws of the church which have fallen into disuse, if he wishes to turn the sacrilege out of the temple, whatever the level, with a spiritual whip, if he wishes to reform those who are called pastors, as well as the priests, the monks, the monasteries, and the churches in a holy zeal [ἐν θείῳ ζήλῳ καὶ δικαίῳ θυμῷ] and a righteous anger, I vow to support him.[7]

Andronikos throws his support behind the patriarch and the church in terms of the classic covenantal Byzantine political ecclesiology, "that they [the priests] may intercede without distraction to obtain for me, and for those who are for me the most dear, health, salvation, and divine help, in order to appease also the anger of the Lord who, because of our numerous sins [διὰ τὰς πόλλας ἡ[μ]ῶν ἁμαρτίας], presses the Christians."[8]

In these brief statements there is a summary of the relationship between the Byzantine *imperium* and the *sacerdotium* as well as a pathetic affirmation of Andronikos' almost total submission to Athanasios' demands. It is clear, however, that Andronikos wanted not only Athanasios back on the ecumenical throne in mid-1303, but also the reform of church and empire, actions well-pleasing to God and assuring God's good will to the Christian empire—a survival of Constantinian quid pro quo in the fourteenth century.[9]

In retaking his old office, Athanasios needed all the support he could muster. He was well aware that he could not rely on the support of bishops and metropolitans, who had to be coerced into accepting his re-establishment and were fundamentally hostile to his reform program. Pachymeres reports, however, much good will on the part of the emperor. On the other hand, Athanasios' feelings toward Andronikos were warm but critical, and in no way does he appear to offer his unqualified support to the emperor.[10] He was obliged in his letters to remind the emperor continually that he was to imitate Constantine in his piety and transfer of authority to the church.[11] It was clear to Athanasios that the emperor existed for the well-being of the church,[12] and, specifically—in this case by suggestion—for Athanasios' reforms. Pachymeres writes that Andronikos fulfilled Athanasios' will as if he were "under his spell." Initially, at least, anyone who displeased Athanasios was sure to meet with Andronikos' disapproval.[13] But as his second patriarchate progressed, Athanasios did not share this perception of Andronikos' support.

Athanasios had to reiterate often the priority of the church almost from the beginning of his second patriarchate. In an undated letter to the emperor, for instance, he wrote: "For this I entreat that [you] should be discreet and we should learn to submit to the church, and not to subject the church, but to be subject to it and its laws and not to stand against it recklessly [παραβόλως]."[14] Carrying on the same theme, he repeated to Andronikos: "I entreat you that during your reign the church of Christ enjoy freedom and not be tied with a string."[15]

All his appeals for the "freedom of the church" will become clearer when we consider, in Chapter 5, Athanasios' struggle against political interference in church life and finances: "as if the worldly rule they hold were not enough, they put their hands on the church; they should not have, but thinking as men, they involved themselves in things they should not have."[16]

The greatest evils are brought about, he warned, by "disregard of the commandments owed to the church."[17] Not serving the church had provoked God's wrath against the people, and was the shame of the empire; it had made the empire prey to foreigners[18] and the smallest of all nations.[19]

## The "Two Powers"

In a letter of a more didactic nature, Athanasios wrote to Andronikos concerning the "two powers," which along with the four elements (fire, earth, air, and water) are given to the people by the grace of God: "the priesthood and the emperorship were given and tied to one another [τὰ ἀλληλένδετα]." God had given the sacrificial priesthood to the people so as to make holy what is earthly (τῆς μὲν ἱερουργίας νοερῶς τῶν γηίνων ἀπανιστώσης βιοτῇ ἁγιοπρεπεῖ μισάσμον) and to make all that is "fleshly" hated (μισάσμον) for the sake of God. The second power, the imperial, was "given to protect the first and also to care for the good."[20]

In another letter, Athanasios urged Andronikos to be concerned for the interest and well-being of the church even before that of the empire. He reiterated essentially what he said elsewhere, but with greater clarity:

> For the priesthood was not granted to the Christian people for the [sake of] the kingship [*basileia*], but the kingship was given for the priesthood, so that by doing what is pleasing to God "the hand which

> is outside" [the state] would strengthen her and take care of her, and by standing with [the kingship], she herself would stand on her own and be increased by God.[21]

Here Athanasios defined the *basileia* as that which is τῇ ἔξω χειρὶ, created by God to serve the church, which is its own end (ἀντικρατύνηται).

With this definition as a given, Athanasios went on to ask the emperor to fulfill this function and send the bishops in Constantinople back to their proper dioceses. Because the patriarch's canonical pressure was not sufficient, it was quite natural for him to call on Andronikos as *epistemonarches* to provide the necessary coercion, and "to staff the church thickly with shepherds."[22] Athanasios was consistent, and the term *epistemonarches* was taken quite seriously as the emperor's premier responsibility—nothing comes before the care of the church.

We can detect a clear affirmation of covenantal principles and a turn from the early Byzantine notion that the church exists to serve the empire and to offer supplication to God, playing an essentially passive role. For Athanasios, the church was the essential substratum without which the empire could not exist. Such an assertion would have been absurd, even inconceivable, during most periods of Byzantine history when the empire was either stronger or the emperor more confident and the church correspondingly less conscious of its own strength vis-à-vis the emperor. Athanasios sounds like a papist! The official policy of the empire and the raison d'être of the emperor were the protection and advancement of the church. Only then, logically, would blessings be guaranteed to the empire and the people.[23] This notion is highlighted by the conspicuous absence of any millennial references, by any warning of the "end of the world," the approaching *eschaton.* Athanasios faced the prospect of the end of the empire and victory by the Turks. Such a victory was quite understandable to him, and he affirmed that their success would be due not to their superiority of arms or strength, but to their moral superiority and the corresponding immorality of the Byzantines.[24] The covenant was being violated, and God, as in the case of Israel, was not obliged to "keep" the nation.

For Athanasios and the succeeding hesychast patriarchs in the mid-fourteenth century, the situation was to be quite different—the empire was not necessarily an *eternal* manifestation of the divine archetype. The frustration of reform and Christian maximalism drove him to this position. Athanasios involved himself in the political and social affairs of the empire as if it were part and parcel of his spiritual duty as "father" of his people, as guardian of the covenant for the earthly partner. He made no artificial distinction between his spiritual and social responsibility. If Christianity was the very definition of the commonwealth, then it was his duty to involve himself in all aspects of the life of the empire. He called on the emperor not only to hear his pleading, but also to enforce the policies he outlined for both the freedom of the church and the well-being of the empire.

## The "Olive Branch" Incident

Athanasios' interpretation of the freedom of the church included the protection of ecclesiastical property and money from alienation and misappropriation. He tried to protect the monasteries, ecclesiastical institutions, and their properties from corrupt secular and ecclesiastical officials, who instead of protecting the administration of monastic goods, and presumably the goods of certain charitable institutions, unduly mixed in their affairs and regulated them to serve their own financial interests. Athanasios held Andronikos responsible for the behavior of these men, reminding him in one place that it was his duty not only to fight heresy but also to see that persons in authority behaved correctly. The emperor, Athanasios wrote, was above all the "benefactor" and must chastise those not doing their duty justly.[25] In general, Athanasios condemned the interference of secular authorities, and in one place associated it with the destructive eighth-century attempts of the Isaurian Emperor Constantine V to impose iconoclasm, which was accompanied by the confiscation of monastic properties.[26]

We can only assume that without an updated census of properties and population it would have been difficult to ensure a regular income as well as detect dishonest tax collectors. The surest source of income for the empire would be the church, where records in general were more accurate than those of the secular authorities and where properties were more vulnerable and available. But there are no accounts of Andronikos' ordering a census of any sort for purposes of taxation.

The immunity the church enjoyed was so central to Athanasios' ecclesiology and his notion of the freedom of the church that he placed violation of it among the sins that were the cause of the loss of Anatolia. He promised Andronikos, sometime shortly after significant reversals in Anatolia in 1302 and before his return to the throne in 1303, that the military situation could be turned about by controlling dishonest fiscal agents.[27] The assurance was timely but not convincing: such military losses continued well into his second patriarchate. In another place Athanasios wrote, in the context of a discussion about episcopal residency, "If then your divine majesty wishes the church of Christ to remain utterly free and untroubled in the spiritual sphere, in which men's souls, churches and monasteries dwell, and exempt from the [taxes] which are owed to the fisc, this would be immediately pleasing to God."[28]

Instead of permitting Athanasios to perform one of his chief duties—guarding the administration of the monasteries and their incomes—the residents of the monasteries themselves forgot the purpose for which these houses had been established. His duty, he affirmed, was to see that their administration was entrusted to persons who were suitable according to the canons (ἐγκανόνως).[29] Speaking of lay officials who were granted certain income in return for administering monastic enterprises, he accused them of appropriating wealth for their own purposes. Because the property of ecclesiastical institutions, including monasteries, was not in itself canonically inviolable, and because its use could be determined within canonical norms by the needs of the church—the local bishops, or the patriarch for those monasteries under his jurisdiction—Athanasios' complaints were clearly justified. Not only were some officials unscrupulous, but their dishonesty so reduced monastic resources that Athanasios could not fulfill Andronikos' mandate to hear complaints and relieve injustices. Preferring to treat the property as their own, the bishops objected to Athanasios' plan to use monastic resources, for example, to ransom captives about to be sold into slavery[30]—a canonical procedure considered among the highest virtues by Orthodox Byzantines.

There was substantial opposition to the patriarch from among almost all categories of citizens, especially among those monastic elements whom Athanasios felt were abusing either their way of life or the wealth that had come into the possession of their communities. It must be remembered that monasteries and pious foundations in general were heavily endowed and often with guaranteed income from areas yet under Christian control (i.e., Slavic territories), especially Russia, and free of Turkish control or assaults. Like the provincial bishops, the monks found the luxuries of the city far more attractive than Athanasios' ascetic discipline and his demands that they live in their monasteries. Nor, it may be assumed, did they like the idea of his confiscating monastic properties in order to fund his social service projects. Athanasios was not a blind defender of ecclesiastical property. He was concerned about ecclesiastical and monastic privileges and sought primarily to protect them from illegal exploitation and theft by corrupt officials, but not to shield them from what he judged legitimate use. As the empire collapsed, the emperor turned to monastic property for ready income to meet military needs and for land to grant to soldiers,[31] with, as we shall see, Athanasios' tentative approval.

Pachymeres records that the Byzantine military system at the end of the thirteenth and the beginning of the fourteenth centuries was collapsing as the soldiers left their *pronoiai*,[32] the land grants that were the basis of Anatolian military strength; consequently, many soldiers had no motivation to fight to protect their own land. Pachymeres attributes the disintegration of the army not only to Andronikos' non-military manner, but also to corrupt officials, who, distant from the capital, appropriated the land and salaries of soldiers. Without shame, he claimed, they were stealing property dedicated to God. He noted that "allowances" may not be given on the pretext of military service to men who had never so much as heard the names of the weapons. This was no doubt written in 1303, when Andronikos was contemplating the policy of confiscating monastic lands for soldiers.[33] Although the emperor had previously attempted reforms to counter this corruption,[34] the reforming general John Tarchaniotes found, for instance, that the best soldiers had lost their *pronoiai* to those who could offer large bribes.[35]

The emperor, having to raise money to fund the army, pay mercenaries, and settle soldiers on their own land, decreed that the proceeds from all ecclesiastical benefices, including the estates of monasteries, should be diverted to military purposes. The goal of this effort was clear: to restore to taxation the properties that had, by pious intention, been exempt from fiscal obligations. Inasmuch as pronoiai were traditionally considered to be the basis of imperial military power, Andronikos tried also to strengthen this base. But lacking sufficient resources to pay the soldiers, he determined to take away the lands given to the churches and the monasteries and to use them to pay the troops. Pachymeres writes:

> Because of critical times and circumstances, it appeared necessary to take the one measure still remaining: releasing from their overlords however much was given in *pronoiai* to the monasteries, the churches, and the imperial entourage, and to make everything, including even lands attached to monks who lived in single cells, into military holdings so that the people could defend their own property.[36]

Such a measure, though desperate, was not unique. It was, however, the first time that it had been contemplated since the reign of Manuel Komnenos (1143–1180), when the needs of the state forced the use of monastic and ecclesiastical holdings.[37] And how did the rigid defender of the freedom of the church respond to this scheme? What we see is not the unbalanced personality so often presented by modern historians. Athanasios did not oppose Andronikos' plans for secularization. Pachymeres records his gesture of approval: "Accordingly, without a word or action the patriarch sent an olive branch to the emperor, from which he was able to derive some encouragement at good things [to come] because of his supreme confidence in the patriarch."[38]

The patriarch was apparently willing to compromise in an area that, according to his logic, involved the freedom of the church. Athanasios understood the primary need of the state, which in 1303 was for military survival; although there is no specific indication that he did so, it would not have been out of character for Athanasios to have inspired such a move. Pachymeres notes that, unfortunately for Andronikos' efforts to reform the army, the redistribution of land never moved beyond the planning stage;[39] nevertheless, the "olive branch" incident increased opposition to the patriarch among the monastic communities, which would have undoubtedly preferred that he take a more rigorously canonical stand, as Patriarch Philotheos did in 1367 in refusing a similar requisition from the Emperor John V.[40]

Though Patriarch Athanasios was a zealous guardian of the rights and freedoms of the church, and sought to protect monastic property from misappropriation and abuse by both lay and ecclesiastical officials, he was not blind to the legitimate uses to which this wealth might be put. He was also well aware of the abuses that monastic wealth had occasioned among the monks of the empire.

## Secularization of the Clergy

As amenable as Athanasios was to the ad hoc secularization of ecclesiastical property and to his own involvement in secular affairs, he was quite adamant about clerical involvement in the secular realm. In one letter he called on the bishops to forbid all priests from civil (ἀρχαῖς κοσμικαῖς) and military service (στρατεία). The priesthood was ordained by God and thus superior to either civil or military occupations.[41] He sternly prescribed suspension for any priest voluntarily leaving his vocation.[42] He even ordered the clergy of St. Sophia to take an oath not to betray their ministry for base gain.[43]

This implacability was also evident in Athanasios' unwillingness to compromise on military service for clerics. Such service was strictly forbidden by Byzantine canonical practice[44] and even occasioned an attack on the Latins by Anna Komnena on seeing the clergy-soldiers of the First Crusade parading past the walls of Constantinople.[45] However, in 1306, when the "warrior" monk Hilarion organized an army of peasants in Bithynia to fight the Turks, he was ordered to Constantinople to defend himself before Athanasios and the synod.[46] He was condemned and forbidden to return to Asia Minor. But the emperor, who needed all the assistance he could muster, gave in to the pleading of the inhabitants of the area and sent him back. Hilarion succeeded in temporarily securing Brusa and its environs. Yet Athanasios remained immovable on questions of the "purity" of churchmen, and no churchman was permitted to draw blood, even in defense of the God-chosen nation.

Athanasios' letter concerning the synodal decision against the priest-traitor John Drimys demonstrates the same theme. The Holy Synod had deposed and excommunicated Drimys for treason against Andronikos II. In attacking the Drimys conspiracy, he included the incongruent juxtaposition of the "stupid" claim one day to be a priest and the next a bearer of swords.[47] The priest was to be the perfect example of what the faithful were to be and was to "demonstrate like a mirror to the faithful what sort of life must be led by those who assert that they are devoted to the true and living and only God."[48] This was not, then, a double standard in the genuine sense but rather a paradigmatic standard, evident in the writings of such monastic activists as Sts. Basil the Great and John Chrysostom. The church was to be the seed for the new life, the new creation and Athanasios maintained this non-identification of the ecclesiastical ministers with the secular order. For all the intimacy of the *hierosyne* with the *basileia*, the church was indeed a separate institution.

## Athanasios and the Emperor

As indicated in the Introduction, personalities went far toward conditioning the nature of Byzantine church–state relationship. Athanasios' concern stemmed not from his sense of the value of the patriarchal office alone, or even from his aggressive nature, but largely from the leadership vacuum created by Andronikos. As the empire decayed morally, politically, and territorially, "the emperor acted as if he were asleep."[49] On the other hand, Athanasios continually expressed his horror at the situation of both the empire and the people, and at times uttered the wish that he was not alive to see the conditions.[50] Complaining to Andronikos that nothing was being done to correct the situation and that "universal lawlessness has, like an irresistible flame, enveloped all the Roman territory twice over; only you, after God, can stop this,"[51] he pursued the theme of right rulership, warning Andronikos that the emperors were "considered after God as gods by their countrymen."[52] A heavy burden to carry! He called for the restoration of the statist tradition of the Byzantine empire, a tradition that distinguished it from the apparent chaos in Western Europe.

Athanasios functioned in this advisory capacity both as patriarch and as spiritual father to the emperor. There was a sincere relationship of affection between the two men, and Athanasios, attempting to convince Andronikos to undertake certain measures, reminded him that there were few persons he could trust, few who were not self-serving flatterers: "you will not find anyone who loves you so much as I, who makes your joy his joy and your salvation his salvation, anyone who, so much as I, sympathizes with the troubles that beset you. . . ."[53] It is not certain, however, to what extent Andronikos acted on Athanasios' suggestions or reports.

Athanasios was too much of a realist to rely solely on the good will of the emperor to achieve his ends, and he played his role of "spiritual father" to the full. Asking Andronikos rhetorically what characteristic (καὶ "τί τοῦτο") is especially common to men who aspire to piety and virtue, he told him the characteristic is to refer everything in life, after God, to your spiritual father and "to converse more frequently with him than all other men."[54] Elsewhere he wrote to Andronikos that one of the essential virtues of good rulership demands that the emperor consult his spiritual father to whom is given "much paternal assurance and assistance and direction, which qualities accrue only to a truly spiritual [father], not to those who speak only to curry favor, and to lightly debase truth and righteousness for worldly motives."[55] In the context of the monastic tradition and Athanasios' extensive experience of that tradition, these demands for a "spiritual father" are less revolutionary than the reader might at first imagine.

Athanasios quite frankly affirmed that Andronikos, almost as a matter of faith, was compelled to follow his advice at all times.[56] Such a tradition of obligation to the confessor was not unknown in Byzantine spiritual tradition, but was more common among monastics where obedience to the *geron*, the elder, was often described as absolute.[57] According to St. John Climakos, obedience was the first virtue a monk had to learn.[58] The relationship of the spiritual father (ὁ πνεύματος πατήρ) and his "children" has long fascinated scholars of medieval and Byzantine history.[59] In fact, studies have indicated that members of the imperial family took advice from "holy men" who presumably possessed, by virtue of this relationship, political influence in the formulation of imperial policy. It is one of the elements in Byzantine history that has provided a virtually unpredictable variable in political and ecclesiastical affairs. The Byzantines were in love with the holy and, more specifically, the holy man.

Moreover, in the *Promissory Letter* Andronikos had already promised Athanasios obedience in his reform efforts. Indeed, both the emperor and the patriarch had an obligation, which Athanasios defined this way: "on the one hand, I should speak and compel and demand what is fitting for you, and, on the other, you ought constantly to show your abundant zeal to heed [me] and carry out [my suggestions]."[60] Athanasios almost represented an outright view of ecclesiastical superiority in every sphere of Byzantine life; here he did not limit his claims to the internal "freedom of the church."

What we see here is a statement of apolitical ecclesiology, formulated as a desperate effort to "force" Andronikos to act on the patriarch's suggestions and demands for justice and righteousness at a time when his influence was waning. In fact, we know that the relationship between the two men did not go as smoothly as Pachymeres recorded, or as Guilland believed,[61] or even as affectionately as Athanasios' assurances to Andronikos suggest. We know, for instance, that during his first patriarchate (1289–1293), Athanasios felt deserted by Andronikos, who was away in Anatolia on a military inspection. In Athanasios' second letter of resignation he complained bitterly that, especially during his first patriarchate, he "found no one to share my grief or to console me."[62] The same complaint was repeated during the latter part of his second patriarchate; it is certainly this perception, as selective as it may have been, that justified his initial demand for the so-called *Promissory Letter.* Many of Athanasios' complaints take on the tone of a melancholic mind rather than of reality. This melancholic sense of doom and helplessness was not atypical of reformers in general.

In several places Athanasios complained about not receiving a response from Andronikos. His letters and memoranda were not answered, and he went so far as to suggest that Andronikos was throwing them away.[63] In another place he noted that although Andronikos responded to some of his petitions, he left the important ones unanswered.[64] He lamented that even his messengers were unwilling to go to the emperor because they were not admitted for long periods of time, were met with silence, and were embarrassed waiting.[65]

In addition to not responding to his letters, the emperor refused to meet with him. On one occasion, Athanasios, filled with self-pity, wrote: "And why have I endured to go hither to you in the hope that I might have a chance to be heard properly by your divine majesty—even though I have never gained [such an appointment]—concerning the total destruction which has befallen the Roman people on account of our lawlessness . . . ?"[66]

Instead of gaining entrance to meet with the emperor and discuss the matters "face-to-face" (στόμα πρὸς στόμα), he was forced to use messengers, who, even if they were honest and trustworthy, should not know what was passing between the patriarch and the emperor "lest there seem to be disagreement between myself and your majesty."[67] Athanasios feared this use of intermediaries would imply a growing enmity that his enemies would seize upon to stir up more trouble for the activist patriarch. He goes on in the same letter, objecting to the use of messengers or intermediaries because of the sensitivity of the matters being dealt with and, again, because of the fear that their use would imply disharmony between the emperor and the patriarch.[68]

As a result of being able to meet with Andronikos only rarely, Athanasios took up occasional residence at the monastery of Chora, near the Blachernae Palace. But despite his physical proximity to the emperor, he was still not permitted an audience as often as he desired: "After spending six days at Chora, as on another occasion ten days, and another time seven or eight, taking no heed of my trouble or the hardships of winter because of my hopes, I returned empty-handed, my face filled with shame and embarrassment and tears."[69]

Athanasios seems to have established Chora as a home base as early as 1304–1305, when he called the bishops there before going on to a meeting with Andronikos at Blachernae.[70] Inasmuch as none, or at best only a few, of these letters of complaint can be dated, it is difficult to trace a degeneration of the amicable relationship that Pachymeres had described in 1303. It is, however, not difficult to imagine that the patriarch, with his incessant petitioning and his fierce sense of justice and righteousness, soon made himself a nuisance, like most prophets and reformers, to an emperor ill prepared to take any action on the innumerable problems that were tearing his empire to pieces.

Athanasios pathetically admitted that he was compelled to make numerous petitions: "Since I take pity on those who have fallen [into misfortune], I am compelled to make petitions especially about those problems that are beyond my power, but are easy, and indeed obligatory, for an emperor." This was the case in spite of the fact that he had managed to submit only a few cases out of thousands (ὅπως ἐκ τῶν μυρίων ὀλίγα προαγόμενοι ἀναφέρειν).[71] Still, he received no reply.

Athanasios' "interference" was an obligation, and this, he explained, was his reason for being angry: "philanthropy and mercy toward the needy are not a mere matter of choice, but rather a necessity and indispensable obligation. . . ."[72] Athanasios' put his predicament simply: "I can neither keep silent nor speak."[73] Thus he was forced, *a fortiori*, to scold Andronikos.

No doubt bewildered by the emperor's failure to respond to his requests, Athanasios assured Andronikos that he did not make these petitions out of self-interest, either before his patriarchate or during it; nor was he courting influence with Andronikos.[74] Finally, allowing for Andronikos' genuine discontent with him, Athanasios demanded that his petitions be answered, if not for his sake, then for the sake of the church; only then would God strengthen the Roman empire.[75] Athanasios, the prophetic reformer, could only consider it unfavorable when his petitions were not answered, for he believed himself to be acting out of the purest of motives, never for personal gain. As is true with reformers in general, Athanasios could not help but sense that a significant number of enemies were working against him around the throne; his paranoia and melancholia were well earned.

What must be admitted, as Athanasios in fact did several times, is that Andronikos was simply tired of the patriarch's endless petitions. Athanasios wrote, by way of justification, that if he had been troublesome to Andronikos, it was only for the emperor's glory: "If I petition in a shameless manner, it is for your glory in both [worlds]."[76] It is not difficult, especially given the lesson of the Old Testament prophets, to imagine that Andronikos found a "household" prophet, continually at his side, a bit annoying. In a letter to Andronikos sometime during the "years of trouble" in the early fourteenth century, Athanasios wrote with the inappropriate sense of guilt common to reformers: "on account of my transgressions your divine majesty does not manifest any zeal for actions which are good and clearly pleasing to God, and this at a time when we need the help of God as never before."[77]

Almost in desperation, Athanasios often blamed Andronikos for the evils that had come on the empire and persisted because of his inaction. Resorting to the Old Testament as prototype, Athanasios exhorted Andronikos to behave as Hezekiah: "the worthy king of the great city of Jerusalem clearly manifested his inner pain at the foolish babblings of Rhapsakes against the great God" (4 Kings 18–19).[78] The emperor is responsible for the empire; therefore, Athanasios concluded propositionally, the terrible warning would "revert to your divine majesty" (πρὸς τὴν ἐκ θεοῦ βασιλείαν σου).[79] He especially faulted Andronikos for not forcing the bishops back to their proper dioceses, and for believing "that it is tolerable for the flock of Christ to remain without shepherds, and to lie pitiably as easy prey for men and demons."[80]

Rhetorically Athanasios asked, "Who makes it his business to ensure that the church and the state are being governed in a manner pleasing to God?" His response was clear: the emperor was the legal authority, established by God to enforce what constitutes "good order" (εὐταξία). The patriarch's logic was prophetic and fearsome: the sufferings of the people and the decline of the Roman state were due to the evils—moral, political, social, and ecclesiastical—that Andronikos permitted.[81] Ultimately, it was up to Andronikos to correct the situation, and it was for this reason that God had made him emperor. As Bréhier has noted, the emperor was concerned not only with the purity of the faith, but also with the good order of the church—the canons, the hierarchy, and the administration.[82]

What is significant is the degree to which Athanasios chose to employ the theme of the commonwealth of church and empire as the new Israel. It was a means of compelling Andronikos' attention to his reports of injustice and his demands for reform. Israel was the archetypical pattern of Christian political existence that Athanasios consistently applied in his letters,[83] and many of his remarks were virtually direct from Jeremiah and Hosea, especially the latter's first six chapters. The immediacy of Israel as *type* is evident as is his syllogistic imperative—as to Israel, so to the Christian empire. Although Athanasios used Israel as archetype, he did not limit himself to it but drew on other scriptural examples. Nineveh was an alternate model of moral repentance (μετάνοια). When Jonah preached, the Ninevites listened (Jonah 3),[84] and Athanasios urged Andronikos to use the Ninevites and their king as an example of repentance.[85] The Ninevites had been convinced by a stranger, Jonah[86]—a fitting reference, especially because Jonah was a "type" (τύπος) of Christ. Nonetheless, Athanasios made no effort to portray Byzantium as a new Nineveh; it was used as an ad hoc model of repentance with no deeper theological significance.

Although Andronikos possessed a peculiarly religious personality that should have led him to act on Athanasios' requests, it is possible that he was simply unable to conform to the pattern of the ruler that Athanasios had in mind; certainly, Athanasios' complaints would lead us to believe that such was the case.

Andronikos' religious, even superstitious, nature is borne out by the sources. Pachymeres offers us an account of a series of earthquakes that did great damage. Andronikos took it as a sign of God's anger and searched seriously for a means to render himself pleasing to God. He determined that the only way to do this was to remove injustices and treat all his subjects equally, regardless of person, station, or gifts.[87]

Andronikos also gave much attention to ecclesiastical affairs, to the exclusion of foreign and domestic matters. It was almost as if he had consciously decided to seek support for his reign in one party within the empire—the church—and then follow through. At one point, Pachymeres informs us, the emperor was approached by a bishop who told him that he must be ready to give orders to the church. Andronikos immediately responded that it was not within his province to give directions to bishops.[88] With such a man on the throne it is not difficult to see why the power and influence of the church grew so significantly during his reign, especially with the right leadership on the patriarchal throne. Athanasios was certainly one of those ecclesiastics whose view of the importance of the church and the patriarchate in the affairs of society bordered on the Gregorian.

In spite of this determination, we find no laws or other regulations designed to bring this about; but Andronikos did establish a standard of justice and a court of twelve judges, including bishops, priests, and senators, who would under oath administer justice fairly.[89] Occasionally Andronikos seemed to hear Athanasios' appeals as well as "divine warnings," so it is strange indeed that he did not heed the warnings of his people's suffering. Pachymeres tells us that Andronikos listened to the patriarch in all things, but we actually have little proof that the emperor initiated any programs for which Athanasios called, with the exception of religious services.

Andronikos' essentially religious character is obvious from his concern for the care of churches, his participation in the liturgical life of the church, and his devotion to the Theotokos. First, with the return of the imperial government to Constantinople, the Byzantines discovered their city looted and largely in ruins.[90] The churches had suffered so greatly at the hands of the Latin occupiers that one of the chief goals of Emperors Michael VIII and Andronikos was the re-endowment of the churches and the monasteries, a sign and symbol of the strength and wealth of the empire. Athanasios urged Andronikos to be generous with the churches and not to allow harm to come to them. He urged him, for instance, not to permit secular buildings to be constructed too close to them.[91] Indeed, Athanasios confirmed, as does Pachymeres, that Andronikos devoted much of his resources to the churches. He praises

Andronikos not only for decorating the churches, but also for presenting gifts of vestments and liturgical utensils to bishops and the patriarch; he even refers to a particular set of vestments as "unique."[92]

Second, the emperor took part in all aspects of liturgical life, which was considerable during the Palaiologan period and part of the Byzantine theocratic phenomenon. In addition, there was a distinct increase in the religious character of court and ceremonial life. This is well illustrated in Athanasios' letters, which, urge the emperor to participate in processions and services. Indeed, there is no community without cult and ritual, and the Byzantines were as liturgical as they were theological—proverbially. Liturgical services increased under Athanasios; especially numerous were vigils and processions. Pachymeres records that Andronikos liked processions and even requested them.[93] Though Athanasios referred to Andronikos as the "lover of festivals and of God" (φιλεόρτω καὶ φιλοθέῳ),[94] in the light of the number of invitations he had to address to the emperor, this pious description may have been an overstatement!

Processions (λιταί) were a common feature of Byzantine life and were designed by Athanasios as a means of appeasing God and offsetting such dangers as earthquakes, which were particularly numerous at the time. Under Athanasios the number of processions of no particular description increased and may be regarded as characteristic of a time of troubles. Indeed, reform movements in the church often had liturgical corollaries. Athanasios increased liturgical activity, and this might be regarded as being at odds with his essentially prophetic character. The Old Testament prophets, however, attacked the rituals of the people only when they sensed that the people had forsaken the faith (Jer. 6:20; Hos. 6:6). Nevertheless, when the people despaired of the faith, the prophets called for a return to rituals.

Athanasios' approach was rather direct: the empire was in a state of desperation, "indicating to us the wrath of God,"[95] because of the sins of the people; the processions he prescribed were a means of demonstrating repentance. He wrote to Andronikos; "If you agree, let us go out with bare feet, especially the monks to hold a procession in contrition with holy icons."[96] He asked Andronikos to share these mortifications and demonstrate his repentance for the sins of the nation.

In addition to processions, Athanasios called on Andronikos to attend services such as those of the evening of Great Friday.[97] In another place, he urged the emperor to have everyone assemble for the Lamentations of Great Friday.[98] He complained to Andronikos that he was greatly vexed by the small attendance at services.[99] Athanasios treated such liturgical participation as a duty of all Orthodox Christians, and he wanted Andronikos to legislate it as essential to the covenantal relationship. All sources indicate that Andronikos himself eagerly participated in these liturgical activities.

Finally, according to Pachymeres, Andronikos showed particular devotion to the Theotokos, regarding her as the protector of the city and crediting her with putting down the treasonous attempts of Alexis Philanthropenos. In her hands, wrote Pachymeres, Andronikos placed his kingdom and the church.[100] Andronikos' devotion extended to declaring that the feast of the Dormition of the Theotokos would cover the entire month of August, rather than the fifteen days through August 15, the actual feast, and the eight-day postfeast denouement. The decree issued by Andronikos determined that the beginning of the feast, August 1, would be celebrated in the church of the Hodeghetria;[101] the actual feast day, August 15, in the Church of St. Sophia; and the end of the feast, on the last day of August, in the Church of the Theotokos at Blachernae.[102] The entire schema designated August, in effect, as a Marian month, a pious exercise that did not survive in the tradition of the Orthodox church, which continues to observe the older pattern of the fourteen-day fast, the celebration of the feast, and the eight-day postfeast, ending on August 23.[103]

Thus, the personalities of the central figures in this chain of events greatly affected their performances in the offices they occupied. Regardless of Athanasios' admittedly limited success in achieving his reform goals, he nonetheless tried to effect change in every aspect of Byzantine life. He was frustrated by the response of Emperor Andronikos, whose sense of urgency was only occasionally aroused to such a pitch that Athanasios' words resonated in his conscience. Any response was largely conditioned by his extreme sense of piety and superstition. Athanasios, on the other hand, appears in his relations with Andronikos as the proponent of the most extreme form of clerical control, albeit embodied personally in Athanasios as spiritual father, over secular power. It was this aggrandizement of the power of the patriarchate of Constantinople that was characteristic of the declining power of the Byzantine *imperium.*

## NOTES

1. Talbot, 61, line 5 (*Regestes*, 1704); see Talbot 104, lines 6–8 (*Regestes*, 1730) for the same theme.
2. V, 230r–232r (*Regestes*, 1589).
3. V, 272v–274r (Γράμμα Ὑποσχετικόν) "Promissory Letter of the Holy Emperor Composed by Him at the Request of the Patriarch, in order that the Patriarch Take His See a Second Time" (V, 272v), edited in Vitalien Laurent's "Serment," 138–39.
4. Laurent, "Serment," 137, lines 46–49.
5. Ibid., 136, lines 34–39: "Ταύτην ὁμολογῶ οὐ μόνον ἀκαταδούλωτον πάντη καὶ ἐλευθέραν διατηρεῖν, ἀλλὰ καὶ ὑποταγὴν πληρεῖν δουλικὴν πρὸς αὐτὴν καὶ ὑποκεῖσθαι αὐτῇ παντὶ νομίμῳ θεαρέστῳ θελήματι καὶ πρὸ τῆς αὐτης προκοπῆς καὶ ἀσφαλείας καὶ ἐπιδόσεως οὐ παίδων, οὐ γυναικός, οὐ φιλίας, οὐ συγγενείας, οὐ πλούτου, οὐ τοῦ ὕψους τῆς βασιλείας αὐτῆς προτιμότερον κρίνω."
6. Ibid., 136–37, lines 39–43.
7. Ibid., 137, lines 45–50.
8. Ibid., 137, lines 55–69.
9. Ibid., 137–38. lines 70–72. See Boojamra, "Constantine and Justinian," 192–94.
10. Pachymeres, 518.
11. Talbot, 82, lines 80–81 (*Regestes*, 1717); Talbot 110, line 29 (*Regestes*, 1735). See Eusebios, "Vita Constantini," pp. 10–11, 492.
12. Talbot, 61, lines 5–9 (*Regestes*, 1704). This idea permeates Athanasios' thinking and borders on Byzantine papism.
13. Pachymeres, 616; see also 579–80.
14. V, 63r–63v (*Regestes*, 1716).
15. Talbot, 57, lines 7–8 (*Regestes*, 1701). He is most likely here referring to local agents who were trying to seize ecclesiastical property.
16. V, 63v (*Regestes*, 1716); the text appears in Gennadius (Arambatzoglou), Ἱστορία τοῦ Οἰκουμενικοῦ Πατριαρχείου (Athens, 1953), p. 309; Gennadius mistakenly notes that ἀρχῇ in the text below refers to the emperor; it most probably refers to civil ruler: "τῇ τοῦ κόσμου μὴ ἀρκεσθέντες ἀρχῇ κἀν τοῖς θείοις τῆς ἐκκλησίας χεῖρα ἐπέβαλον, οὐχ ὡς δέον, ἀλλ' ὡς αὐτοῖς ἐφετὸν λογισμοῖς ἀνθρωπίνοις καὶ ὧν οὐ δεῖ κατάρχειν ἐπέβησαν. . . ."
17. Talbot, 104, lines 11–12 (*Regestes*, 1730).
18. V, 20v (*Regestes*, 1692).
19. V, 64v (*Regestes*, 1716). See also Dan. 3:1–57.

20. V, 62[r] (*Regestes* 1716); "τῆς δὲ δευτέρας προσνεμηθείσης εἰς ἀσφάλειαν τῆς προτέρας καὶ συντήρησιν καὶ ἐπίδοσιν τῶν καλῶν."

21. Talbot 104, lines 25–28 (*Regestes*, 1730): "οὐ γὰρ διὰ τὴν βασιλείαν ἡ ἱερωσύνη ἀπεχαρίσθη τῷ Χριστωνύμῳ λαῷ, ἀλλὰ διὰ τὴν ἱερωσύνην ἡ βασιλεία, ἵνα πρὸς τὸ ἀρέσκον Θεῷ τῇ ἔξω χειρὶ κρατύνουσα ταύτην [the Church] καὶ περιέπουσα καὶ συνιστῶσα, ἀντικρατύνηται πάλιν αὐτὴ καὶ συνίσταται αὐξομένη ὑπο Θεοῦ." My translation of this passage differs from Talbot's.

22. Talbot, 61, lines 48–54 (*Regestes*, 1704); Athanasios is referring here to the bishops as true shepherds, not as "enemies of the cross," which many of them were described as being.

23. Talbot, 61, lines 41–45 (*Regestes*, 1704).

24. Talbot, 13, lines 5–9 (*Regestes*, 1610). See also Talbot 36, lines 16–20 (*Regestes*, 1639), where he mentions the sins of Israel on a one-to-one basis with the sins of the Byzantines as the source of their respective destruction.

25. V, 62[r]–62[v] (*Regestes*, 1716); for the text, see also Gennadios, "Ἐπιστολιμαία διδασκαλία τοῦ οἰκουμενικοῦ πατριάρχου Ἀθανασίου Α′ πρὸς τὸν αὐτοκράτορα Ἀνδρόνικον Β′," *Orthodoxia* 27 (1952), 137–79.

26. See Warren Treadgold, "The Revival of Byzantine Learning and the Revival of the Byzantine State," *The American Historical Review* 84 (December 1979), 1264. See also, Bréhier, *Institutions*, pp. 349–50.

27. Talbot, 37, lines 16–27 (*Regestes*, Appendix 7).

28. Talbot, 69, lines 182–85 (*Regestes*, 1614). Inasmuch as this letter was written in 1303, Athanasios still had significant influence over Andronikos, especially in his self-assumed role of seer or prophet.

29. Talbot, 83, lines 9–35 (*Regestes*, 1718); see Canon 49 of the Council in Trullo (Rhalles and Potles, II:423) for one example of the prohibition of the alienation of monastic property.

30. Talbot, 25, line 6 (*Regestes*, 1613).

31. See George Ostrogorsky, "Pour l'histoire de l'immunité à Byzance," *B*, 28 (1958), 165–254, for a description of these attempts.

32. Pachymeres, 390. "There were no troops to meet the enemy. The army was not only weak, but the soldiers, abandoning their holdings [*pronoiai*], turned to the West, trying only to save their lives."

33. Talbot, 83, lines 53–56 (*Regestes*, 1718).

34. Pachymeres, 208–209.

35. Pachymeres, 258.

36. Pachymeres, 390–91. For differing interpretations of the meaning of Andronikos' project, see Peter Charanis, "Monastic Properties and the State in the Byzantine Empire," *DOP*, 4 (1948), 56–58, who suggests that the passage involves monks defending their own properties; and Elizabeth Fisher, "A Note on Pachymeres' 'De Andronico Palaeologo,'" *B*, 60

(1971), 232. I cannot believe that a Byzantine emperor would call on monks to fight, even in self-defense.

37. For previous examples, see Ševčenko, "Cabasilas," 154, and Charanis, "Properties," 69–72.

38. Pachymeres, II:390.

39. Pachymeres, II:390–91.

40. Miklosich and Müller, I:507–508. Philotheos did point out that the emperor could take the villages he requested on his own authority: he had given them to the church. The use of ecclesiastical goods and property for the purposes of raising an army was not unknown in Byzantine church history. See, for instance, Franz Dölger, *Regesten der kaiserurkunden des oströmischen Reiches*, 4 vols. (Berlin: Beck, 1960), I:165, under Heraclios in the seventh century, and II:1085, under Alexios Komnenos. See also F. Chalandon, *Essai sur la règne d'Alexis Comnène* (Paris: Picard, 1900), pp. 80–81, 120.

41. V, 139r (*Regestes*, 1747). He refers to Canons 3 and 7 of Chalcedon (Rhalles and Potles, II:230, 232) which anathematize any priest who engages in administrative or military functions. In spite of this, Theodore Balsamon, the late twelfth-century canonist and patriarch of Antioch (1186), commenting on the fifth-century Canon of Carthage, concluded that the emperor could dispense clergy to exercise civil functions (εἰς κοσμικὰς ἐνεργείας); see Balsamon's commentary on Canon 16 of Carthage (Rhalles and Potles, III:344).

42. V, 139v (*Regestes*, 1747).

43. V, 211r–v (*Regestes*, 1761); the same appears in V, 209v–210r (*Regestes*, 1765).

44. See Canon 7 of Chalcedon (Rhalles and Potles, II:232) and Canon 83 of Apostolic Canons (Rhalles and Potles, II:107). The idea of holy wars was all but absent in Byzantium, and Athanasios reserves the expression πόλεμος ἱερός for the struggle against social injustice; see Talbot 12, lines 32–34 (*Regestes*, 1676). On the dual standard for clergy and monastics in Byzantine spirituality and canon law, see chap. 4 below.

45. Vitalien Laurent, "L'Idée de guerre sainte et la tradition byzantine," *Revue Historique du Sud-Est européen*, 23 (1946), 71–98. On the Byzantine sense of horror when faced with arms-bearing clergy, see Anna Komnena on the Latins of the first crusade: "For the rules concerning priests are not the same among Latins as they are with us [the Byzantines]. For we are given the command by canonical laws and the teaching of the Gospel, 'Touch not, taste not, handle not! For thou art consecrated.' Whereas the Latin barbarian will simultaneously handle divine things, and wear his shield on his left arm, and hold his spear in his right hand and . . . he communicates the body and blood of God, and looks murderously and becomes 'a man of blood.' " Anna Comnena, *The Alexiad*, 10.8, trans.

Elizabeth Dawes (London: Routledge & Kegan Paul, 1928; repr. 1967), pp. 256–59. In fact, although there were specific and clear prohibitions against the bearing of arms by priests in the Latin West, they were ignored in practice.

46. Pachymeres, 596. To the very end of the empire, the Byzantines maintained the prohibition against clergy and monastics taking up arms. In 1168, for instance, a synodal sentence (*Regestes*, 1078) suspended and deposed a priest for shedding human blood. See Canon 10 of I Nicea (Rhalles and Potles II:587–88) and Canon 7 of Chalcedon (Rhalles and Potles, II:232). The latter canon excommunicates, rather than deposes, a priest so involved because, as Balsamon and Zonaras explained, it deals with clergy who had already yielded their clerical office; therefore, no double punishment was involved (Rhalles and Potles, II:232–33).

47. Talbot, 81, lines 46–53 (*Regestes*, 1636).

48. Talbot, 81, lines 19–23 (*Regestes*, 1636).

49. Pachymeres, II:412.

50. Talbot, 15, lines 19–23 (*Regestes*, 1611).

51. Talbot, 49, lines 14–15 (*Regestes*, 1695): "τῆς γὰρ κοινῆς ἀνομίας ἀνυποίστου δίκην φλογός, τήν ὅση ὑπὸ Ῥωμαίους δραττομένης διττῶς."

52. Talbot, 92, lines 30–31 (*Regestes*, 1724): "τὸ μετὰ θεὸν ὁραθῆναι τῷ ὁμοφύλῳ θεούς."

53. Talbot, 59, lines 26–31 (*Regestes*, 1703).

54. Talbot, 92, lines 14–18 (*Regestes*, 1724).

55. Talbot, 92, lines 31–34 (*Regestes*, 1724).

56. Talbot, 92, lines 7–11 (*Regestes*, 1724). This letter dates from the latter part of Athanasios' second reign; he may here have been desperately trying to regain control over the emperor.

57. St. Basil, *Regulae brevius tractatae*, in PG, 31:1161. See also John Klimakos, *The Ladder of Divine Ascent*, trans. L. Moore (London: Harper, 1959), p. 69.

58. *Ladder of Divine Ascent*, p. 69.

59. Rosemary Morris, "The Political Saint of the Eleventh Century," in *The Byzantine Saint*, ed. Sergei Hackel (London: Fellowship of St. Alban and St. Sergius, 1982), p. 46. I. Hausherr, "Direction spirituelle en Orient autrefois," *Orientalia Christiana Periodica*, 31 (1955), 144. It is not unusual that a spiritual father was also patriarch. For spiritual fathers in this period, see Salaville, "Lettre," 101–15; and Vitalien Laurent, "La Direction spirituelle des grandes dames de Byzance," *REB*, 8 (1950), 64–84.

60. Talbot, 92, lines 7–11 (*Regestes*, 1724): "τὸ μὲν λέγειν ἡμᾶς καὶ βιάζειν καὶ ἀξιοῦν ἁρμόζον ὑμῖν, τὸ ὑπακούειν δὲ καὶ πληροῦν διηνεκὴς αὐτῇ καὶ πλοῦτος καὶ σπούδασμα. . . ."

61. Guilland, "Correspondance," p. 160.

62. Talbot, 115, lines 136–41 (*Regestes*, Appendix 11).

63. Talbot, 49, lines 106–107 (*Regestes*, 1695).
64. Talbot, 80, lines 28–32 (*Regestes*, 1715).
65. Talbot, 99, lines 15–19 (*Regestes*, 1726).
66. Talbot, 14, lines 11–18 (*Regestes*, 1677); see also Bănescu, "Athanase," 28–56, and Laurent, "Serment," 129.
67. Talbot, 24, lines 7–11 (*Regestes*, 1623).
68. Talbot, 24, lines 7–11 (*Regestes*, 1623).
69. Talbot, 14, lines 39–45 (*Regestes*, 1677).
70. Talbot, 23, lines 12–13 (*Regestes*, 1621). The monastery of Chora is identified with the Kariye Djami, which was restored in the early part of the fourteenth century by Theodore Metochites. The monastery church still exists today, and considerable attention has been given to its study and restoration; see Paul A. Underwood, *The Kariye Djami* I (New York: Pantheon, 1966), p. 3. On Chora, see also Raymond Janin, *La Gêographie ecclêsiastique de l'empire byzantin.* III. *Les Églises et les monastères* (Paris: Institut français d'Études byzantines, 1964), Part I, pp. 537, 545–53.
71. Talbot, 99, lines 11–14 (*Regestes*, 1726).
72. Talbot, 99, lines 18–22 (*Regestes*, 1726).
73. Talbot, 99, lines 23–24 (*Regestes*, 1726).
74. Talbot, 58, lines 7–11 (*Regestes*, 1702).
75. Talbot, 60, lines 55–60 (*Regestes*, 1654).
76. Talbot, 58, lines 27–31 (*Regestes*, 1702).
77. Talbot, 7, lines 18–22 (*Regestes*, 1597). One author comments: "Saints who are larger than life belong to folklore, not the real world. . . . A dead holy man, whose holiness can be verified according to objective criteria, is preferable to a live one, whose eccentricities only confuse the issue" (Paul Magdalino, "The Byzantine Holy Man in the Twelfth Century," in *The Byzantine Saint*, ed. Sergei Hackel [London: Fellowship of St. Alban and St. Sergius, 1982], p. 60.
79. Talbot, 15, lines 20–24 (*Regestes*, 1611).
80. Talbot, 49, lines 56–60 (*Regestes*, 1695).
81. Talbot, 49, lines 96–100 (*Regestes*, 1695); see *Epanagoge*, 1.1, in Zepos and Zepos, p. 242.
82. *Institutions*, p. 349. At the beginning of the thirteenth century, the canonist Demetrios Chomatianos, archbishop of Bulgaria, reiterated the common belief that imperial power was absolute and could innovate and intervene in ecclesiastical administration. See Zepos and Zepos, V, Responsio 2. See also Gasquet, *Authorité*, p. 119.
83. This issue is raised in Steven Bowman "Two Late Byzantine Dialogues with the Jews," *Greek Orthodox Theological Review*, 25 (Spring, 1980), 83–93. The Byzantine Orthodox rationalization of the events of 1453 closely paralleled the Jews' reactions to Titus' victory in A.D. 70.

84. Talbot, 3, lines 25–29 (*Regestes*, 1673). On the use of Jonah in a reform age, see Michael McGiffert, "God's Controversy with Jacobean England," *The American Historical Review*, 88 (December 1983), 1153.

85. Talbot, 49, lines 111–15 (*Regestes*, 1695). See also Talbot, 3, lines 39–43 (*Regestes*, 1673).

86. Talbot, 70, lines 2–5 (*Regestes*, 1710).

87. Pachymeres, 235.

88. Pachymeres, 159.

89. Pachymeres, 236–37. A few days later, Andronikos issued a chrysobull; see Boissonade, *Anecdota Graeca* II, pp. 85–86.

90. A. Heisenberg, *Aus der Geschichte und Literatur der Palaiologenzeit* (Munich: Bayerische Akademie der Wissenschaften, 1920), p. 85; Nicol, *Last Centuries*, p. 46.

91. Talbot, 66, lines 68–73 (*Regestes*, 1709).

92. Talbot, 66, lines 46–50 (*Regestes*, 1709). For a new type of Byzantine embroidery to which Athanasios may have been referring, see Talbot's commentary, p. 377.

93. Pachymeres, 420–21.

94. Talbot, 71, lines 9–14 (*Regestes*, 1711). Laurent in *Regestes* lists two letters (1711 and 1653) as corresponding to Talbot's 71; actually only 1711 corresponds to Talbot's text.

95. Talbot, 70, lines 7–11 (*Regestes*, 1710); see for discussion Guilland, "Correspondance," p. 137.

96. Talbot, 70, lines 13–17 (*Regestes*, 1710).

97. Talbot, 71, lines 10–14 (*Regestes*, 1711).

98. Talbot, 52, entire letter (*Regestes*, 1697). See also Talbot, 53, lines 19–23 (*Regestes*, 1698).

99. Talbot, 54, lines 19–23 (*Regestes*, 1699).

100. Pachymeres, 231, 255.

101. See Janin, *Géographie*, 208–16. The church of the Theotokos Hodeghetria was very popular among the Palaiologan house and Michael VIII carried the icon of the Hodeghetria at the head of his triumphal entry to Constantinople on August 15, 1261. See Pachymeres, 160.

102. The very significant Novel 39 is contained in the works of Nikephoros Choumnos in Boissonade, *Anecdota Graeca* II, pp. 107–37; as well as in Zepos and Zepos, p. 568–79, and PG, 161:1095–1108. The decree was probably addressed to Choumnos as mesazon. Dölger, *Regesten*, No. 1296, dates it to July or August 1296. For extensive discussion of the act, see V. Grumel, "Le Mois de Marie des Byzantins," *EO*, 31 (1932), 257–69. Grumel dates the act somewhere between 1294 and 1309.

103. See K. A. Heinrich Kellner, *Heortology* (London: Paul, Trench, Trubner, 1908), p. 227.

# 4

# Foundations of Athanasios' Reforms

AS SOON AS ATHANASIOS BECAME PATRIARCH, he directly attacked everything he regarded as contrary to Christian ethics and good order, εὐταξία. In fact, ἀταξία, disorder, was for him the source of the Byzantine dilemma.[1] Theoktistos, one of his two biographers, wrote that Athanasios assumed responsibility for "the church which had been put to laziness for a long time and lay fallow due to anarchy; he first, with rigor, tamed the morals of the people."[2] Athanasios' letters offer a picture of the social and ecclesiastical decay that, until their discovery, was known only through passing references made by narrative historians or from the detached observations of such aristocratic social observers as Nikephoros Choumnos and Nicholas Kabasilas. In addition to his efforts at moral and ecclesiastical reform, Athanasios eagerly tried to set the pattern for social justice, philanthropy, and political reorganization. Every day, wrote Kalothetos his biographer, Athanasios taught, educated, and protected the poor, widows, and orphans; he reintroduced laws on marriage and celibacy and worked for justice.[3] He was not, as Pachymeres pointed out, a man of patience or subtlety.

Athanasios was not simply a moralist making tiresome, pious, and melancholic exhortations, but a man who saw a threat to the church and the empire. It is this vision that marks him as a genuine reformer. He noted in one of his letters, "The Christian empire is being destroyed in two ways, from without by enemies, and from within by excessive injustice and depravity."[4] Athanasios believed himself to be the spiritual and moral guardian of Byzantine Christian society, and, like all reformers, felt a personal responsibility for a good deal of the social and political faults of the empire. The function of the monk from the social perspective was to work for the well-being of God's people, through prayer and service. For the monk-patriarch Athanasios, the struggle consisted of rebuilding Byzantine society on the pattern of (*a*) the monastic ideals of social mutuality of the cenobitic community, (*b*) the demands of the "first" sacrament (baptism), and (*c*) the ever-present reality of the Old Testament categories of obedience and punishment. Such had been the goal of Sts. Basil the Great and John Chrysostom. Only within the context of this cenobitic intention and the tradition rooted in baptism and viewed through Old Testament typology can Athanasios' programs be understood. In addition to the political basis of reform—the intimate association between *basileia* and *hierosyne*, and ecclesiological freedom of the church—Athanasios' writing exhibits a spiritual foundation, mutualism, regeneration in baptism, and the warning of the Old Testament prophets.

## The Monastic Impulse

Athanasios was not only a recognized master of the monastic life (βίος θεωρητικός), but also one of the outstanding moralists and ethical thinkers (βίος πρακτικός) of the Byzantine Church; one of his limitations, apart from his universally recognized harshness of personality, was the lack of a systematic approach in his teaching or a plan of action. The object of this book is to illustrate from Athanasios' correspondence that he was a mature, albeit unsystematic, ethical thinker with deep roots in both the scriptures and the traditions of the Byzantine Orthodox Church, and to provide some system to his thinking and his programs.[5] He represents—as indeed did Basil the Great, the first bishop to unite episcopacy and monasticism in one social mission—that salient Byzantine thrust from the ascetic/monastic to the social activist/church politician.[6] In spite of claims to the contrary, monasticism, both Eastern and Western, is intimately associated in principle with the idea and practice of reform. Ladner, in fact, focuses on monasticism as one of the roots of early church reform.[7] In the early Christian centuries, monasticism was the principal means of realizing the idea of reform in the church and in society. Such was the case with Basil of Caesarea, the father of Eastern cenobitic monasticism, who, rooted in the more generalized reform ideals current in Asia Minor, expressed the evangelic-apostolic life of the Acts of the Apostles in his monastic rule.[8] Is this some sort of religious schizophrenia? Was the mystical life opposed to social involvement? Not at all; it was quite logical for Athanasios to use monastic self-abnegation as the basis for service to others and involvement in the political affairs of the empire.

The origins of Christian monasticism, in fact, coincide with the church's confrontation with new secular tasks and dangers. This was possible because the church had become a power in both the material and the spiritual arenas. From the beginning of monasticism those who followed the monastic life "were the principal agents of reform in the Christian world."[9]

It is unfortunate that many historians dismiss Athanasios' reform efforts precisely because they were motivated by an ascetic-rigorist tradition of Byzantine monasticism and as such did not adequately take into account the facts of history. His reforms did not last, having been largely abortive efforts to redirect the movement of an entire empire away from what now appears to have been a sickness unto death. The immediate success or failure of his measures, however, must not be the issue; we must of necessity judge Athanasios and his work by what he intended to accomplish, what insight he brought to the problems afflicting the Byzantine Church and empire, and what influence he had on later ecclesiastical developments.

It has rightly been observed that few Byzantines had dealt with the problem of the eremetical or "theoretical" life in light of the reality that every Christian had to face. In the post-patristic age Byzantines gave little attention to ethical thinking. Theological affirmations and clarifications remained largely the fare of the day, with no real effort on the part of theologians to relate these fruitfully to the active life of the Orthodox population. This is not to say, however, that ethical thinking was completely absent in either a formal or an informal sense. Certainly it was present during this period—the turn of the fourteenth century—and Athanasios is an outstanding witness to it. Nevertheless, I maintain that Athanasios' monastic tradition was the impetus for his political and social reforms. They were based on the sense of mutualism that characterized the monastic cenobium, communal life, which from the time of Sts. Basil and Pachomios came to characterize the essence of Byzantine monasticism.[10]

It is significant that in Athanasios' sense of reform, in this striving for social and cenobitic mutuality, he was the precursor of hesychasm. Ladner's study has shown that the image/likeness parallel and dichotomy of Genesis 1:26 is at the roots of patristic reform. The distinction is also the basis of Byzantine monastic spirituality, particularly that of the Alexandrian fathers. For Gregory of Nyssa, reform on earth is the return to a spiritual paradise and the recovery of the likeness to God. In fact, this recovery, for Ladner, is the most thoroughgoing reform because it amounts to the process of deification (ϑέωσις). It was also, although he does not demonstrate this, a basis of social reform: "It would be quite wrong to assume that the idea was so highly individualistic that it could not or did not influence civilization."[11]

In a letter urging the emperor to compel good deeds and thus properly govern the empire, Athanasios wrote: "For, if we lived in this way, it was hoped that 'when Christ, Who is our life, shall appear, then shall ye also appear with Him in glory.' Blessed be this deification [ϑέωσις]. I pray that we may not fail to attain it; nor from now on let us prefer shameful action."[12]

The association between a mimetic pattern and reform in the Christian church has not been missed. Karl Morrison has noted: "the strategy of mimesis demanded reform, not as a single act, but as a continual process, since a symmetry between idea and actuality could never be resolved into equivalence."[13]

But the Christian reformation of humankind in the image of God far transcended a mimetic referral to a mythical golden age. Athanasios makes no such reference to paradise. The mimetic tradition, in the Byzantine eucharistic liturgy, as reflected in the image/likeness distinction of Genesis 1:26, had both a past and a future orientation.[14] Reform was for Athanasios a future-directed process of deification implied in the fortuitous application of the word ὁμοίωσις.[15] It was not merely a *return* to the *image* of God, to a paradisaic state of social harmony and justice, but a growth into the likeness of God, the creator and sustainer. Reform for Athanasios is more than a mimetic movement in which reality seeks to copy an eternal pattern or return to a primordial purity; it is rather a movement forward which seeks to share in the heavenly kingdom. It is this latter definition of reform that enables me to associate Athanasios' reforms with Palamite spirituality. Athanasios' hagiographer, Theoktistos the Studite, in his "Oration on the Translation" of his relics, refers to Athanasios' reforms as μίμησις πραγματεύεται.[16]

One of the remarkable features of this period is that even during what has been described as a decline in the political capacity of the empire and the growth of the influence of the monastic element, Byzantium manifested a socio-ethical renaissance, closely associated with the rise of Palamite hesychasm. One author has commented that "un examen attentif de ses institutions m'a persuadé que ce conservatisme est toujours doublé d'une lente révolution."[17] It would seem that Byzantium was immune to a sudden death. Thus, at the turn of the fourteenth century and well thereafter, we detect the development of social literature as well as a spiritual-ascetic renaissance, which was to reach its brilliance in the theology of the hesychast fathers of the fourteenth century.[18]

St. John Chrysostom, to whom Athanasios has often been likened,[19] tried to rebuild and reorder the Christian society of Antioch and Constantinople on the basis of the commonality of the apostolic-evangelic way of life. Ernst Troeltsch has noted that it was John Chrysostom's goal to turn Antioch and Constantinople into "a communistic fellowship of love like the monastic life."[20] Specifically, John sought to extend the monastic community of possession to Christian society at large. For John, all Christians had the same obligations as monks. They did not have to retreat to the wilderness to be Christians. He applied the apostolic pattern from Acts to monks and then to everyone. If everyone lived this way, the *oikoumene* would be converted without any need for miracles. Basil took the same approach, applying the principles of the monastic *cenobium* to the church at large and to Christian society.[21] In monasticism, Basil and John had found an agency of reform according to the image of God. Athanasios sought the same foundations as Sts. Basil and John: there was to be a single standard for monks and seculars alike. All this showed itself in the demand for an ordered existence in both society and the church.

It is in this social and political outreach that we see Basil of Caesarea (379) as a direct ideological antecedent. His conceptions of Christ's double commandment to love God and neighbor as self (Matt. 22:37–39) and the human person as "active agent" are the foundation for his conception of monastic life as fundamentally cenobitic; praise of God and service to one's brothers and sisters are, almost paradoxically, a twofold aspect of glorifying God. This patristic affirmation, so powerful in St. Basil of Caesarea, of the person as active agent and social being is the basis for the continuing and creative tension in the corporate life of the Byzantine Church between the internal and the external, between the church and the world, between *theoria* and *praxis.* It is in Basil's "Detailed Rules" that Athanasios read the poignant words, "Whose feet will you wash? For whom will you care? If you live by yourself to whom will you come last?"[22] Although there are few explicit references to Basil in any of Athanasios' letters, it is impossible to imagine that a monk of Athanasios' stature was not familiar with Basil's rules. In fact, his monastic rule closely paralleled Basil's.[23]

Constantelos has noted the intimate association between the mystical life and social involvement for one of Athanasios' contemporaries, Theoleptos, Metropolitan of Philadelphia (ca. 1250–1324/25), who successfully led the defense of his city against the Ottoman Turks (1304–1305). Theoleptos had the same background, spiritual training, and activist mentality as Athanasios, and he paralleled in many ways in Philadelphia what Athanasios was doing in Constantinople. During the siege of his city, Theoleptos organized communal meals, serving as cook, baker, and waiter.[24]

Not altruism but a sense of monastic solidarity inspired Athanasios, and without this dynamic notion of social mutualism and dynamic Christian personhood, his concerns for human suffering would have been no more than the aristocratic condescension or bourgeois altruism that characterized most of his contemporaries. Were it not for Athanasios' monastic and specifically cenobitic commitment, he would indeed have been merely a "deflector" of social tensions.

Matschke develops an interesting thesis, although from a Marxist perspective, that Athanasios' social reforms played the reactionary role of maintaining a failing Byzantine social structure.[25] Although Athanasios may have played an important role in heading off social upheaval, Matschke does not give credit to the patriarch's genuine compassion for the people of Constantinople, or adequately take into account the fundamental inertia of the Byzantine social system. From a Marxist perspective, Athanasios failed in his reforms because he did not use "creatively" the instability of the period to bring about the birth of a new social order. Yet Athanasios was concerned, not with social revolution, but with meeting immediate and individual needs. Matschke makes a rather clumsy distinction between Athanasios' sympathy for the "suffering masses" and his sympathy for the "struggling masses." According to him, Athanasios sought to ameliorate the suffering of the people by preaching, moralizing, threatening, and, finally, taking action, but his failure to identify with the radical aspects of the unrest rendered his reforms a failure.[26]

Athanasios saw a return to the monastic ideal of mutuality as the only salvation for the church and the empire; in fact, the concept and practice of mutuality offers a congruent rationale for his social thought and programs. Athanasios was fundamentally a reformer, and his reforms had their origin in the monastic *cenobium.* There is no hint in his letters of the type of revolutionary calls common in the Latin West of the period; no idealization of poverty or blanket condemnation of wealth; no cry for a coercive redistribution of the "goods of the earth." There are no Dolcinians and no *fraticelli.* Athanasios as an ascetic reformer provides a striking contrast to the revolutionary spiritual movements being spawned in the West in opposition to the decadent Avignonese papacy.[27]

Like Basil and John Chrysostom before him, Athanasios saw restructuring the empire on a monastic basis as the goal of his reforms. Indeed, he would have liked to turn the empire into a monastery. Pachymeres, for instance, reported that many of the clergy, especially those of St. Sophia, were anxious lest Athanasios force them to follow his severe monastic lifestyle.[28] Athanasios was troubled by the conduct of the priests of the cathedral, who, he claimed, did not fulfill their responsibility, and his conflict with them eventually reached the point that they went on strike when he withheld their salaries.[29] They wrote a letter in answer to the patriarch's accusations and asked that it be read in the synod of abbots where his attack had been made.[30] The priests charged that Athanasios had created his own regulations and wanted them to live like monks, a demand, they said, that would require them to close the churches to the people and give up their families. Monks, they claimed, had no practical cares to keep them from their liturgical services.[31] Athanasios probably wanted the secular priests merely to pattern their personal as well as liturgical lives after the monastic *cenobium*, creating out of the clergy of St. Sophia a type of semi-monastic brotherhood; it is difficult to imagine that he wanted them to put their families aside. There was, however, no tradition of *vita communis* for the secular clergy in the East as there had been in the West from the time of Augustine.[32]

There is a tendency in every reform "movement" to surround itself with a fringe of the uncontrollable and unreasonable.[33] Unlike early American religious reformers, there was no evidence that Athanasios held the naïve view that the mere exposition of problems and evils coupled with an appeal to innate goodness would be sufficient to bring out correction. Athanasios, no fool, was well aware of the limiting effects of human sin. From the start, according to Pachymeres, Athanasios was surrounded by a group of monks who "came from nobody knows where" and installed themselves around him.[34] Sharing his concerns, these monks formed a type of inquisitional body and instituted a reign of terror over their brother monks, who, they decided, were living contrary to monastic simplicity. Pachymeres, angered by these activities, compared this body of monks to a scorpion that leaves its habitat and stings everyone in its path.[35]

This band of zealots reproached other monks for the money they spent, for having new habits, for owning two or three tunics, for wearing crosses of gold or silver, for taking two meals a day during Lent, and for going to doctors when they were sick. Often these attacks were more than verbal reproaches; these zealots physically assaulted wrongdoers, arrested some, and confined others in prisons with no chance of reprieve.[36] Pachymeres was quick to report that it was the monk Sabbas, who did nothing without the consent of Patriarch Athanasios and unofficially acted as his agent, who attacked all sorts of "imagined" evils. After visiting certain monasteries, Sabbas withdrew revenues from them and condemned their inhabitants for their "crimes," presumably a reference to their wealth. The officials of these houses, who in some cases were bishops who had been granted them as a residence or as a subsidy, were outraged by the loss of income as well as by the implicit judgment on their manner of life.[37]

Athanasios demanded that the monks sever their attachments to family and friends, and especially to wealth. In an encyclical addressed to all the monks and nuns throughout the empire, he wrote that they were to practice poverty, live in humility, renounce all pleasure and self-will, and forgo all relationships of friendship and family in order to keep company only with Christ.[38] He attacked those monks who "only cut their hair without at the same time renouncing carnal passions or the will."[39] He was not, however, contemptuous of the secular world; in his writings, there was no millennial call for an escape to the desert. Athanasios stated quite explicitly that the monastic state was in no way superior to other Christian states, and was in fact second in dignity to that of baptism, which all Orthodox enjoy.[40] Therefore, the call to sever all social ties in no way exempted the monks from performing charitable acts or from sharing their often considerable wealth with the needy in "the world outside." In one letter addressed to an abbot, Athanasios wrote that the obligation of the monks to eat no more than once a day would save enough food and money to feed and care for a substantial number of poor persons in Constantinople.[41]

Athanasios was aware of the special needs of the laboring brothers and allowed them to take bread and water at the sixth hour during the time of sowing and to double the ration during the summer heat. He warned the brothers enjoying this to keep in mind that a little suffering was the source of great joy.[42] In spite of such attention to the daily life of these laboring monks, Athanasios' letters do not speak about the monasteries as working communities. This aspect of Byzantine monasticism was fundamental and was "by no means a secondary or even subsidiary element,"[43] according to Florovsky. Work was necessary, not only because idleness was a source of evil, but also because work provided for the needs of the monastery and of others. According to St. Basil, "in labor the purpose set before everyone is the support of the needy, not one's own necessity."[44] Such an idea, although not explicit in Athanasios, certainly comes close to his programs of social and political reform and his attention to the needs of the working brothers.

Athanasios felt that the reordering of monastic life was the beginning of the reordering of society. In order to set an example of practical Christianity, the church had to reform itself, in part by sacrificing its wealth to the needs of the larger community. Such a program was not to be popular among Byzantine churchmen. In reforming the social and political order, Athanasios did indeed make personal enemies and was denounced almost as often as he denounced others. Pachymeres' history recorded many attacks provoked by Athanasios' rigorous asceticism and maximalism.[45] This opposition led to his two resignations, in 1293 and in 1309.

## The Baptismal Imperative

There had been, throughout the early Christian period, an association of baptism, individual penance, and the idea of reform. "The ideas of religious conversion and of individual spiritual regeneration through baptism are closely connected, but not identical, with the Christian idea of reform."[46] In fact, baptism and personal renewal are the *sine qua non* for the idea and actualization of reform. Baptism for Athanasios was the sacramental basis of Christian reform, both personal and social. Given this, the post-baptismal process of realization of the initial act provided occasion for a series of new starts, reform "windows," as it were. For Athanasios there was an intimate tie between reform and baptismal regeneration—a process highlighted by periodic reforms.

What is remarkable by its absence is any reference to a eucharistic imperative. Athanasios spoke little of the eucharist, and when he did, his use of the traditional τὰ ἅγια, the *holy things*, was general enough that a reader might not be aware of the term as a eucharistic reference.[47] He focused instead on baptism as the foundation for ethical and spiritual life. I suggest that his silence on the eucharist and emphasis on baptism was not uncommon among Byzantine ascetics.[48]

Recognizing a tension between the imperfect social and ecclesiastical order, on the one hand, and the possibility of a nearly perfect life based on the pattern of the monastic *cenobium*, on the other, Athanasios sought to rebuild the social system and the ecclesiastical structure to reflect his conception of "right order" in the empire, an earthly reflection of the heavenly archetype. His repeated references to the discrepancy between the baptismal oath and the failure of the clergy and the people to actualize it in their lives were attempts to apply monastic principles to Byzantine society as a whole. In other places he saw the baptismal promise as the basis for the monastic life. Athanasios focused on baptism, the teachings on baptism, and the reality of baptism as a basis for Christian reform. Athanasios concerned himself especially with the proper celebration of and instruction about baptism, demonstrating an ethical understanding of the sacrament of initiation. In one letter, he announced to the bishops that their first concern must be the proper teaching about "the mystery [sacrament] of the triple immersion," in particular making its meaning clear to the clergy in their charge.[49]

Athanasios, like many Greek fathers before him, interpreted baptism in a dynamic sense: baptism is not only an "event," but a "process" extended throughout the life of the Christian, and, as such, carries moral implications. The condition for salvation is twofold: to be baptized and to live in accordance with that baptism. He wrote, for instance, "Let us not lose the holiness which we have received at holy baptism."[50] He urged the people not to forget "to live according to holy baptism,"[51] for "what grace is there to an insensitive infant who goes through the holy washing but does not fulfill what belongs to baptism once [the infant] becomes an adult?"[52] Athanasios' is an existential approach, with little room for speculation.

Relying on scriptural support, he explained the centrality of baptism in terms of ethical and moral behavior. Baptism, he warned, is not sufficient for salvation, as some believe; only penance and good works can make baptism a reality in the life of the individual. The duty of the bishop and the priest is to teach the people how to live and to perform penance in proportion to faults committed. Athanasios referred to the "mystery of baptism" as an obligation of both "word and work" (ὀφειλῆς ἔργῳ καὶ λόγῳ). In fact, the conjunction of *logos* and *ergon* recurs in his letters as the basic principle of Christian life and the basis of personal and social order, τάξις. As an introductory remark to one letter, Athanasios noted that in the restoration of that primordial purity, "faith without works is dead" (James 14:17).[53] His fundamental existential treatment of an essentially theological category reveals him to be a practical theologian, a theologian of the *Lebenswelt*, in the prophetic tradition of Jeremiah (see Jer. 32:1–5) and of St. John Chrysostom. Athanasios met the people, in sound prophetic fashion, in the city, not only at the altar.[54]

## The Old Testament Paradigm

The themes of right order (εὐταξία) and justice were tied in Athanasios' mind to the identification of the empire with Israel.[55] He used Old Testament typology as a paradigmatic and didactic device to make sense out of Byzantine experiences and to assist him in understanding the reality of Byzantine election and decline in a meaningful way.[56] This theme, readily discernible in his letters, is not mentioned by any modern authors. Without an understanding of the role of Israel as paradigm or typos for the Byzantines and especially for Athanasios, his reforms and exhortations make little sense.

Athanasios was a reformer and, like all reformers in Byzantium, knew nothing of revolution. The Byzantine system was the earthly copy of the divine archetype; it was the commonwealth of God, for which the closest earthly paradigm was that of ancient Israel (τὸν παλαιὸν Ἰσραήλ),[57] which was an essential feature of the Byzantine treatment of Israel. He possessed a clear sense of the unity of church and empire as *basileia* and *hierosyne*, but he was enough of a churchman to realize that the church could exist without the empire should the sins of the empire lead to victory by the Turks. There was no dire warning of the millennial end, cataclysmic consummation, or the death of the church. As the continued existence of the empire appeared increasingly problematic, however, the tie between the empire and the church became a less viable option for Byzantine churchmen. If Athanasios was indeed haunted by the paradigm of Israel, it was because of the threat of the loss of God's protection and election.

Athanasios' reform thinking was ruled by the parameter of (*a*) Old Testament prophecy, (*b*) prophetic form, (*c*) emphasis on ritual purity, (*d*) typological identification, and finally, (*e*) a legal morality. The fifth point I intend to consider in a future work. The first four aspects will be examined here as playing an intimate and intertwining role in Athanasios' preaching and letters and in his interpretation of Byzantine political, social, and ecclesiastical life. No historian can hope to understand Athanasios without this Old Testament matrix. Byzantium in Athanasios' letters was identified with Israel, the people of God (ὁ τοῦ Θεοῦ λαός): God, he wrote in a letter to Andronikos, substituted the Orthodox people for the people of ancient Israel; their claims have been abrogated and transferred to Byzantium, which God brought into existence and granted the *hierosyne* and the *basileia.*[58]

As has been pointed out, Athanasios formulated the essential Hebraic identification of the terms for church and empire: "For *Christianity* is being destroyed in two ways, from without by enemies, and from within by excessive injustice and depravity."[59] In fact, for Athanasios "Christianity" appeared as one and the same bipolar reality as Israel of the Old Testament. It is clearly inadequate to translate or interpret τὰ τῶν Χριστιανῶν as "Christianity"; rather, it is more adequately rendered as the "Christian polity," the mutual commonwealth of empire and church. The Byzantines, and correspondingly the emperor, were a special people and would be judged according to their election by God. This election separated the Byzantines from other nations. Athanasios referred to Andronikos as rescuing the "patrimony of Christ" (κλῆρον Χριστοῦ), which had been completely overwhelmed by troubles.[60] Taking up the theme of Byzantium as a new Israel, he warned Andronikos to heed the warning to first-born Israel (προτότοκον Ἰσραήλ)[61] that the kingdom will be taken from it if it does not bear fruit (Matt. 21:43) and be given over to the Gentiles (τοῖς Ἔθνεσι).[62] Without this identification of Byzantium and its cosmic paradigm, Israel, Athanasios' political philosophy cannot be understood. God was a Byzantine, and God and Byzantium were in a covenant whose conditions were spelled out in legal, ethical, and ritualistic terms—just as they were in Leviticus. He called on the emperor to reform the nation and purify it. In one letter he referred to the priest Eli (Sam. 2–4) who had allowed the immorality of his sons to go unpunished. Athanasios may have seen himself as Eli and Andronikos as one of his sons, or he may have been warning Andronikos not to behave as Eli and suffer the wrath of God.[63] It was probably the former, because Athanasios continually reminded Andronikos that he was a "son of the church" (υἱέα τῆς ἐκκλησίας).[64]

God was not necessarily a Byzantine, and the kingdom could be taken from the Romans and handed over to "others." Just as Israel had forfeited the promise, so too could the Byzantines; for their crimes, they would lose God's protection and be treated even more harshly than the Israelites of old.[65] This Old Testament identification is fundamental to an understanding of Athanasios' sense of urgency for social and political reform. Athanasios could not escape the Hebrew paradigm, the sense of prophetic urgency, or the call for ritual purity. Referring to the apocryphal extension of Daniel 3:1–31, the so-called Song of the Three Children or Song of Azarias, he wrote: "Not being joined together by holy things, we have become smaller than any nation and we are become nothing and humble on account of our unlawful deeds, especially today."[66] The Song of Azarias was read in the Byzantine lectionary every Great Saturday morning and must have rung all too true to Athanasios as he looked about him in Constantinople: "For we, O Lord, are become less than any nation, and are kept under this day in all the world because of our sins."[67]

The relationship between God and the empire was convenantal and therefore conditional. As long as the commandments of Christ were kept (along with the Orthodox faith), "prosperity will last as long as the empire," until the end of the world, "as has been announced." This was the belief commonly held by the Byzantines. Not so Athanasios; the empire was a contingent reality. With the prophet Hosea (4:1), he might have cried, "The Lord hath a controversy with the inhabitants of the land, because there is no truth, nor mercy, nor knowledge of God in the land."[68] Byzantium *was* the New Israel, not just an analogue or parallel of the Old. It was this that made his prophetic warnings and his prophetic references more than moral exhortations; they were dire warnings. If Byzantium had replaced its paradigmatic predecessor as Yahweh's convenanted partner, then, as it had happened to the Israel of the Hebrews, he warned, it would happen to the Israel of the Romans. This identity with Israel and the Old Testament explain the emphasis on purity in his reforms; this is especially evident in his call to ritual purity for the priesthood[69] as well as his Old Testament warnings of false shepherds.[70]

In Athanasios' writings, as in Byzantine thinking in general, there was, however, a paradox, an antimony, with the paradigm of Israel. Any model, typology, or dogma is limited. Athanasios represented the Byzantine schizophrenia toward Israel. He seemed to reject, for instance, Old Testament ceremonial law in Eastern tradition (as in the use of τὰ ἄζυμα), but he affirmed ritual purity from the same Old Testament source. This is the context in which we can place his prohibition against the secularization of priests and monks. The traditional Byzantine dual standard for priest and laity allowed for the setting aside of the clergy, who, for instance, could never shed blood, as prohibited by the Levitical regulations. On the one hand, he appropriated the title and promise of Israel to the Byzantines and nullified the "old" dispensation; on the other, he selectively affirmed aspects of the old Levitical prescriptions. For instance, the law regarding the eating of strangled meats was affirmed, as it was at the Council of Jerusalem (Acts 15:29). In several places he called upon the bishops to excommunicate anyone who drank the blood of any animal.[71] This love/hate relationship was a fundamental contradiction in both Byzantine ecclesiology and political thought.[72] It seems the Byzantines chose what they wanted, having read both Leviticus and St. Paul.

Athanasios made great use of what might be called paradigmatic preaching, continually identifying groups, individuals, and the empire with Old Testament *typoi.* For instance, Andronikos was a "new Moses," and "Hosea even from afar speaks to us"; Byzantium was the New Israel, and Athanasios himself was Hosea or Jeremiah. Athanasios continued this Old Testament identification, not only in his extensive references to and personal identification with the prophets, but also in his passion for ritual and moral purity among the people, especially among the priests. Like the sacrificial priesthood of Israel, he continually criticized the Orthodox clergy for betraying the people.[73] His emphasis on Israel and the Old Testament notions of ritual purity in his reforms were necessarily part of his sense of the identification of Byzantium with Israel.[74] The typology is inescapable and not at all revolutionary; it was common in Byzantine writing.

It takes no great theological sensitivity, however, to realize the syllogistic imperative of his argument. Byzantium as the New Israel, as God's chosen people, bore a great ethical and moral burden. Athanasios proclaimed the inevitable warning attached to such an identification. The form of payment, as in the Old Testament, was set by Hebrew law—a rule-based morality and law-abiding piety. Indeed, Athanasios' was a rule-centered morality. As McGiffert notes with regard to Jacobean England, so Athanasios with regard to Andronikos.[75] If all the people, led by the example and the legislation of the emperor, would repent, then Anatolia would be restored. But if repentance were only partial, then God's beneficence would also be partial.[76] The ultimate punishment would be the loss of the land and the empire: "Lo, I will bring a nation upon you from afar, O house of Israel" (Jer. 5:15). For Athanasios, this threat was both immediate and unpleasant.

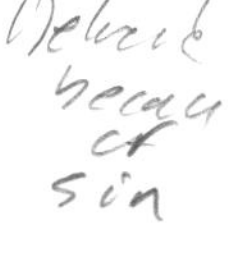

Again and again, Athanasios warned that the Byzantines were being delivered over to the hands of Ishmael on account of their adultery, incest, and perverted passions, sodomy, pederasty, blasphemy, sorcery, and injustice.[77] Inasmuch as their misfortunes were occasioned by their social, political, and personal sins, the only salvation was repentance and a turning to justice. Nothing else would save the city or the empire. Quoting Psalm 126 (127):1, he made the point: "except the Lord keep the city, the watchman watches in vain."[78] The people of God must be exhorted and exalted to live a lawful life in order to overcome its defects. Athanasios told Andronikos to proclaim virtues if he were to be considered a true son of the first Orthodox ruler, no doubt referring to Constantine, whose time for Athanasios represented a "Golden Age."[79] The patriarch singled out three essential virtues as the basis for governance of the Byzantine state: justice, moderation, and mercy.[80]

Athanasios read Byzantine history, as many before him did, especially Eusebius the historian, through the prism of the Old Testament. Without the strength of the paradigm, both historical and theological, Athanasios as a reformer would have been lost in whimsy and pious exhortations. Israel as paradigm tied Byzantium together; correspondingly, its military and territorial demise held his social and political reforms together.[81]

In his correspondence with both the emperor and church officials, Athanasios' attention was focused on the need for establishing right order and freedom in the church and justice and righteousness in the empire. These were the fundamental points of his reforming zeal. Only in this sense can his scrutiny of every aspect of Byzantine life be considered radical: he sought out the roots of social and political decline and made them known to the emperor. For Athanasios the well-being of the Byzantine commonwealth, as the Israel of God, was in very practical terms inextricably bound up with social justice and a well-ordered ecclesiastical life. Deliverance of the nation from the multi-faceted internal and external threats was almost in mathematical proportion related to the degree of repentance, which in Athanasios' thought meant a *metanoia* of both thought and behavior. If the whole people, led by the emperor, would repent and give the church its due, then not only would the Eastern regions be regained but "the rebellious Ishmaelites" (τοὺς ἐπαναστάντας Ἰσμαηλίτας) would be crushed.[82]

As we shall see, the ultimate responsibility for effecting the reforms belonged to Andronikos, because he had been given the necessary coercive power to deal with the violations. Athanasios' role was largely limited to investigations, reports, prophetic exhortations, and warnings directed at the people and the emperor, but he did not, however, hesitate to demand that the emperor use force and enact legislation whenever simple exhortation failed.

## The Role of the Emperor

Athanasios' letters detail the horrors of the domestic decline of the Orthodox commonwealth: "I hoped to be counted 'among those who sleep in their tombs' before seeing these misfortunes that have befallen the Christian people, or, second best, to crawl into a dark hole underground these days . . . rather than to manage the affairs of the Church of Christ my God."[83] What are the "misfortunes" of the Christian people? He wrote:

> As I sit here in the midst of a crowd of unhappy people who are quarreling with each other, I see one man in tears, another who has been struck by someone, another bemoaning his bloody clothing, still another the loss of his property, yet another suffering from oppression especially at the hands of those who collect the public taxes (who have an obligation to treat justly those who are in any way suffering), not to mention those who escape half-dead from the Ishmaelites [Turks] and the very Italians [Catalans?]—and then are mercilessly stripped by their own countrymen.[84]

Athanasios depended on Emperor Andronikos to implement his reform of social and political life. So during his first patriarchate, Athanasios focused his attention on the emperor, believing that God's grace toward the empire depended directly on the emperor's faithfulness to the task of righteous leadership. Justinian's sixth Novel specifically stated that the empire would be restored to its full geographical extent as a result of the *symphonia* between the *imperium* and *sacerdotium*.[85] Athanasios often made the same promise, *mutatis mutandis*, to Andronikos: God will restore the full extent of the empire to the "Romans," who have become, through their unfaithfulness and injustice, the laughingstock of their neighbors.[86] Athanasios, of course, established the conditions for this restoration, the first of which was the emperor's support of his programs. The emperor's duty, Athanasios repeated with numbing regularity, was to effect the reforms outlined by the patriarch.

For Athanasios, the solution to the problems was to return to Christian morality, the abandonment of which had led to the horrors of injustice, exploitation, and political corruption and indirectly to the evils that God had sent by way of chastisement. The process of social disintegration that Athanasios described was, according to his logic, inevitable without acts of repentance. In sound prophetic style, he affirmed that "if we did not sow these troubles, we would not be reaping their fruit."[87] He repeatedly called on Andronikos as the "pious ruler" to impose a return to Christian morality and repentance (ἐπιστροφὴ καὶ μετάνοια), the only virtues that could save church and empire.[88]

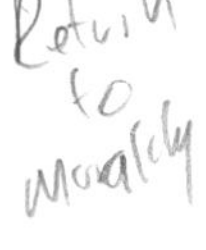

Following the theme of chastisement and repentance, Athanasios quoted the prophet Jeremiah: "And let it not be said about us, 'O Lord, thou hast scourged them, but they have not grieved; thou hast punished them, but they would not receive correction' " (Jer. 5:3).[89]

The same letter, citing Jonah's warning, urged the Byzantines to reject the example of the Sodomites, who disregarded God's warnings and were both condemned and destroyed (Gen. 19), in favor of the example of the Ninevites, who showed repentance and were saved from impending doom (Jonah 3).

But simple repentance was not sufficient, and the evangelical imperative was clearly one of action for the reform-minded patriarch. He wrote, paraphrasing James 2:26: "Without acts, the faith is a dead body." He urged Andronikos not to "confound only by words the sins of the schismatics,"[90] but to use the power given to him by God; for what good is a lion that has no "teeth and claws"?[91] In another place he wrote, "Rouse yourself to provide justice for the wronged and punishment for sinners."[92]

Again, he urged the emperor, "Do not shout down wickedness with words, but destroy it manfully with actions."[93] Athanasios did not stop at pious exhortations and dire prophetic warnings of the punishment of God, but made specific suggestions about the way Andronikos should govern the empire, defend the people, and bring about moral regeneration.[94] Athanasios called on Andronikos to wage "this holy war" against injustice (τοῦτο καὶ πόλεμος ἱερός), fulfill appropriate petitions, and scorn those who betray the truth and, through greed, cause injustice.[95] Again the imperative: "Let us rescue both poor man and beggar from hands stronger than theirs."[96]

The patriarch, with his incessant petitioning and his fierce sense of justice and righteousness, soon made himself a nuisance to an emperor ill prepared to act on the empire's innumerable social problems. In a letter to Andronikos, Athanasios admitted that his interference in the affairs of the empire could annoy the emperor. Nonetheless, Athanasios said he was under a moral obligation to interfere, and that this obligation was the reason for his own anger. He stated: "Philanthropy and mercy for the needy are not a mere matter of choice, but rather a necessity and indispensable obligation."[97] Elsewhere, he wrote: "If on occasion I appear to make petitions in a shameless manner, it is because of my desire for your glory in both worlds."[98] Again, Athanasios' predicament was simple: "I can neither keep silent nor speak."[99]

Over and over, Athanasios outlined the importance he ascribed to his office. He was the sole representative of the people before God and the emperor; it was his duty to meet their needs as well as to make those needs known to the emperor: "One worships God by attending to these matters [the correction of injustice], but if they are not reported, or are neglected even after the report is made, this angers God exceedingly."[100] He also complained that Andronikos threw many of his letters away and ignored his reports and complaints. Elsewhere he warned Andronikos not to put off his petitions; God would not allow the emperor to escape punishment because power had been granted to him to do justice. According to Athanasios' way of thinking, it was the indispensable duty of the emperor (and of each Christian) to rescue those who called upon him, and it was the patriarch's duty to bring all these matters to the emperor's attention.[101]

The emperor, it seems, often refused to meet with Athanasios, who would then move into the monastery of Chora to await an audience.[102] It is clear that the social conditions and crises of the empire were beyond Andronikos' capacities to govern. Though the emperor respected and even loved Athanasios, his talents and his will were not adequate for the tasks outlined by the patriarch. Athanasios' personal austerity exaggerated what he could reasonably expect the emperor to do. Like reformers of every age, Athanasios was a trial to his friends because his work by its nature forced him to "disregard the peace and proprieties of the social world."[103]

It is unfortunate that many historians dismiss Athanasios' reforming efforts, because they were motivated by an ascetic-rigorist tradition of Byzantine monasticism and as such were inappropriate to the *Lebenswelt.* Even though his reforms were largely abortive efforts to redirect the social life of the empire, their success or failure must not be the issue. Athanasios' efforts should rather be judged on the basis of his mimetic intentions, his keen insight into the fundamentally evangelical nature of social and political issues, his faithfulness to Old Testament patterns of reform and renewal, and the urgency of baptismal promises. These categories would come to play a significant role in the developing Palamism of the fourteenth century.

## Notes

1. KVA, 487. Ahrweiler, *Idéologie*, pp. 129–47. On the meaning of ἀταξία, καινοτομία, and εὐταξία, see Nicol, *Church and Society*, pp. 24–25. The entire Byzantine polity was permeated with the urgency of "good order," εὐταξία, as foundational to social, political, and ecclesiastical life. Such was the power of the myth of the heavenly archetype in the Byzantine mind.

2. TVA, 63.

3. KVA, 483.

4. Talbot, 6, lines 12–15 (*Regestes*, 1675). "Christianity" is an essentially abstract term; hence, my change in Talbot's rendering of the Greek text.

5. The Greek monastic distinction between πράξις or πρακτική φιλοσοφία and θεωρία does not oppose the practical to the theoretical. It is πράξις in the sense of struggle against vice and for virtue. See T. Camelot, *Foi et gnose: Introduction à l'étude de la connaissance mystique chez Clément d'Aléxandrie* (Paris: Vrin, 1945). Theodore Metochites wrote on the difficulty of reconciling the two lives. See Hans-Georg Beck, *Theodoros Metochites, die Krise des byzantinischen Weltbildes im 14. Jahrhundert* (Munich: Beck, 1952), pp. 26–29.

6. William K. Lawther Clarke, *Basil the Great: A Study in Monasticism* (Cambridge: Cambridge University Press, 1913), p. 17, writes: "Basil was the first bishop who united episcopacy and monasticism in one social mission." As a bishop, Basil saw it as his duty to enable the church to realize its diaconal dimension. Basil of Caesarea organized Byzantine monasticism and demonstrated, as Lawther Clarke has noted, the unity of the ascetical and the social functions. See Ernest F. Morison, *St. Basil and His Rule* (Oxford: Clarendon, 1912); W. K. Lawther Clarke, *The Ascetical Works of St. Basil* (London: SPCK, 1925). See also Keith Bridston, "The Future of Mission as Ecumenical Activity," *Greek Orthodox Theological Review*, 26 (Winter 1981), 325–32. On Basil as a reference point for reform see Margaret Murphy, *St. Basil and Monasticism* (New York: AMS, 1971), pp. 83–86. Finally, see Basil's brilliant affirmation of the social nature of Christian spiritual life in "Regulae fusius tractatae," Interrogatio 7, *PG* 31:927.

7. *Reform*, p. 313; Constable, "Renewal," p. 39–41. The Byzantines lacked the discipline of the monastic orders that were common in the West and were often, as in the case of the thirteenth-century Franciscans, designed to promote renewal. This goal was fostered through the spread of "daughter" houses.

8. Jean Gribomont, "Le Monachisme au IVe siècle en Asie Mineure de Gangres au Messalianisme," *Studia Patristica* II (Berlin: Akademie, 1955), pp. 400–16.

9. Ladner, *Reform,* pp. 32, 319–20.

10. See the classic work of Eric Osborn, *Ethical Patterns in Early Christian Thought* (Cambridge: Cambridge University Press, 1978), p. 11. See Stein, "Institutions," 137, who writes that Byzantine unlike Western monasticism did not recognize the need to act in human affairs and make "un juste usage de sa raison." He largely dismisses Byzantine Christianity as an administrative organ of the state, excessively ritualistic, and largely unresponsive to the needs of actual life. See also Beck, *Theodoros Metochites,* p. 32, for a discussion of the social function of Byzantine monasticism; and Georges Florovsky, "The Social Problem in the Eastern Orthodox Church," *Christianity and Culture* (Belmont, Mass.: Nordland, 1974), pp. 131–42.

11. Ladner, *Reform,* p. 106.

12. Talbot, 49, lines 81–85 (*Regestes,* 1695).

13. *The Mimetic Tradition of Reform in the West* (Princeton: Princeton University Press, 1982), p. 392.

14. See *Service Book of the Holy Orthodox-Catholic Apostolic Church,* trans. Florence Hapgood (Englewood, N.J.: Antiochian Archdiocese of North America, 1965), p. 104.

15. Ladner does not develop the use of ὁμοίωσις, although he notes the dynamic nature of the Greek terms as opposed to others and to the Hebrew original.

16. See "Oration" in Talbot, *Healing,* p. 70, lines 19–20.

17. Zakythinos, *Crise,* p. 149.

18. Ostrogorsky, "Palaeologi," p. 340. See also Basil Tatakis, *La Philosophie byzantine* (Paris: Presses Universitaires de France, 1959), p. 228; Tatakis points out that the centers of this renaissance were Constantinople, Thessalonica, Mistra, Nicea, and Trebizond. See Rodolphe Guilland, *Essai sur Nicéphore Grégoras* (Paris: Geuthner, 1926), p. 69, who outlines the theological work of men such as Nikephoros Xanthopoulos, John Glykys, Maximus Planudes, and Constantine Akropolites.

19. For instance, see Talbot, 2, lines 15–19 (*Regestes,* Appendix 2). Andronikos refers to Athanasios as having the moral virtue of John Chrysostom; see Gregoras, 246.

20. *The Social Teaching of the Christian Churches* I, trans. O. Wyon (London: Stewart, 1931), p. 127.

21. John Chrysostom, "In Epistolam ad I Corinthinos, Homily VI," section 4, in PG 61:52–54. John Chrysostom, "In Matthaeum, Homily VII," section 7, in PG, 57:81–82. See L. Meyer, *Saint Jean Chrysostome, maître de perfection chrétienne* (Paris: Beauchesne, 1933). On St. Basil, see Jean Gribomont, "Les Règles morales de saint Basile et le Nouveau Testament," *Studia Patristica* II (Berlin: Akademie, 1957), p. 417; see also Osborn, *Ethical Patterns,* p. 108.

22. St. Basil, "Regulae fusius tractatae," in PG, 31:905–1052. See also Osborn, *Ethical Patterns*, pp. 84–113. Athanasios' Ὑποτύποσεως Γράμμα (V, 176ᵛ–178ʳ) is compared with Basil's rules in Boojamra, *Church Reform*, pp. 172–81. For Basil there is a distinct corporate aspect to Christian perfection. This social theme in monasticism is brought out by Paul J. Fedwick, *The Church and the Charisma of Leadership in Basil of Caesarea* (Toronto: Pontifical Institute of Mediaeval Studies, 1979), p. 21.

23. Athanasios quotes the Basilan canon in at least two passages; see V, 158ᵛ (*Regestes*, 1749) and V, 142ᵛ–143ʳ (*Regestes*, 1747). More specifically, in his *hypotyposis* the prohibition against private ownership repeats Basil's. Compare V, 173ʳ (*Regestes*, 1595) with Basil the Great, *Ascetica* II, in PG, 31:881.

24. Constantelos, "Mysticism and Social Involvement," 49–60. Philadelphia held out until 1390 before falling to the Turks. The man of prayer as the man of action is Constantelos' theme. We are told by Nikephoros Choumnos, the famous enemy of Athanasios, that Theoleptos was a "father and provider to his flock." See Nikephoros Choumnos, "Epitaphios to the Metropolitan of Philadelphia, Theoleptos," in *Anecdota Graeca* V, ed. J. F. Boissonade (Hildesheim: Olms, 1962), pp. 229–31.

25. Matschke, "Politik und Kritik," p. 482*n*56. Matschke writes that Athanasios "damit verbunden war jedoch das Bemühen, die sozialen Spannungen zu entschärfen, ihren gewaltsamen Ausbruch zu verhindern, die Unterschichten eng an den Staat und die Klasse, die ihn trug, zu ketten." Athanasios is in fact anti-revolutionary, an "effective instrument of state power." Ibid., p. 483. Matschke's discussion approaches the absurd when he explains Athanasios' atavistic economic thinking with regard to rising forms of capitalism as the reason for his isolation and lack of support from among the higher clergy, nobility, and land-rich monastics; see p. 486. There are far more congenial explanations for his unpopularity among the powerful of the empire!

26. Ibid. Athanasios, for Matschke, was a truly tragic figure; he was, however, "despite the shipwreck of his life work one of the greatest men of his age."

27. Geoffrey Barraclough, *The Medieval Papacy* (London: Thames & Hudson, 1968), pp. 144–50.

28. Pachymeres, 643–50. The priests of St. Sophia complained that the patriarch wanted them to lead a monastic life, even though they had wives and children. On his prolonged conflict with the clergy of the great church, see Boojamra, *Church Reform*, pp. 128–38.

29. Pachymeres, 642.

30. Pachymeres, 647.

31. Pachymeres, 648. See Boojamra, *Church Reform*, p. 131.

32. Ladner, *Reform*, 352, No. 10. Ladner correctly notes that "the rareness of the *vita communis* among eastern Christian clergy is no doubt

connected with the fact that contrary to the west the east did not insist on general clerical celibacy. . . ." Augustine, for instance, had a strong sense that priests and their bishops should live a common life as monks do, having everything in common. See Possidius, "Vita Sancti Aurelii Augustini," 24–25, PL 32:53ff.

33. See the treatment of nineteenth-century United States reform movements in John M. Blum, et al., *The National Experience* (New York: Harcourt, Brace & World, 1963), pp. 245–46.

34. See TVA, 59–61, where Athanasios' disciples are discussed.

35. Pachymeres, 148.

36. Pachymeres, 148–49.

37. Ibid. See also Pachymeres, 614, where he claims Athanasios renders punishments disproportionate to minor faults.

38. V, 174v–175r (*Regestes*, 1755).

39. V, 94r (*Regestes*, 1651), "τὴν τρίχα γὰρ μόνην κειρόμενοι, οὐ συναποβαλλόμεθα καὶ τὰς ἐπιθυμίας τὰς σαρκικάς, ἢ τὸ θέλημα." See V, 269r (*Regestes*, 1658).

40. V, 269r (*Regestes*, 1658).

41. V, 96v–97r (*Regestes*, 1651). The intimate association between fasting and social responsibility was made early in the history of the church, when, for instance, Hermas notes that "on the day on which you fast you will taste nothing but bread and water; and having reckoned up the price of the dishes of that day which you intended to have eaten, you will give it to a widow or an orphan, or to some person in want." Hermas, *The Shepherd*, trans. C. Taylor, 2 vols. (London: SPCK, 1903, 1909), Similitude 5.4.

42. V, 99r (*Regestes*, 1736).

43. Florovsky, "Antinomies," p. 86.

44. See note 10 above.

45. Pachymeres, 150; see also 164, where his harshness is attacked. Gregoras noted that Athanasios was forced out of office the first time (1293) because of the complaints of bishops, monks, and laypersons concerning his melancholic temperament (Πνευματικὴ σκυθρωπότητα); See Gregoras I:182, 191.

46. Ladner, *Reform*, p. 32. In the Christian East and in the Christian West, from the very beginnings of Christianity, "reform was regarded as an important and indispensable supplement to prebaptismal conversion and to baptismal regeneration." Ibid., p. 319.

47. Talbot, 47, lines 35–39 (*Regestes*, 1633). To the same point, see Talbot, 44, lines 22–25 (*Regestes*, 1665), where he urged Andronikos to punish those who do not attend matins, vespers, and liturgy on important feast days, but made no mention of eucharistic participation as necessary or enabling for the ethical or spiritual life.

48. See, for instance, J. Gouillard, "Quatre procès de mystiques à Byzance (960–1143)," *REB*, 36 (1978), 5–81; and Magdalino, "Byzantine Holy Man," p. 62, where baptismal sufficiency and its condemnation are discussed.

49. V, 138v (*Regestes*, 1747): "καὶ πρώτως διδάξωμεν τί τὸ τρισσὸν ἐν τῇ καταδύσει μυστήριον τοῦ ἁγίου βαπτίσματος."

50. V, 223v (*Regestes*, 1776); "μὴ οὖν ἀπολέσωμεν τὸν ἁγιασμὸν ὅν ἡγιάσθημεν ἐν τῷ ἁγίῳ βαπτίσματι."

51. V, 224r (*Regestes*, 1776): "πρὸς ἅπερ ἐν τῷ ἁγίῳ βαπτίσματι συνεταξάμεθα ζῆν, μὴ ἐπιλανθάνεσθε."

52. V, 205r (*Regestes*, 1660): "ποία γὰρ χάρις νηπίῳ ἀναισθήτῳ τυχόντι τοῦ Θείοῦ λουτροῦ, εἰ μὴ ἀποπληροῖ ἀνδρωθέν τὰ ὀφείλοντα τῷ βαπτίσματι."

53. V, 133r (*Regestes*, 1747): "ἔργων χωρίς, τὴν πίστιν, νεκὰν εἰπών."

54. I am indebted to Rev. Dr. Paul Tarazi of St. Vladimir's Seminary for references to the prophets and particularly to Jeremiah.

55. For a fascinating discussion of antinomial typologies, see Alexander Webster, "Antinomial Typologies for an Orthodox Christian Social Ethic for the World, State, and Nation," *Greek Orthodox Theological Review*, 28 (Fall, 1983), 221–54. One of the antinomies of Byzantine thought was the rejection of matzo in the eucharist because of its Jewish association and the maintenance of the sabbath as a liturgical eucharistic day. See Canons 11 and 60 of Trullo, which deal with matzo and the prohibition of fasting on the Sabbath respectively (Rhalles and Potles, II:324, 425). See Smith, *Bread*, pp. 31–32, for an excellent treatment of the Byzantine reaction to the use of azymes. The Byzantines traditionally charged that the Latins were Judaizers, as in the fierce mid-eleventh century controversy among Humbert, Niketas Stethatos, and Leo of Ochrida. See Smith, *Bread*, p. 148. Among church fathers there were no common guidelines for the treatment of the Levitical regulations. Israel here appears to be a paradigmatic and heuristic tool by which the Byzantines sought to understand their own place in history.

56. George Mouly, *Psychology for Effective Teaching* (New York: Holt, Rineholt & Winston, 1962), pp. 326–27.

57. V, 19r (*Regestes*, 1692).

58. V, 19r–v (*Regestes*, 1672).

59. Talbot, 6, lines 12–14 (*Regestes*, 1675).

60. Talbot, 82, lines 5–9 (*Regestes*, 1717) = κλῆρος; Talbot, 81, lines 162–66 (*Regestes*, 1715) = κληρονομία.

61. Talbot, 69, line 2 (*Regestes*, 1614).

62. Talbot, 82, lines 22–25 (*Regestes*, 1717); Athanasios here includes a number of ominous scriptural warnings, especially that of the barren fig tree. See V, 272v, for New Israel.

63. Talbot, 49, lines 5–8 (*Regestes*, 1695).

64. Talbot, 49, lines 39–44 (*Regestes*, 1695). See also Talbot, 18, line 10 (*Regestes*, 1679).

65. V, 25[r] (*Regestes*, 1692). Athanasios goes to the extent of describing how the empire has already suffered after the fashion of Old Israel; survival is now an immediate question. See Bănescu, "Athanase," 48.

66. V, 63[v] (*Regestes*, 1716). See also V, 82[r] (*Regestes*, 1735).

67. "The Song of Azarias" or "Song of the Three Children" is sung on the morning of Great Saturday and would be commonly heard by all faithful Orthodox. It appears in the Septuagint Apocrypha. See *The Septuagint Version of the Old Testament and Apocrypha* (London: Bagsters, n.d.), p. 131.

68. Talbot, 110, lines 43–47 (*Regestes*, 1735).

69. Boojamra, *Church Reform*, pp. 135–36. Note especially the reference to the priesthood, which parallels the prescriptions of Leviticus 21, especially 21:7, 13–15. See below, chap. 5.

70. See V, 134[r] (*Regestes*, 1747), where he paraphrases Hosea 10:5 and 6:9. He quotes Joel in V, 134[v] (*Regestes*, 1747); and Zachariah 11:5 in V, 135[r] (*Regestes*, 1747). This letter deals largely with Old Testament references and uses Zachariah as a warning to those clergy who do not do their job or are unjust. See Boojamra, *Church Reforms*, pp. 102–104; chap. 5, below.

71. V, 143*v* (*Regestes*, 1747); and 158[r–v] (*Regestes*, 1749). See Canon 83 of Apostolic Canons (Rhalles and Potles, II:107) and Canon 67 of Trullo (Rhalles and Potles, II:439), which prescribed the deposition of a cleric and excommunication of a priest for eating the flesh of a strangled animal or drinking the.blood of an animal. A judaizing tendency is evident early in Byzantine ecclesiastical thought and practice; on the other hand, Canon 11 of Trullo (Rhalles and Potles, II:328–30) proscribed the eating of matzo. See Boojamra, *Church Reform*, p. 136.

72. The occurrence of this apparent contradiction between the Old Testament affirmation of ritual purity in Athanasios' letters and a rejection of the ceremonial practices associated with Israel such as the Latin use of ἀζύμα in the eucharist represents a fundamental contradiction in Byzantine ecclesiastical practice and thought. This would be a fruitful area for investigation. It may be that Athanasios based his opinions on those aspects of the law reaffirmed by the Council of Jerusalem (Acts 15), such as strangled meats (Acts 15:20). In this case, of course, the practices are rooted in apostolic, not Hebraic, tradition. This does not, however, apply to the ritual purity he insists on applying to his clergy. There is, in fact, no consistent pattern of application among Byzantine Christians. There was a similar problem in the West, where the demand for clerical celibacy was based in part on Old Testamental requirements for ritual purity. Because

daily Mass was the norm, sexual abstinence would be required. In this case, temporary sexual liaisons would be preferable, in principle, to marriage!

73. See V, 229*v*–230*r* (*Regestes*, 1778).

74. See for instance, V, $158^{r-v}$ (*Regestes*, 1749) and V, $140^{r}$ (*Regestes*, 1747) where the violation of a priest's wife is sufficient cause for him to give up the priesthood or for separating himself from her. See also V, $192^{v}$–$193^{v}$ (*Regestes*, 1760) where second marriages are forbidden to the clergy. See also Boojamra, *Church Reform*, pp. 136, 138.

75. McGiffert, "God's Controversy," 1153: "The ultimate sanction was the doom of Lo-Ammi—not my people." See Hosea 1:9; one of Hosea's sons was named for the judgment of God, "for you are not my people and I will not be your God."

76. Talbot, 37, lines 23–26 (*Regestes*, appendix 7).

77. Talbot, 36, lines 8–12 (*Regestes*, 1639).

78. Talbot, 82, lines 69–73 (*Regestes*, 1717).

79. Talbot, 82, lines 76–80 (*Regestes*, 1717): He refers to Andronikos as the "son of Constantine," rather than the "new Constantine," a common title. See Talbot, 112, lines 12–15 (*Regestes*, 1666) where he refers to Constantine as Andronikos' "spiritual father."

80. Talbot, 29, lines 10–15 (*Regestes*, 1687)

81. See Boojamra, *Church Reform*, pp. 102–104, 120, 127.

82. Talbot, 37, lines 23–27 (*Regestes*, Appendix 7).

83. Talbot, 14, lines 1–6 (*Regestes*, 1677).

84. Talbot, 46, lines 13–17 (*Regestes*, 1639).

85. See Justinian, Novel 6, Preface, *Novellae*, edd. Schoell and Kroll, p. 35; and Dvornik, *Political Philosophy* II, pp. 815–16.

86. *V*, 230*r*–232*r* (*Regestes*, 1589).

87. Talbot, 14, lines 33–38 (*Regestes*, 1677). See also Talbot, 15, line 15 (*Regestes*, 1611).

88. Talbot, 15, lines 7–11 (*Regestes*, 1611).

89. Talbot, 3, lines 21–26 (*Regestes*, 1673).

90. Talbot, 6, lines 5–9 (*Regestes*, 1675).

91. Talbot, 7, lines 12–16 (*Regestes*, 1597).

92. Talbot, 6, lines 2–5 (*Regestes*, 1675).

93. Talbot, 7, lines 64–65 (*Regestes*, 1597).

94. For example, see Talbot, 78, lines 39–43 (*Regestes*, 1638); Athanasios' concerns included military, economic, and political matters as well.

95. Talbot, 12, lines 36–40 (*Regestes*, 1676).

96. Talbot, 5, lines 23–27 (*Regestes*, 1674).

97. Talbot, 99, lines 18–22 (*Regestes*, 1726): "εἰ δὲ μὴ αἵρεσις ἡ φιλανθρωπία καὶ σπλάγχνα τοῖς χρήζουσιν ἀνοιγόμενα, ἀλλὰ μᾶλλον ἀνάγκη καὶ ἀπαραίτητον ὄφλημα. . . ."

98. Talbot, 58, lines 27–32 (*Regestes*, 1702).
99. Talbot, 99, lines 23–27 (*Regestes*, 1726).
100. Talbot, 12, lines 16–21 (*Regestes*, 1676).
101. Talbot, 46, lines 23–27 (*Regestes*, 1693).
102. Talbot, 23, lines 39–44 (*Regestes*, 1621).
103. Blum, *Experience*, p. 245.

# 5

# Athanasios' Reform Measures

## Public and Ecclesiastical Corruption

The civil services, the episcopal hierarchy, and the military were the backbone of Byzantine stability. The decay of these three areas both was symptomatic of the decline of the empire and accelerated that decline. Athanasios refused to accept the civil and ecclesiastical chaos that characterized the "time of troubles" at the turn of the fourteenth century. He attempted to apply with full rigor the laws and canons of the church as if nothing had happened or was happening, and he represented one of the few centripetal forces in the empire.

Athanasios had an elevated view of the value of his patriarchal office and used the influence of that office to ensure integrity in public affairs. Both spiritually and politically he became the protector of a centralized state, whose elements had for a thousand years guaranteed the stability of the Byzantine empire, population, and Orthodox Church; determined to redirect the empire according to his reform principles, he would reaffirm the statist controls and services that had created the stable and well-ordered Byzantine state in the "modern" sense of the word. Using his position, he became involved in such matters as fortifying the city, maintaining its grain supply, and hiring the Catalan Grand Company as mercenaries, as well as monitoring the behavior of bishops and priests.[1] He addressed numerous, unsolicited reports to Andronikos, singling out particular abuses and injustices. He did not stop at general abuses, but actually named names, including those of members of the imperial hierarchy, whose behavior was not above his reproach.[2] Athanasios saw all this as well within his competence as patriarch; it was his duty to set the moral and spiritual life of the empire and the church in right order: "If then we wish to save ourselves and the world, let each of us recognize our own [duties] and those toward the community, especially those who administer public affairs [οἱ διοικοῦντες τὰ δημόσια], both worldly and spiritual."[3]

In attacking the misbehavior of the civil and ecclesiastical hierarchies he applied Old Testament prophetic warnings. As the prophets lamented for Israel, so they now weep for the Romans.[4] He continued the attack on ecclesiastical and civil leaders with references to Micah and David, who warned that Israel could not be built on blood and that leaders must not mingle with evil and injustice.[5] Athanasios complained the immorality was especially rampant in the army where soldiers, instead of marching with Christ, were indulging in adultery and thievery: "How will they be victorious?"[6] Athanasios took it upon himself to check into the functioning of city affairs, including the actions of both private and public officials; he could easily accomplish this with the large number of loyal monks committed to his rigorist bent of mind and eager to seek out malfeasance. He sought, in effect, to function much as the old prefect of the city had functioned with regard to food, weights, and measures. The good will of the merchants was not enough to rely on, and persuasion and coercion had to be included.[7]

## Public Officials

Byzantine social life was characterized by large-scale corruption, not an unusual corollary of political and military decline. The cases that Athanasios heard of were usually instances of exploitation by civil and ecclesiastical officials and by merchants. In a letter to Andronikos, Athanasios revealed a profound Christian political philosophy:

> When men to whom the great God has not given an emperor are wronged by certain people, they are consoled by the expectation that they will be avenged in the world to come; but when through the grace of Christ, men have been granted an emperor . . . they perish of sorrow if they do not see him defending truth and righteousness.[8]

Referring to officials, he went on to say that the emperor must restrain the wicked (τὸν ἀναχαιτισμὸν τῶν κακῶν) from exploiting the people and the church.

Holding Andronikos responsible for the behavior of public officials, Athanasios wrote that it was the emperor's duty not only to fight heresy, but also to see that men in authority behave correctly; further, the emperor was above all the "benefactor" and should chastise anyone not doing his duty justly.[9] Bréhier, summing up the Byzantine tradition, notes: "la loi civile doit donc prêter son appui à l'Église, respecter ses privilèges et les défendre au besoin, même contre les agents impérieux."[10] Athanasios warned Andronikos to find men who could do their jobs honestly, in a God-pleasing manner. If the emperor was not able to find such men, Athanasios himself would make recommendations or find them. During the famine of the winter of 1306–1307, Athanasios suggested the names of several men, monastic and lay, to staff a grain-supply commission for the city.[11] This call for mutuality, which was the underpinning of both Athanasios' social and his ecclesiastical reforms, confirms my thesis that he sought to impose monastic categories on the whole of the Byzantine society.

Athanasios complained bitterly about those officials who opposed necessary reform measures and whose habit was always to postpone until "tomorrow." He assured Andronikos that he was complaining not of inconsequential matters, but of those "that will cause destruction to both body and soul."[12] This concern was well within Athanasios' purview not only as the spiritual father of the emperor and the empire, but also as a judicial agent commissioned by the emperor, before he re-assumed the patriarchal throne, to hear cases of injustice and report on them.[13]

Athanasios' most vehement attacks fell on tax agents (οἱ ἐνεργοῦντες) who were not investigated as he had recommended but allowed to persist in their injustices and exploitation of the people.[14] However, the patriarch allowed for the possibility that Andronikos might have been misled by some of his ministers who advised him against corrective measures. At one point, after he had praised Andronikos' good works, Athanasios urged him not to curtail them because of ambition, family, or friends, or the inhumanity (φορολόγων ἀνανθρωπία) of tax collectors, but to require that tax agents conform to the law and cease "milking" the people to build their personal fortunes. Athanasios advised: "The collection of taxes should not be entrusted to the heartless . . . who are little or no better than 'cornrust and locust'; they have brought nothing but unbearable misfortunes upon the common people."[15]

Writing to Andronikos about monastic properties and their taxes on their rents from dependent peasants, Athanasios reminds him that it is the obligation of the emperor to regulate the affairs of monasteries but only insofar as they relate to secular affairs (τοῦ κόσμου εἰσὶ δουλεῖαι). The monastery had to be protected from illegal taxation on lands it did not hold and from which it received no income. His letter seems to imply that poor recordkeeping enabled tax agents (οἱ ἐνεργοῦντες) to collect and pocket taxes at the expense of the imperial treasury.[16] These tax collectors, he warned, wanted to destroy the Roman state and people, and only Andronikos could save the empire by enforcing the laws of the nation and restoring τάξις.

Among the poorest of the poor in Constantinople were the Anatolian and Thracian refugees who were filling the city after the military defeats of 1302 and the Catalan rampages. Athanasios complained that Andronikos never ordered an investigation of certain charges he had made; and he particularly lamented the lack of action and the veniality of the hetaeriarch, the official who dealt with refugees: "How often, when I have reported to you about the matter, has your divine majesty ordered the hetaeriarch either to accompany me in an investigation of the truth, or to arrange a just and true redress of things which I have reported, not to satisfy my personal desire, but because this is the will of God and brings glory and honor . . . to your majesty."[17]

Athanasios probably wanted the official to go with him to investigate refugee problems, and perhaps the lack of housing and food; instead the hetaeriarch devoted his time to personal gain and to deceiving the emperor under a guise of meekness, a brand of hypocrisy particularly abhorrent to Athanasios. In the end Athanasios suggested that the hetaeriarch's absence was preferable, for he would simply try to search out personal gain in the suffering of others.[18]

Athanasios was especially angered by Nikephoros Choumnos, the prefect of the scriptorium (ὁ Κανικλείου), who was appointed to the office around 1295[19] and later became one of Andronikos' most trusted advisors as mesazon or chancellor.[20] Choumnos was one of the many intellectuals with whom Andronikos surrounded himself (others were Theodore Metochites and Nikephoros Gregoras) and one whom Athanasios accused of using his authority harmfully. Proclaiming the need to do penance and to return to a practical faith, Athanasios wrote to Andronikos: "Do not allow ourselves to be guided by our appetites, as the prefect of the scriptorium who does not seek to reconcile himself with God for all the wrong he committed in the exercise of his power, but only to contract marriages, as if they were able to wrest him from the hands of God."[21] In fact, Athanasios may be referring to Andronikos' several attempts to get Irene Choumnos married off. The first, and unsuccessful, attempt was to Alexis, the king of Trebizond, and the second, successful, to his own son, John the Despot, despite the opposition of the empress.[22]

Athanasios seems to have had a special emnity for Choumnos, who, as *mesazon*, occupied a powerful position and undoubtedly undermined the patriarch's influence with the religious and superstitious Andronikos. Choumnos, a classicist and humanist who possessed great influence around the imperial throne, may have been one of these officials working against the patriarch; inasmuch as his influence dates from Athanasios' first patriarchate, he may have had a hand in the patriarch's initial resignation.[23]

From his Marxist perspective, Matschke suggests that Athanasios' hostility was motivated by his opposition to Choumnos as a representative of a group of feudal nobles who were opposed to the centralized state he was attempting to reinforce.[24] In spite of the author's tendentious treatment, the point is well made that all Athanasios' efforts at reform also served the purpose of centralized state control; only such a state, in Athanasios' thinking, would or could serve the needs of the people and maintain good order in state and church. This was certainly one of his reasons for so violently attacking unjust officials who had no concern for the well-being of the empire or the people.

The hostility seems to have been mutual, and Choumnos, after Athanasios' second resignation, made fantastic charges of simony against the retired patriarch.[25] The charges were false and no doubt the result of vicious rumors and distortions. Nonetheless, in the context of his attack on Athanasios, Choumnos reported that Athanasios was the leader of a faction that had broken communion with him.

Athanasios repeatedly condemned court officials who loved presents, sought compensation, and did not judge fairly the cases of orphans.[26] He urged Andronikos to "teach the officials not to be 'companions of thieves,' or to succumb to bribes and gifts,"[27] to tour the walls of the city and to investigate cases of guards who, unable to bribe their supervisors, had lost their jobs. He specifically questioned the wisdom of "farming" out such positions of defense to the highest bidder, who then had to extort money from his underlings to recover his initial investment.[28] Athanasios also mentioned an incident in which agents were ordered to conscript men to row the ship of the grand duke. But these agents conscripted more men than were required, "as many as they could take captive." They then extorted money from the conscripts to be allowed to go free. This horrifying injustice assured the loss of God's protection.[29]

Athanasios concluded that if the Byzantines truly wanted to save both themselves and "the world," all—"especially those who administer public affairs, both ecclesiastical and civil"[30]—would have to recognize their own duty toward the community. Such was the pathetic level of the Byzantine civil service at a time when Athanasios felt that all elements of society had to pursue justice and righteousness vigorously.

In a typical linking of the themes of social and ecclesiastical reforms, Athanasios lamented that if the officials of the state were bold with the things that belonged to the church, how then would they treat the poor and simple, already "weighed down by injustice," who had no one to defend them?[31] The ecclesiastical institutions—churches and monasteries, orphanages and almshouses—were relatively well endowed with holdings by pious individuals in areas under Christian, albeit not imperial, control. This was especially true of Athonite monasteries. After the restoration of Constantinople as an imperial capital in 1261, both Michael VIII and Andronikos II, because of the destruction of records and confiscation of church properties, had to reaffirm the numerous holdings of ecclesiastical institutions. Such was the case both with the monastery of Karakala, which, at the request of Athanasios, was confirmed in its properties and immunities (ἐξκουσσεία) from imposts and taxation,[32] and with the monastery of Xeropotamou on Athos.[33] These two examples are typical of a broader movement toward consolidation of ecclesiastical holdings, wealth in ecclesiastical hands, and increase in fiscal immunities, and these came at a time when imperial wealth and power were on the decline. As might be expected, this wealth became the object of abuse by both ecclesiastical and secular officials, whom Athanasios faulted for their greed.

Ševčenko has developed evidence that there was a great deal of pressure on ecclesiastical property and wealth from provincial civil and military aristocracy, pressure that had formerly been ascribed to the zealot revolutionaries of the mid-fourteenth century.[34] The church had always to be attentive to efforts to alienate its property for secular purposes. It was Isaac Komnenos who, in gratitude to Patriarch Michael Kerularios (1043–1057) for bringing him to power, gave the Byzantine Church greater autonomy over its own property, a policy that he soon tried to reverse by turning ecclesiastical property into coinage without the approval of the church.[35] This continued to be a source of ecclesiastical irritation with civil officials, especially in the early fourteenth century, when the church and its various institutions—monastic, charitable, liturgical—came into possession of more and more wealth from sources outside the empire, such as Russian and Balkan Orthodox princes.

In another letter, Athanasios referred to tax agents who pillaged the goods of the church and violated its legal immunity.[36] The immunity that the church enjoyed was so central to Athanasios' ecclesiology that he placed violation of it among the sins that were the cause of the loss of Anatolia.[37] Within imperial territory, although little income and property were left to the church, immunity was significant. Athanasios sought to stop any additional drains on these reserves: "Since on account of my sins the church has been stripped by a barbarian gale" and only a mouthful was left, Andronikos must appoint an overseer to protect the church, "so that state officials may not mercilessly devour the property of the church."[38] Only with the establishment of such an administrator, wrote Athanasios, would civil officials cease to abuse ecclesiastical goods. He implied that the officials would no longer have an excuse (their personal distaste for him) for ignoring his demands. And why this animosity? Athanasios' prestige was at a low ebb.

Athanasios no longer had any credibility among public officials, who resented him "because of the charges I make against them." All respect for the church, he claimed, had been lost and these functionaries whom he did not name were shamelessly exploiting and misappropriating the goods and property of the church. He mentioned specifically that he had attempted to take action against a man who had stolen eighteen hundred *modioi* of wheat, but to no avail. Annoyed by agents who abused the goods of the church, Athanasios attacked Nikephoros Choumnos, claiming that Choumnos, for whom he had no affection, was among a number of corrupt officials who made their fortunes by abusing their power. He complained that the suffering did not fall on the monks, priests, or officials, but on the common people, who were least able to bear the burden. Referring to Byzantine lay and ecclesiastical officials, he wrote that their love of gifts led them to devour the people as "loaves of bread" (Ps. 14:4).[39] Finally, in a voice characteristic of reformers, Athanasios wailed that if he could not protect the church from such men, how could he defend the people "weighed down by injustice"? He seems to have assumed a personal burden of guilt for the evils of society, and to have felt driven to do something about it.

### *Ecclesiastical Officials*

Athanasios did not limit his attacks to secular and civil officials; he fiercely attacked those leaders of the church who betrayed their duties. The principal objects of this attack were the bishops illegally resident in the capital city and, with few exceptions, exploiting the relative comfort it offered them.

The patriarch classified many of his objections to ecclesiastical life under the category of the decline of the church and its loss of internal freedom. This had been a steady process since the time of Constantine, and he reminded Andronikos that he must help to ensure proper order in the life of the church. He repeated the same guarantee that followed his exhortations to social justice: God will restore his empire and protect his people, bringing back the flock from those who have taken it away.

Athanasios also attacked church officials for their abuse of the people and of ecclesiastical and particularly monastic property, complaining that these men were appointed to their spiritual offices, not from among those who were the most dignified and worthy but from among the highest bidders. He wrote to Andronikos that the iniquities of the people, particularly of priests and monks, were bringing God's condemnation on the Byzantines.[40] These officials, particularly the bishops, had forgotten their spiritual vocation and were occupying themselves with such private affairs as obtaining a higher rank in the church, accumulating large sums of money, and taking bribes for rendering decisions in the *synodos endemousa.*

He also accused the inhabitants of monasteries of forgetting the purpose of these houses. His duty, he affirmed, was to see that the administration of the monasteries and of their income was entrusted to persons who were suitable, according to the canons (ἐγκανόνως).[41] Speaking of lay officials (χαριστικάριος) who were granted income for administering monastic enterprises, he accused them of personally appropriating the wealth.[42]

Besides the wealthy citizens and the secular officials who opposed him, Athanasios endured the opposition of those monastic elements whom he had criticized for abusing their way of life or for misusing the wealth that had come into their possession. Like the provincial bishops, the monks did not like Athanasios' ascetic disciplines or his demands that they live in their monasteries as prescribed by secular laws and ecclesiastical canons. Moral decline had struck the convent: "never had such license for corruption been granted to nuns and monks."[43] The decline of monastic life, indeed the decline of social life in general, was largely due to the military and political chaos. Nor it may be assumed, did they like his idea of confiscating monastic properties for philanthropic purposes.[44] The opposition to the patriarch was so strong among certain monks, we are told by Pachymeres, that on his second accession to the patriarchate in 1303 many of their number fled to Latin religious houses in Pera.[45]

Pursuing the theme of monastic mutuality into the social order, Athanasios attacked the bishops who had fled their dioceses and taken up residence in Constantinople for "robbing the poor." He identified ecclesiastical income with the money that properly belonged to the poor and should have been used to meet their needs:

> If each of the bishops was rightly compelled to remain in the see assigned to him and if all of them [were compelled to] pasture their sheep, and not themselves, rather than dining luxuriantly off what rightly belongs to the poor [ἐκ τῶν πτωχικῶν ἔχειν] . . . then God would remove all cowardice from us, and would show us His great works in us in right council.[46]

He complained, for instance, of the bishop of Bitzyne, who lent out church funds for eight hundred gold pieces annually.[47] He chastised the emperor for permitting the bishops to remain uncanonically in Constantinople and to collect church funds to use for evil purposes such as partying with the self-exiled patriarch of Alexandria, Athanasios II.[48] Not only were many of these bishops and secular officials unscrupulous, but their dishonesty so reduced monastic resources that Athanasios could not fulfill Andronikos' mandate to hear complaints, relieve injustices, and provide social services. Athanasios was equally concerned about the quality of monastic administration in the hands of inexperienced monks.[49]

Because selling ecclesiastical goods and even liturgical items to ransom prisoners and assist captives had a long and well-established history among Byzantine Orthodox, Athanasios considered this a good means of assisting the needy and providing an example for the wealthy to follow. But the bishops, rather than support his efforts, bitterly fought the patriarch's use of ecclesiastical funds, claiming the property did not belong to him.[50] They were partially correct, but he was the patriarch and in principle responsible for the disposition of the affairs of the church. Athanasios made it clear that he was ultimately responsible for all ecclesiastical, including monastic, property. This, however, was a responsibility usually distributed among several officials in a diocese and not left to the bishop alone, though the power of the bishop over diocesan property was early tied to his pastoral responsibilities. Canon 41 of the Apostolic Canons notes: "for if he is to be entrusted with the precious souls of men, much more are temporal possessions to be entrusted to him. He is therefore to administer them all of his own authority, and supply those who need."[51]

Athanasios attacked the bishops for a variety of reasons. In general, he combined specific offenses with Old Testament warnings, finding the book of Zechariah ideally suited to wayward bishops: it spoke of Judah, God's beloved, as a flock without shepherds (Zech. 10:2–3). Similarly Jeremiah, the prophet Athanasios most resembles, lamented that because of the sins of the leaders the flock would be scattered and the vineyard would become a desert (Jer. 10:20–22; Hos. 5:1). Athanasios warned the bishops, "We should become wise from the example of the terrible things that happened to [the Old Testament priesthood]."[52]

As the prophets had lamented for Israel, he wrote, so they now lament for the empire of the Orthodox. "Though far from Jerusalem, the prophet Hosea (6:9) speaks to us: 'the priests and the [civil] leaders are become like a net to entrap from their positions.' "[53] In a relatively long didactic letter (*didascalia*) addressed to the "Christian people," he listed the two main categories of his reform efforts: moral violations and the exploitation of the poor, widows, and orphans. Athanasios mourned that no one speaks a word about it or punishes offenders; "quite the contrary, the priest has become one of the mob," doing the same evils.[54]

In his attacks on ecclesiastical and civil leaders, he also referred to Micah and David, who warned that Israel could not be built on blood, nor its leaders mingle with evil and injustice. Joel as well, he warned, spoke out against the sacrificial priesthood, which had led the holy nation of Israel astray.[55] Urging the bishops not to liken themselves to the sacrificial priests of Israel who said "Blessed is the Lord and we have become rich" (Zech. 11:5),[56] he applied to these men the reproving words that Ezekiel (34:2, 8) directed at the priesthood: "They feed themselves and not the sheep."

## *Refugee Influx*

In Bithynia, on July 27, 1302, the Osmanli Turks defeated Andronikos' son, Michael IX, at Bapheus. Afterward, many Bithynians who survived the battle and ensuing massacre fled to Constantinople and the islands of the Propontis.[57] All that was left in Anatolia were the armor-fortified cities of Nicomedia, Brusa, Nicea, Philadelphia, and Magnesia. Pachymeres described the conditions:

> The situation in the east declined and worsened so that every day more dire reports came to the emperor. . . . Between the enemy and us there was only the narrow sea. The enemies attacked without restraint, destroying all the lands, the most beautiful churches and monasteries, and some of the fortresses, and they burned the most beautiful of these. They reveled daily in murdering and in dreadful enslavement such as had never been heard of.[58]

The leading cities of Bithynia resisted Turkish attacks for another two decades, with Brusa falling in 1326, Nicea in 1331, and Nicomedia in 1337. Each conquest was accompanied by violent displacements of both rural and urban populations and by the collapse of what had been highly structured military, civil, and ecclesiastical affairs. Anarchy prevailed, nullifying all efforts at gaining an advantage over the seemingly undefeatable Turks. Even the meager opposition of those remaining loyal lacked leadership, for many of the civil and ecclesiastical officials had fled to the relative security of Constantinople. Nothing so catastrophic had ever struck the patriarchate of Constantinople before.

It is virtually impossible to determine either the overall population figures for the period or the number of persons who were forced to migrate westward. Nevertheless, we can assume that there had been a large and stable Orthodox population in Anatolia,[59] for there was a sizable number of bishoprics in the territory and, by canon law, a bishopric could be established only in a well-populated city (πολυάνθρωποι).[60] We can in no way understand the history of the Byzantine Church in that period or the account of Athanasios' activities without assuming a substantial shift in population from what had been the wealthiest and numerically strongest part of the church.

Turkish invasions in the eleventh and twelfth centuries produced insignificant population movements. Anatolia was still largely Hellenized and Christian at the time of Athanasios' first patriarchate. Vryonis notes that at the end of the thirteenth century the largest source of income for the occupying Turks was the tax paid by Greek Christians.[61] This is certainly supported by Athanasios' claim that the Orthodox population in the area had been deserted by the civil servants and the bishops, who had fled the area. Regardless of earlier settlements, the fact is that "this late thirteenth and early fourteenth-century period is the period of final, critical change in the ethnic and religious configuration of Anatolia."[62]

As Anatolia slipped away from the empire and the church, a large number of refugees fled to the capital. Athanasios nowhere mentioned the number of refugees in Constantinople or the number in need of housing, but what is clear is that as the territory of the empire shrank, the population of the city increased.[63] André Andréades was the first to study the population of the city systematically, and he concluded that it rarely fell below half a million and often approached 800,000.[64] For the period from the end of the twelfth century to the fall of the city, however there was a steady decline from 800,000 to 140,000, and for the period of Athanasios' patriarchates the population may have been somewhere between 150,000 and 200,000.[65]

After 1290, there was great disruption in western Anatolia as the Osmanli began to consolidate their territory. Between 1290 and 1300 Osman extended his boundaries until they were contiguous with the Byzantines'. The missionary zeal of the Osmanli, which distinguished them from other Turkish groups, as well as their strategic location in Bithynia, gave them a more aggressive character than that of other Turks.[66] In settled areas under older Turkish control, Christians had reached a modus vivendi; this was not so in the newly conquered areas, from which large numbers of Byzantine Christians fled. We know that the Maeander was severely depopulated by the early fourteenth century.[67]

Following the defeat of Michael IX at Baphaeus, and for twenty-five years thereafter, there were considerable population shifts. When Michael, who had taken refuge behind the walls of Magnesia, decided to leave, his army was followed by men, women, and children "who paid for the preservation of their lives with a long march and much sorrow."[68] The exodus was massive; as one author notes; "Ainsi la région, que quelques années auparavant était parmi les plus habitées, présente des la fin du XIIIᵉ et le début du XIVᵉ siècle l'aspect d'une contrée quasi déserte et ruinée."[69] Some went to fortified cities in Anatolia, but most moved across the Bosphorus to Constantinople. Pachymeres wrote that the Osmanli, whom he called "Persians," were "attacking the lands of the Rhomaioi," and they "transformed them in a short time into another desert encompassing the length and width of the land from the Black Sea to the Sea by Rhodes."[70] Muntaner, the Catalan chronicler, noted that refugees fled before the Turks to coastal regions, interior fortified cities, and, if lucky, to Constantinople. Pachymeres wrote:

> You saw at that time a pitiful sight: namely, those who were carrying away their possessions and crossing over to the city [Constantinople], who had despaired of their salvation. And the straits received a throng of people and animals daily who had not been freed without the greatest of tragedies. There was no one who did not lament the loss of the members of his family, one recalling her husband, another her son or a daughter, another a brother and a sister, and another the name of some relation.[71]

Pachymeres notes that "the ruin of the countryside gave birth to want in Constantinople"[72] Constantinople received such sizable numbers of refugees that the population soon became oppressed by famine and plague. Traditional services and controls that had given the city the appearance of a modern state weakened and finally collapsed. Besieged by Turks on the east and Catalans on the west, and troubled by social turmoil, the urban population was prepared neither morally nor financially to support the refugees and in no mood to open homes and larders.[73] But Athanasios was not about to accept anything short of sharing all available goods.

Athanasios demonstrated throughout his letters a genuine concern for the refugees flooding the city, and in the process of meeting their needs, he necessarily assumed many civil duties that had previously devolved on other officials. His warning was clear: should the people and the emperor continue in their refusal to help the needy, and particularly the refugees, the result would be total ruin of the nation.[74] Muntaner, an essentially hostile outsider, agreed with Athanasios' observations on the suffering, noting that because of Catalan charity and the absence of it among the Greeks, more than two thousand poor Greeks whom the Turks had plundered joined the Catalans:

> When we were at Constantinople, the people who had fled from Anatolia because of the Turks, lived and lay among the rubbish heaps and called out that they were hungry, but there was no Greek who would give them anything for the love of God, and yet there was a great market of all kinds of victuals.[75]

The state machinery was too disorganized for Andronikos to rally its limited resources to action. In fact, Athanasios' demands for assistance often went unheeded, and his was the only voice calling for assistance. Is it any wonder that the poor of the city looked to him as a saint, whereas the officials and the wealthy sought his resignation?

The immediate problem was food; although it was not in particularly short supply, it was being sold at exorbitantly high prices due to inflation, the debasement of the traditionally stable Byzantine coinage (*hyperperon*), hoarding by foreign and Byzantine speculators, and the export of grain to Italy where it brought higher prices.[76] The Byzantine grain market was almost totally dominated by Italian merchants, particularly the Genoese, who controlled the fish and corn markets of the Black Sea.[77]

In the winter of either 1305–1306 or 1306–1307, Athanasios tried to compel the wealthy of the city to assist in the relief of the refugees. He asked that Andronikos read an encyclical letter to all the "powerful" (δυνάμενοι) of the city assembled in the imperial palace, outlining in what manner and to what measure (ὅσον καὶ οἷον) they were to contribute. He requested that all take into their house for the winter as many refugees as possible. If this was not possible, then each should give funds toward the support of the refugees:

> It seems good to those who fear God to become heirs of the divine voice which commands: "I was hungry, and you gave me food," and to save their souls from the pitiable and terrible sentence which

> decrees: "Depart from me, ye accursed ones . . . for I was hungry and you did not feed me" [Matt. 25:35, 41–42]. Wherefore I ask that rich and poor, laymen and monks, gain the blessing of God, and be saved from the abominable sentence, and assume responsibility for the support of a number of fellow believers in proportion to the prosperity which was granted you by God, and inscribe these names in the present letter, so that I may know which ones are left out, and may petition my mighty and holy emperor to make provision for them.[78]

In another letter, addressed "to the great and small alike," Athanasios called on the people to practice almsgiving. Referring to the refugees, he wrote: "The life of the Byzantines is no more than a dream. All have lost someone—parents, friends, and acquaintances; many have abandoned their futures and land to the enemy, leaving their homes without knowing where they are going." These refugees had to be cared for, and all were expected to share their earthly goods without the pretense of poverty. Always the moralist, he urged that the people use the fate of the refugees to reflect on the "value of earthly things."[79] All were urged to offer the refugees lodging and any extra food and clothing. Again he asked that those who were able should charge themselves to care for one or two refugees; the others should give alms according to their means, with joy.[80] In still another place, he urged all those who were well off and comfortable to share with the poor, and he offered himself and the patriarchate as a clearing house for the distribution of supplies. Many of the poor were actually lodged by the patriarch in the secularized church of St. Mocius the Great Martyr,[81] despite, it seems, an earlier letter forbidding residence in a church building.[82]

Athanasios also attempted to rouse the people to assist those taken captive in Turkish raids. Western Anatolia in the late thirteenth and early fourteenth centuries was the center of a flourishing trade in Christian slaves. Matthew of Ephesus wrote, "Also distressing is the multitude of prisoners, some of whom are miserably enslaved to the Ishmaelites and others to the Jews. . . . Those [prisoners] arising from the enslavement of Rhomaioi through the capture of their lands and cities from all times by comparison would be found to be smaller or at most equal."[83]

In one place Athanasios suggested that prosperous Byzantines should contribute money for the relief and release of captives: "For example, there is within the city a great number of captives, and those who have the means should help them, each in the way he prefers."[84] He suggested two ways in which the wealthy could assist (δύο γὰρ ζητῶ): "either that each assumes the support of as many [captives] as he can until summer, or that he give as much as he wishes."[85] He addressed the faithful directly and urged them to contribute money, bread, and clothing to the prisoners as they were able and to take in as many as possible.[86] He set up the same conditions for the relief of prisoners as he did for the refugees. The Byzantine church throughout its history had encouraged the relief of captives. Gregoras noted that Irene Choumnos, on becoming a religious, gave up much of her wealth to both prisoners and the poor.[87] Athanasios himself gave, through his servant Christdoulos, one *nomisma* to each prisoner in the city.[88]

The situation was aggravated by a serious miscalculation: in the winter of 1303–1304 Andronikos had brought the Grand Catalan Company, led by Roger de Flor, to the empire to assist in clearing Turkish-occupied lands and to relieve the besieged Anatolian cities.

Athanasios had opposed the employment of the Catalan mercenaries. His letters demonstrate that he had news of Roger's men maiming the Byzantine population of Anatolia. He outlined their successes, but also listed their atrocities. In spite of their successes, he urged Andronikos not to rely on foreign armies; "even if the whole West, if it were possible, were to join to help us," it would do nothing.[89] Athanasios was angered by Andronikos' refusal to heed his warnings regarding the Catalans. He disliked the Catalans not only for their violence and their Latin Christianity, which he feared would be foisted upon Orthodox believers, but also because they represented a deceptive solution to the Byzantine predicament. To Athanasios, military might was not what was needed; rather, only social justice would win God's pleasure and God's assistance. In addition, it soon became evident that any benefits the Catalans brought to the empire not only were ephemeral but were severely limited by their plundering of the people they were hired to protect.[90]

Besides their plundering and the threat of conversion, the Catalans represented a tremendous financial strain on the empire. They were, after all, mercenaries. In the early autumn of 1304, their leader demanded payment in compensation for booty lost when the Byzantine population locked them out of Magnesia.[91] Money was not readily available, and Andronikos was forced to institute a new tax, the *sitokrithon* (σιτόκριθον). The emperor ordered that every peasant give six *modioi* of wheat and four of barley to the treasury. In addition, one-third of the salary of every Byzantine official was deducted to meet the Catalan demands.[92] Pachymeres recorded that early in 1305, when the emperor was trying to raise 100,000 *modioi* of grain for the Catalans, both imperial and Catalan agents were put to the task of making the collection.[93] Although Athanasios agreed that taxes had to be collected, he insisted that the "bloodthirsty" Catalans must not be allowed to collect them. More serious was Andronikos' effort to palm off on Roger's men a debased silver coinage as pay. This move backfired when the cheaper money was eventually passed on to the Byzantine population and fisc.[94]

### *Provisioning the City*

Another of Athanasios' concerns was to provision the people of the city. Throughout the history of the empire, the political threat inherent in famine was sufficient reason for the food supply to be a central concern of the imperial administration; the capital was heavily populated for most of its history and its foodstuffs often had to come great distances.[95] Andréadès, in an effort to determine how applicable the term "monopolistic paradise" was for Byzantium, concluded that the state traditionally exercised control, not only of the fiscal but also of economic and commercial policies as well. Neither work nor commerce was free in Byzantium.[96] Brătianu wrote that statism and controls "le plus absolu présidait aux échanges commerciaux et en règlementait minutieusement tous les détails."[97] Although free wheat ceased to be distributed in the seventh century, the government continued to control prices.

The commercial gains made under the reorganization of Michael VIII were lost during the weak leadership of Andronikos. In 1265, Michael VIII signed a treaty with Venice fixing the rules for commerce in wheat; in 1285, the same regulations were repeated in a treaty by Andronikos.[98] Both stipulated that grain could not be exported unless the price fell below a certain level. By 1304, the export of wheat grown on Byzantine territory, though small indeed, was forbidden. Wheat grown in the Black Sea area not under Byzantine control could, however, be freely traded. Although completely enfeebled and fallen from its former grandeur and incapable of military efforts, the empire nonetheless pursued "la politique étatiste en matière d'approvisionnement, qu'il avait héritée du règne autoritaire et ambitieux de Michael VIII."[99] Although the treaty of 1285 would certainly lead to this conclusion, the fact is that by the early fourteenth century, Andronikos no longer had the means to enforce such a policy on export sales or on the storage of cereals in state warehouses. The export restrictions of 1265 and 1285 were unenforceable. Athanasios' letters offer a picture of the empire in which these statist policies and the guild structure of the former years had collapsed. The empire could not assure itself of a stable income; nor could the people expect goods at fair prices. Hence, by the beginning of the fourteenth century, there was virtually no state control over the Byzantine economy.

Athanasios insisted that such controls be re-established, but the problem that both he and Andronikos faced was not so much the shortage of as the speculation in wheat, which pushed its price out of the reach of the lower classes. The fact that Athanasios worked so hard to re-establish this statist policy indicated that the emperor was hard-pressed to control prices, exports, and the warehousing of cereals. Attempts to control prices were the last line of defense.[100]

Athanasios reacted vigorously to exploitation by Italian merchants who, from the end of the eleventh century, had dominated much of Byzantine grain traffic.[101] In a letter to Andronikos, he violently attacked grain dealers and profiteers: "those who are enriched by Mammon have not hesitated to hoard grain and wine which God has furnished for the support of the people . . . to the ruin of the poor." He even threatened to read the letter in St. Sophia and excommunicate the dealers.[102] Pachymeres records that the letter was read publicly, but to no avail; it was not followed, however, by the threatened excommunication.[103] His vita reports that he actually "ordered" that the warehouses of the rich, merchants, and other speculators be opened "through words and persuasion" and the population fed in public kitchens.[104]

Athanasios asked rather bluntly that Andronikos "not yield to bribes, either through the disease of greed or simple friendship." It is evident that Athanasios blamed Andronikos for the condition of the people and for the fact that Latin merchants had the upper hand in the Byzantine marketplace. Commenting on government controls of supplies, he remarked in 1304:

> [Controls] will contribute much to the incomparable blessing of good order. For the state is suffering great harm from the famine, since

> the Romans' [Byzantines'] fortune, both gold and silver, has almost all ended up in the hands of the Latins. But worst is their arrogance as they laugh at us haughtily, and despise us so much that they boast of receiving favors from the wives of citizens in payment for grain. . . . For this reason I ask that your majesty see to it that they not gloat anymore in such undertakings.[105]

The Latins referred to here are no doubt the Genoese of Pera, whose ships monopolized the Black Sea grain traffic.[106] Food was available, but the Latins and the Byzantine speculators wanted either to export it to Italy or to hold it until prices increased. This hoarding, together with inflation and the debasement of the once stable Byzantine monetary coinage, brought on shortages and famine.

The Byzantine and Western agents amassed large quantities of wheat in their warehouses; it was stored until the price rose and then, without thought to the harm, held for release at still higher prices.[107] This was not a unique form of profit-taking or exploitation but it was one that was particularly distasteful to the patriarch. Especially acute during Athanasios' second patriarchate, it was aggravated after 1305, when buying Thracian and Black Sea grain became difficult because of a Bulgarian blockade.[108]

Athanasios appealed to Andronikos to end these speculative practices. His letters are filled with moralistic demands for the emperor to legislate moral life so that evils will be lifted from the people to ensure justice. He should punish all officials who saw the rise in prices, the inflated currency, and the decrease in supplies as opportunities to profit, fulfill his obligation to be the good steward of what God had granted him, and demonstrate this stewardship with deeds.[109] He called on Andronikos to put to shame those who considered the trade in grain "a source of profit and luxury and perpetual glory to raise the prices on all necessary provisions." He continued: "It is for the sake of these people that God decreed men should be ruled by men, lest like fishes the stronger swallow up the weaker with impunity."[110] He went on in another place to say that only the emperor could end this "plague," the monopoly of victuals; no priest, no levite, no official could remedy this, only the emperor, to whom he referred as ὁ Μωυσῆς, the one who strikes the rock and gives water to his people.[111]

Besides appealing to the emperor, Athanasios went directly to the people and made appeals for acts of pious charity. All must eventually answer the charge of the St. Matthew's Gospel (25:31–

46).[112] He noted that all who give to the poor, give to God (δανείζει Θεῷ).[113] "Let us give to these who are hungry, let us dress Christ through the poor."[114] Anyone who speculated on the misery of the times to earn more would groan in the future life: "cursed [δημοκατάρατος] be he who raises the price of wheat, and blessed be he who is honest in his dealings."[115] "Let us feed, house, and clothe those without anything; let us care with deed and word as is within our power for those who are widows, orphans, and ill."[116] Otherwise, he wrote, we shall be thought of as having killed (ἀπέκτειναν) them.[117] "Those who wish to do good in this way, let them write it down on paper and the whole people will pray for them."[118] This list was to be read in church, but, he noted, it would be better not to have one's name listed, not to yield to human vanity.

In the summer of 1305, after the defeat at the Battle of Apros, the large number of refugees as well as the monopoly of grain supplies strained the resources of the capital. Athanasios issued a letter calling on all the people, both religious and lay, to offer the patriarch all they were able—oil, wheat, wine, fish, cheese, vegetables, and other victuals. In addition, he called for clothing to be distributed.[119] We do not know how he distributed these supplies, but it is likely that he set up distribution centers at the gate and doors of monasteries and churches throughout the city.[120]

The monks and nuns of the empire were not exempt from these social demands. In a general letter written during the winter of 1306–1307, Athanasios called on them to observe the fast days and periods and to eat only once a day during the two days of the week not designated fast days, that is, Wednesdays and Fridays. The money and food thereby conserved in this way would be distributed to the hungry and needy in the city.[121] Certainly one of the reasons why he demanded *stabilitas loci* for monks and nuns of the empire was that they too easily took up residence in the homes of the wealthy as professional divines and domestic "holy men"; they became part of the very problem he sought to solve. Pretending to be "holy men," they were, in effect, nonproductive consumers of the wealth that could have been put to the service of the poor.[122]

There was nothing revolutionary in Athanasios' call. Byzantine social activists, such as the zealot revolutionaries of Thessalonica (1342–1350), knew nothing of genuine revolution or of a revolutionary movement beyond their own city, despite the existence of parallel movements in parts of Thrace.[123] Even some minor initial anti-ecclesiastical episodes ended quickly when they were opposed by the people.[124] The only affirmation beyond the charitable is the salvific in which Athanasios identified the salvation of the giver with the treatment of the poor and hungry (Matt. 25:35–45). The social structure was to remain unchanged because, as the eternal metaphor of the kingdom of God, it was in no need of change. Reform was essentially future-directed: "For the sake of [the Kingdom of God] the Lord thought it just to have rich and poor in the world, so that He might make the former heirs of His Kingdom on account of their mercy and compassion, and the latter through a thankful and patient spirit."[125] "It is in our power," therefore, Athanasios wrote, "to gain heaven or hell through our works."[126] According to him, it is the poor who teach the glorious how to live by their requiring to be fed and housed;[127] riches are a great danger, not in themselves but in their use or misuse. All this he encouraged with the story of Lazarus and the rich man's storehouses (Luke 16:20–23).[128] In another place, he warned that the people should not regard the story of Lazarus as a μύϑος.[129] The reference point for reform is always the Kingdom of God. Revolution and radical change do not flow from the essentially conservative attitude that had characterized the Byzantine ecclesiastical and political life since the eighth century.

In addition, Athanasios' attitude toward property was relatively traditional and rooted in the patristic tradition. He directly challenged the notion of private property as absolute, as "sacred."[130] With its roots in the Roman legal tradition of *res privata*, capitalism had rooted itself in the primacy of property or capital. The fathers of the church, such as Sts. Clement of Alexandria, Basil the Great, and John Chrysostom, challenged Roman law and practice. For them, the cause of poverty was to some degree the private appropriation of what had been created as common; therefore, property could be described as "injustice," "theft," and "robbery."[131] In Athanasios there was nothing abstract: his concern was as immediate as the obvious disparity between the wealth and the poverty of Constantinople. He even complained that some of the bishops, by using the income of the church for their own benefits, had actually taken what properly belonged to the poor, and in patristic tradition, he affirmed human solidarity and mutuality, against which an absolute sense of private property was a threat. Athanasios was no innovator; he stood firmly in the patristic tradition of the Orthodox church in his teaching on wealth, property, and poverty. Needless to say, this patristic teaching was received well neither in the fourth nor the fourteenth century.

All his pleading brought no action by the emperor and no recorded responses from the wealthy of the city. For whatever reason, Andronikos was incapable of re-establishing traditional food controls in the city. Athanasios was clearly angry in the spring of 1306, when cargoes of Genoese Black Sea grain reached the city for transshipment and were stored in warehouses during a famine. In fact, much of the food shortage was artificial, and wheat continued to be exported to the West. Athanasios reported that on walks through the city, the poor and the hungry "complain as if with one voice about the grain, and almost everyone entreats me piteously that it not leave the capital."[132] He promised the people that he would urge the emperor to forbid Genoese merchants to export grain to Italy.

Athanasios received little support from Andronikos, and his anger increased accordingly:

> In the present circumstances, since the whole people has been shipwrecked, I do not simply petition for the relief of a general disaster, but I insist and am adamant [ἀξιῶ καὶ καταναγκάζω], and if I am not heeded, I will get angry, trusting in my own conscience.[133]

He wrote impatiently, probably in the critical period late in 1306:

> Although up to this time, I have not gone so far as to force your divine majesty to fulfill my petitions, but have only made reports referred to your discretion, now, so that good order and righteousness may firmly abide in the Queen of Cities, not only do I supplicate and demand, but I will not cease to demand, that above all the honest purchase of grain and bread be carefully controlled, and that this supervision be carried out by a man noted for his honesty.[134]

Athanasios found the corruption of the food control so offensive that he asked that nothing with regard to provisioning the city be done without his permission. Athanasios demanded, in short, control of grain prices, the exclusion of Byzantine and Italian middlemen—black marketeers—and the restoration of the state monopoly. He thanked the emperor for adopting his idea and establishing a grain commission, so "that the ships which transport the grain could be closely supervised, so that public buyers of grain and grain dealers do not buy up cargoes, but rather that the needy individual should be able to procure it directly."[135] The people of the city were to have immediate access to supply ships and the profit-taking middlemen were to be cut out. The grain commission was charged with surveillance of all that concerned the provisioning of the capital. To fulfill this charge, Athanasios told Andronikos that there was no one "more honest, nor more trustworthy than Dermokaites, the Sebastos, whose selection will bring about good order" (ὑπὲρ εὐνομίας καὶ εὐθύτητος).[136] Athanasios asked "that no other official except the pious man I mentioned [Dermokaites] be permitted to control the administration of grain supply." He then requested that one of his own monks be added to the proposed commission.[137]

Part and parcel of Athanasios' emphasis on the grain commission was the need to control weights and measures, as well as distribution and prices. In a letter asking that two of the demarchs, Antiocheites and Ploummes, be selected for the commission, he asked for controls on the use of double weights. Closing the letter, he added: "And I ask that these measures be maintained perpetually, to the glory of God who is extolled through good order . . . for careful and provident governing of all your subjects."[138] The call for standard weights and measures became a theological theme in the context of the God who abhors injustice.

The urban bishop traditionally was the one to oversee the reliability of weights and measures in each city.[139] But with the collapse of the guild system, it was difficult to determine and control who was functioning in what capacity. The government had lost control of the bakers' trade.[140] Athanasios' call for the grain commission, as well as for various regulations to supervise bakers, and for the direct sale of wheat and victuals from ships to the poor was part of his essentially conservative policy to restore a statist system. Only such a system would ensure protection to the oppressed poor of the city and guarantee the equitable distribution of the limited resources available to the urban population.

Byzantine wealth, according to Athanasios, was pouring into the hands of the Latin merchants because they controlled the shipping and marketing of necessary foodstuffs during a time of famine and inflation. Athanasios' persistent passion (everywhere evident in his letters) for the proper functioning of the Orthodox commonwealth shaped his policy of traditional Byzantine statist economic controls. His call for state control of grain sales and of weights and measures was an attempt to return the empire to its previous policy as outlined in the tenth-century *Book of the Prefect*.[141]

Life in the already beleaguered empire was further complicated when the Catalan leader was assassinated by one of Michael IX's troops.[142] Berengar de Rocafort promptly assumed leadership of the Catalans and announced that all ties of allegiance to Andronikos were terminated, and the territory of the empire was now subject to plunder. For two years Thrace was ravaged by the Catalans who encountered almost no opposition from imperial troops. The Catalans besieged Constantinople, painfully revealing the full extent of imperial impotence and occasioning civil disorders in the city in May 1305.[143] Andronikos' unwise dissolution of the Byzantine fleet early in his reign now became an explosive issue as he became unable either to defend or to provision his capital. It was clear to many that, from an economic point of view, the Byzantines should go into the shipping business themselves to recapture the grain trade. The Genoese fleet, which the Byzantines previously had relied upon for defense, was unavailable during the Catalan siege, for the Genoese had made peace with the mercenaries in exchange for freedom to navigate the Hellespont and Propontis.[144]

Andronikos made no attempt to defend the countryside, where, within sight of the city, fields, orchards, and vineyards were destroyed indiscriminately. Attempts to buy off the new Catalan leader, de Rocafort, failed; his demands were astronomically high.[145] The horror of Asia Minor was being repeated at the walls of Constantinople.

At the same time as they attacked the cities in the area, the Catalans lived off the land. Muntaner observed that "we sowed nothing nor ploughed nor dug over the vineyard nor pruned the vines, but took, every year, as much wine as we wanted and as much wheat and oats."[146] He agreed that the terror that the Catalans created among the Byzantine population at this time was so extreme that the very word *Frank*, a generic term for Westerners, was sufficient to send the people into flight.[147] It was indeed a pathetic picture: the inhabitants of the suburbs, countryside, and Pera, along with the Anatolian refugees, crowding the fortress-capital, already beleaguered by famine.

One of the most significant issues that confronted the emperor and the city was the collapse of the Thracian grain supply. Although the capital had suffered from food shortages since 1302, the worst threat came in the winter of 1306–1307 as a result of Andronikos' political decision to destroy the Thracian grain supply—a rare occasion of a firm stand and independent action on the part of the emperor. At this time the city relied on its Thracian and Black Sea grain supplies. The alliance of Berengar de Rocafort and Svetoslav closed off Bulgarian grain supplies and ports to Byzantium. Andronikos had to institute a special police force in July 1305 to accompany the peasants out of the city to cultivate their fields threatened by marauding Catalans.[148]

It occurred to Andronikos that, in spite of the threat of famine and the vigorous opposition of Athanasios, one way of ridding Thrace of the Catalans was to leave the land fallow and to suspend the policy of sending peasants out to their fields under police protection to cultivate crops. There is no evidence that crops were sown in the fall of 1305. The danger of course was clear: the population of the overcrowded city might face starvation well before the Catalans retired from the region in search of food and plunder elsewhere.[149] Andronikos, even though he did not always act on Athanasios' constant suggestions, had at least *listened* in the past. On this occasion he was out of character in his determination; he would not retreat from his order to destroy the crops and leave the fields uncultivated. Pachymeres recorded that the people did not dare leave the city for fear of the Catalans and, in addition, because the emperor's order forbade them to venture far from the walls. He wrote, "Those around the emperor had seen best to forbid the sowing, so that the peasants would not sow for the enemies [to harvest] next year. For this reason the plows remained idle and our people were menaced by the most severe famine."[150] The vita of Kalothetos recorded the severe famine of 1306–1307: "Famine had struck Constantinople, famine more terrible than any ever recorded, so that whole families were extinguished. Dead people were lying in piles in the streets. So weakened were men by this famine that those who carried the dead fell themselves into the tombs."[151] Athanasios' letters also indicate that the idea was that of the emperor's advisors. Athanasios asked Andronikos to let the peasants go back to their fields to cultivate crops.[152] What had been rich and productive farmland between the Marcia River and the walls of Constantinople was totally wasted,[153] thus aggravating the already severe famine in the overcrowded capital.

Although this policy to drive out the Catalans was eventually successful, it was violently opposed by Athanasios, who was more concerned with the immediate implications of the famine in the city than with the distant possibility of the departure of the Catalans:

> Leaving the land unplanted, Holy Emperor, will bring more destruction than profit, seeing that it is our sins which force the goodness of God to deliver us over to various misfortunes, or even to the sword. And instead of demonstrating substantial conversion and marked repentance . . . we rather indulge in oppression of the poor [and] kindle the injustice and greed of those who rage in such [oppression].[154]

He plainly suggested that some merchants in the city encouraged this scorched-earth policy in order to enhance their own dishonest gain: "And would that you did not yield to those who yearn for this sort [of profit]," but punish them rather than forbid the people "to till the soil in order to earn their living."[155] As usual in Athanasios' letters, he returned to the primary cause of Byzantine suffering—sin and the failure to offer repentance. Pachymeres said that the people wanted to return to the fields and believed them to be safe from the marauding Catalans because of the patriarch's prayers. It is not our food, Athanasios said, that attracts the enemy, but the baseness of our souls. "Therefore urge us to do good deeds, either by persuasion or force, and in any case do not prevent the people from tilling the earth."[156]

Andronikos held to his plan and was vindicated by the departure of the Catalans in the summer of 1307, when they found things very expensive and suffered from a severe lack of food.[157] They decided to move into Macedonia. The severity of the famine was, however, averted because Svetoslav had allowed Black Sea grain to reach the city.[158]

Athanasios deplored the lack of action on his own part—his failure to share even "the crumbs from his table" (Matt. 15:27).[159] During the same winter (1306–1307), he took another step beyond noisome appeals and prodding of the civil authorities. He actually initiated a program of establishing, staffing, and supplying soup kitchens at various locations about the capital. His vita describes him in the same terms he had used to inspire Andronikos—the "new Moses."[160]

It was this famine that apparently occasioned an incident of a miraculous nature. Theoktistos, his biographer, reports that Athanasios sought to lend relief to the victims by opening his own limited supplies of grain and money to the public. He ordered his faithful servant Christodoulos to give thirty modioi of wheat to each of the poor convents in the city, even though his stores totaled only fifty modioi. As he distributed the wheat, his supplies miraculously held out, as in the multiplication of the loaves (Matt. 14:17–20; Mark 6:38–44), to supply all the poor convents. In a second incident, he similarly ordered Christodoulos to distribute one measure of grain to each poor person—with the result that a total of six measures sufficed for two thousand persons.[161]

The dating of the kitchens can be determined internally. Both Athanasios' letters and his biographers indicate that they were opened in the period of the most severe famine as well as the most severe winter; all evidence indicates that this period corresponded to the winter of 1306–1307.[162] In a letter to the emperor, he quoted Matthew 22:37–40 concerning the two great commandments, and then went on: "And what was my charity to the poor?" He described how he had decided to set up locations to boil a gruel for the needy and the miserable.[163] In another letter dating from about 1306–1307, he wrote, detailing this effort,

> We thought of setting up cauldrons from whatever chanced to be [available], or even to provide boiled wheat for the people who are in a bad way [τοῖς ἀθλίοις]. Therefore I ask the poor and rich, and laymen and monks, to assist us by contributing to the cauldrons whatever each one has in abundance: oil and wheat, and wine, fish, and cheese, and vegetables, all kinds of food, and [also to donate unneeded] shoes and clothing they happen to have.[164]

How was he to supply these kettles? He called upon the people of the city to make contributions. In a didactic letter, he called on all—clergy, monks, and laity—who had extra resources to offer to the patriarch all that they were able: oil, wheat, wine, fish, cheese, vegetables, and other things to be distributed, as well as clothing. Only in this way would they share the kingdom of the Father, for they would have nourished Christ in the persons of the poor.[165] From his vita we learned that he offered vegetables seasoned with oil and other condiments by the bowl or potful to the needy.[166]

Because of the impoverishment of the church, it was not easy to keep such an operation supplied with victuals. In addition, wood was in very short supply either because little or no money was available to purchase it or because the emperor had forbidden all workers to leave the city. Athanasios begged the emperor: "I soon ran out of even enough wood to keep the fires going. Therefore, I entreat your Divine Majesty to order the keeper of the domains in the hills to be free to bring me wood."[167] The wood was eventually received to keep the fires burning.

Where, in fact, did Athanasios obtain his funding for his social services? He nowhere mentioned his income, only his problems with funding. The destitution of the church was not apparent. Indeed, we may assume that considerable wealth, if not in specie, then in properties and manufacturing facilities, was at the disposal of the patriarchate. The clergy of St. Sophia, in an incident already discussed in Chapter 4, expressed tendentious doubts about it, claiming that Athanasios reduced their salaries unjustly. They demanded to know by what canons they were permitted to starve. Significantly, they also demanded that Athanasios prove to them that the church was in fact poverty-stricken, as the patriarch claimed in reducing their salaries.[168] We can assume that as archbishop of Constantinople he obtained the income typical of any diocesan bishop. As patriarch, of course, he had income due to the patriarchate from suffragan bishops, at least some of whom held dioceses in prosperous areas. The loss of Asia Minor—the economic, military, and ecclesiastical heartland of the empire—was a severe shock to the empire and the church.[169]

Russia, and indeed to a lesser extent the Balkans, offered an economic and ecclesiastical safety valve for the Byzantines.[170] Finally, we know that Athanasios took seriously his control over the property of monasteries and churches in his diocese. In one location, he affirms that he was appointed by a divine mandate to control the church and to manage it and its property as he felt best, "either to sell it or to give it away."[171] Such an attitude was well founded in canonical literature.

Anatolia had had an elaborate ecclesiastical organization of metropolitanates, archbishoprics, and bishoprics, all of which were subordinate to the see of Constantinople. After the disasters beginning late in the eleventh century and continuing until the period under consideration, the territory under obedience to the patriarchate became subject to the same dismemberment as the imperial territory. The poor financial condition of the empire and the church was not due simply to mismanagement or misappropriation, but also to the loss of the large, income-producing areas of Anatolia. The Church of Constantinople lost not only its patrimony but also its income from the dioceses in Anatolia that had formerly supported its many social functions.

In fact, in spite of the pauperization of the Church of Constantinople through the loss of Anatolia, the patriarchate, it may be surmised from late evidence, received significant income from its ecclesiastical dependencies in the Slav lands to the North—Serb, Bulgar, and Russian. Even though the Metropolitan of Kiev was extremely powerful and controlled a vast territory, he occupied only the sixtieth place in seniority and was moved to seventy-second under Andronikos II.[172] Since 1299, the Metropolitan of Kiev resided in prosperous Vladimir on the Klyazma. The see then moved to Moscow, keeping the title of Vladimir and Kiev. Just as the Metropolitan of Kiev received income from his suffragans, we may assume the Patriarch of Constantinople received a regular income from the Metropolitan of Kiev and all Russia, a "very populous nation" (ἔθνος πολυάνθρωπον). As Meyendorff concludes: "The rich revenues of the [Kievan] metropolitanate were of substantial interest to the impoverished Byzantine authorities."[173] The very extent of the country, the piety of its princes, and its large population guaranteed income to the economically strained Byzantine church. It is likely that the Metropolitan could and did influence the Russian princes to send additional gifts and contributions to Constantinople. Meyendorff notes that although concrete evidence for these contributions, such as patriarchal *acta* vis-à-vis the Balkans and Russia, is lacking, it can be surmised that such contributions to the patriarchate were regular. There are, however, several examples of donations for extraordinary reasons, among them Symeon of Moscow's gift in 1347 to John VI Kantakouzenos for the restoration of the collapsed apse of St. Sophia.[174]

Athanasios' reforms focused on the corruption of officials, both secular and ecclesiastical. They cut across all aspects of Byzantine social life and focused on the abuse of the church and the people of the empire. The key to reforming the abuses was the emperor's enforcement of the laws of the empire and the pursuit of righteousness, mutuality, and justice. They were largely reforms rooted in traditional statist controls of essential social services and canonical controls on the behavior of bishops and clergy and the functioning of ecclesiastical institutions. Only the proper application of the canons and laws of the church and empire could ensure the freedom of the church and right order in the Christian empire.

## Notes

1. Talbot, 94, entire letter (*Regestes,* 1608 = Catalan). Talbot, 17, lines 10–14, 42–44 (*Regestes,* 1612 = fortifications). Talbot, 72, lines 1–33 (*Regestes,* 1649 = famine and food supply).

2. See Talbot, 107, entire letter (*Regestes,* 1732), where Athanasios urges Andronikos to chastise his son, the despot Constantine, who caroused at night with the son of the prefect of the city; this was improper given the time (probably Lent) and the desperate situation of the people. He also advised on marital problems between Andronikos and his wife, Irene; see Talbot, 75, entire letter to Irene (*Regestes,* 1629); and Talbot, 97, entire letter to Andronikos (*Regestes,* 1647).

3. Talbot, 37, lines 16–22 (*Regestes,* Appendix 7).

4. V, 134[r] (*Regestes,* 1747).

5. V, 134[v] (*Regestes,* 1747).

6. Talbot, 36, lines 14–18 (*Regestes,* 1639): "καὶ πόθεν ἔξουσι τὸ νικᾶν."

7. Talbot, 100, lines 14–18 (*Regestes,* 1727).

8. Talbot, 18, lines 1–7 (*Regestes,* 1679).

9. Talbot, 17, lines 78–85 (*Regestes,* 1612).

10. *Institutions,* p. 349.

11. Talbot, 100, lines 14–19 (*Regestes,* 1717); and Talbot, 93, lines 13–17 (*Regestes,* 1652).

12. Talbot, 49, lines 28–32 (*Regestes,* 1695).

13. Talbot, 17, line 28 (*Regestes,* 1612).

14. Talbot, 18, lines 28–32 (*Regestes,* 1678). See also Talbot, 36, lines 28–32 (*Regestes,* 1639).

15. Talbot, 68, lines 8–12 (*Regestes,* 1624).

16. Talbot, 27, lines 1–4 (*Regestes,* 1686). Athanasios is careful to point out that the emperor's proper concern is for the secular aspects of administration of monasteries (τοῦ κόσμου εἰσὶ δουλεῖαι). Although the reason for the letter and its content is confused, the complaint is clear. The monks, it appears, would lose the rent from land transferred to the peasants and would be taxed on that land as if they yet held it, while the peasants' tax or rents would go directly into the pockets of the tax collectors.

17. Talbot, 60, lines 62–68 (*Regestes,* 1654); Guilland, "Correspondance," p. 61; on the hetaeriarch, see Kodinos (Pseudo), *Traité,* pp. 178, 186, where the office is described as minor and assistant to the grand hetaeriarch. Laurent assumes that Athanasios here is attacking the grand

hetaeriarch, who would have had direct contact with the emperor; see *Regestes*, 1654, and Dölger, *Regesten*, No. 2266.

18. Talbot, 60, lines 68–75 (*Regestes*, 1654). See Matschke, "Politik und Kirche," 483.

19. Talbot, 37, lines 33–37 (*Regestes*, Appendix 7).

20. Raymond Loenertz, "Le Chancelier imperial à Byzance au XIIIe et au XIVe siècle," *Orientalia Christiana Periodica*, 26 (1960), 275–300; see Kodinos (Pseudo), *Traité*, chap. 5, where the office is described as the actual seat of power and not merely an aulic distinction. In Jean Verpeaux, "Contribution à l'étude de l'administration byzantine," *Byzantinoslavica*, 16 (1956), 276–91, the title is traced to the reign of Michael VIII. Under Andronikos II we can distinguish three men who functioned as mesazon.

21. Talbot, 37, lines 33–39 (*Regestes*, Appendix 7).

22. Bănescu, "Athanase," 55. In spite of his dislike for Choumnos, Athanasios sent a touching letter of consolation to Andronikos, and through him to Irene Choumnos; see Talbot, 96, entire letter (*Regestes*, 1664).

23. Pachymeres, II:192.

24. Matschke, "Politik und Kirche," 483; Matschke pursues a simplistic approach to Patriarch Athanasios. Athanasios was most likely opposed to Choumnos as a classicist and humanist. Choumnos may also have been working against the influence of the patriarch with the emperor, for he represented the decentralizing interests of a landed aristocracy. This is likely: Athanasios demonstrates no open hostility toward classical learning, which Jean Verpeaux, *Nicéphore Choumnos* (Paris: Picard, 1959), p. 192, overstates as a characteristic of monks. Athanasios was opposed to those who sought the salvation of the empire apart from repentance and social justice.

25. Choumnos, "Ἔλεγχος κατὰ τοῦ κακῶς τὰ πάντα Πατριαρχεύσαντος," in *Anecdota Graeca* V, ed. J. F. Boissonade (Hildesheim: Olms, 1962), pp. 255–88, esp. 259–60. Vitalien Laurent, "Les Grandes Crises religieuses à Byzance: La Fin du schisme arsenite," *Académie Roumaine, Bulletin de la Section Historique*, 26.2 (1945), 284, affirms that Athanasios lost his throne because of Theophanes.

26. Talbot, 17, lines 63–67 (*Regestes*, 1612).

27. Talbot, 3, lines 58–62 (*Regestes*, 1673).

28. Talbot, 17, lines 42–51 (*Regestes*, 1612). See also Pachymeres, II:559–61, who mentions a certain Dositheos, who had been so treated.

29. Talbot, 8, lines 16–23 (*Regestes*, 1593).

30. Talbot, 37, lines 16–20 (*Regestes*, Appendix 7).

31. Talbot, 87, lines 38–40 (*Regestes*, 1719).

32. Paul Lemerle, "Un Chrysobulle d'Andronic II Paléologue pour le monastère de Karakala," *Bulletin de Correspondance hellenique*, 60 (1936),

440. See Dölger, *Regesten*, No. 2166; and Ostrogorsky, "L'Histoire de l'immunité," 165–254.

33. *Actes de Xéropotamou*, ed. Jacques Bompaire, Archives de l'Athos, 3 (Paris: Lethielleux, 1964), pp. 13–15. For the effects of this increase in wealth on monastic life, see Boojamra, *Church Reform*, pp. 149–53.

34. See Ševčenko, "Cabasilas," 153–60, who has re-evaluated the conclusion of Tafrali, *Thessalonique*, passim, that the "Anti-zealot Discourse" of Nicholas Kabasilas was actually directed at civil officials who took liberties with ecclesiastical properties, and not against the zealot revolutionaries of Thessalonica (1342–1347). See also Charanis, "Properties," 65*n*31; Ostrogorsky, "L'Histoire de l'immunité," 165–254; Boojamra, *Church Reform*, 155–158.

35. Emilio Hermann, "The Secular Church," *Cambridge Medieval History* IV.2, ed. Joan Hussey (Cambridge: Cambridge University Press, 1967), p. 115. Seen against the long struggle between church and state over the rights of sacred property, Kerularios reacted in frustration, assuming an imperial insignia—purple slippers. See Romily Jenkins, "A Cross of the Patriarch Michael Cerularius," *DOP*, 21 (1967), 237. On Michael's use of the "Donation of Constantine" of which he learned from Cardinal Humbert, see Smith, *Bread*, p. 102.

36. Talbot, 87, lines 1–5 (*Regestes*, 1719).

37. V, 62[r–v] (*Regestes*, 1716); for the text see also Gennadios Arabantzoglou, "'Επιστολιμαία," 173–79.

38. Talbot, 87, lines 26–30 (*Regestes*, 1719).

39. V, 65*r*–65*v* (*Regestes*, 1715); also Talbot, 17, lines 35–49 (*Regestes*, 1624).

40. Talbot, 37, lines 1–5 (*Regestes*, Appendix 7).

41. Talbot, 83, lines 9–13 (*Regestes*, 1718); see Canon 49 of the Council in Trullo (Rhalles and Potles, II:423) for one example of the prohibition of the alienation of monastic property to laypersons.

42. Joan Hussey, "The Later Macedonians, the Comneni, and the Angeli," in *The Cambridge Medieval History* IV.1, ed. Joan Hussey (Cambridge: Cambridge University Press, 1966), p. 219. The Charisticarioi were no longer in existence in fourteenth century but the effective practice was still in effect. See Emilio Hermann, "Charistikaires," in *Dictionnaire de Droit Canonique* III (Paris: Letouzey et Ané, 1939), cols. 611–17.

43. Talbot, 36, lines 11–15 (*Regestes*, 1718).

44. Byzantine canon law permitted the sale of ecclesiastical property and liturgical vessels for the ransom of captives only; see Nomocanon II, 2 (Rhalles and Potles, I:108–9) and Novella 65 of Justinian. That Athanasios felt himself personally responsible for the property of the church, see Talbot, 77, lines 16–20 (*Regestes*, 1714).

45. Pachymeres, II:518–21; Gregoras, I:258–59.

46. Talbot, 14, lines 19–27 (*Regestes*, 1677).
47. Talbot, 25, lines 13–17 (*Regestes*, 1613).
48. Talbot, 7, lines 42–46 (*Regestes*, 1674).
49. Talbot, 83, lines 57–61 (*Regestes*, 1718).
50. Talbot, 25, lines 6–10 (*Regestes*, 1613). Ecclesiastical canons, in general, did not permit the alienation of ecclesiastical property in the Eastern Church for any reason. Nonetheless, on numerous occasions property was voluntarily or involuntarily given up to meet social or military needs. The basic thrust of Byzantine nomocanonical legislation was defensive, protecting church from the misappropriation of its goods. Ecclesiastical property and its disposition in the Byzantine empire had been a greatly underestimated factor in Byzantine ecclesiastical and political life. This notion has recently been corrected by the excellent work of John Philip Thomas, *Private Religious Foundations in the Byzantine Empire* (Washington, D.C.: Dumbarton Oaks Press, 1987), esp. pp. 193ff. Ecclesiastical property, because of its sheer quantity and extent, if for no other reason, was the object of attack, abuse, misuse, and misappropriation for centuries. Questions of control and legal alienation were raised from time to time in legal and ecclesiastical documents by such as Justinian's Novel 120, which permitted the sale of ecclesiastical *keimelia* (sacred vessels) for the ransom of prisoners only (544). Heraclius resorted to the use of the wealth of the Church when attacked by Slavs and Persians in 626 and justified it by references to Justinian's Novel 120. Justinian's law was merely a floodgate for the emperors, to be used and adjusted at will. Isaac I Comnenos (1057–1059) successfully made a move on ecclesiastical property, as did Alexius I (1081–1118), who had recourse to such property and *keimelia* to fight off the Normans in 1081 and the Patzinaks in 1087, each time promising restitution and "never again." See Dölger, *Regesten*, No. 1085. The text appears in *Novella de sacris vasibus in publicum usum non convertendis* (1082); see *Jus graeco-romanum* III, ed. K. E. Zachariae von Lingenthal (Leipzig: Weigel, 1856), pp. 355–58. This did not go unopposed; witness the famous case of Leo of Chalcedon, who accused the emperor of iconoclasm because of his apparent disregard of things and images in his effort to gain liquidity in the 1080s. See John P. Thomas, "A Byzantine Ecclesiastical Reform Movement," *Medievalia et Humanistica*, 12 (1984), 1–16. The supporters of the imperial efforts were not few, as Anna Comnena (*Alexiad* 5.2) and Psellos (*Chronographia* 7.60) make clear. On the support of Patriarch Eustatios Garidas, see Michael Attaliates, *Historia*, ed. I. Bekker (Bonn: Corpus Scriptorum Historiae Byzantinae, 1853), pp. 60–62. Thomas refers to the opposition of Leo of Chalcedon as a part of a "reform" movement. Reform is a strong word, and the author does little to support or define it. He apparently has in mind "reform" in the sense of Western reform and the limitation of lay power and influence within

the Church. Reform in the case of Athanasios and the late Palamites takes on a more systematic and systemic appearance. In general, Athanasios was fighting an age-long battle against the Byzantine tendency to see religious institutions, whether liturgical or charitable, as sources of both profit and piety.

51. Talbot, 83, lines 1–6 (*Regestes*, 1718). He could dispose of the goods of his church at his own will according to Apostolic Canon 38 (Rhalles and Potles, II:52). Measures were, however, taken to ensure there would be no abuse by establishing commissioners to oversee ecclesiastical property. See Canon 26 of the Council of Chalcedon (Rhalles and Potles, II:276).

52. *V*, 134*r*, 136*r* (*Regestes*, 1747).

53. *V*, 134*r* (*Regestes*, 1747). This is a paraphrase of several verses from Hosea; see, for instance, the congruency with Hosea 10:5 and 6:9. Almost every reference Athanasios made to judgment and chastisement, including military losses, are taken from Hosea. McGiffert, "God's Controversy," 1153.

54. *V*, 19*r* (*Regestes*, 1692).

55. *V*, 134*v* (*Regestes*, 1747).

56. *V*, 135*r* (*Regestes*, 1747): "καὶ οἱ πωλοῦντες αὐτά, εὐλογητὸς κύριος καὶ πεπλουντήκαμεν ἔλεγον."

57. Pachymeres, 327, 334–35.

58. Pachymeres, 338.

59. Speros Vryonis, *The Decline of Hellenism in Asia Minor and the Process of Islamization for the Eleventh through the Fifteenth Century* (Berkeley: University of California Press, 1971), p. 25. Population estimates for Asia Minor during this period are around six million.

60. See ibid., p. 27, for a discussion of the population requirement for the establishment of an episcopal see. What is clear here is that a large and stable population was necessary. Canon 57 of Laodicea prescribes πλῆθος ἀνθρώπων for the appointment of a bishop; see Rhalles and Potles, III:222–23, commented on by Balsamon. The Council of Chalcedon established in 451 that only "cities" might be episcopal seats. Later the terms "city" and "bishopric" became interchangeable; on this see Heinrich Gelzer, "Ungedrückte und ungenügend veröffentlichte Texte der *Notitiae episcopatum*," *Bayerische Akademie der Wissenschaften. Abhandlungen der philosophisch-philologischen Klasse*, 21 (1901), 546.

61. Vryonis, *Decline*, 170, 182. Marco Polo testified that Anatolia was yet largely Christian, both Greek and Armenian. See *The Book of Ser Marco Polo the Venetian Concerning the Kingdoms and Marvels of the East* I (London: Murray, 1903), p. 43.

62. Vryonis, *Decline*, p. 258.

63. Ibid, pp. 1–2.

64. André Andréadès, "La Population de l'empire byzantine," *Actes du IVe congrès international d'Etudes byzantines* (Sophia: Institut archaéologique bulgare, 1935), p. 117.

65. Andre Andréadès, "De la population de Constantinople sous les empereurs byzantins," *Metron*, 1 (1920), 68, 104.

66. Henry A. Gibbons, *The Foundations of the Ottoman Empire* (London: Cass, 1968) p. 28. Ibn Batoutah offers a detailed picture of the principalities that arose on the remains of Seljuk and Byzantine rule; see *Voyages d'Ibn Batoutah* II, edd. C. Defremery et B. R. Sanguinetti (Paris: L'Imprimèrie nationale, 1914) pp. 255–354.

67. Pachymeres, 310–11.

68. Pachymeres, 412.

69. Hélène Ahrweiler, "L'Histoire et la géographie de la région de Smyrne entre les deux occupations turques (1081–1317), particulierement au XIIIe siècle," in *Travaux et Mêmoires* I (Paris: De Boccord, 1965), p. 28.

70. Pachymeres, 318–19.

71. Pachymeres, II:415; see ibid., 102, where he refers to the Turks in classical terms as Πέρσαι. Ramon Muntaner, *The Chronicle of Muntaner* II. trans. Lady Goodenough II (London: Hakluyt Society, 1921), p. ccii, reports that the Turks would have taken Constantinople had they had the ships.

72. Pachymeres, 402: "καὶ λίαν ἐδεῶς ἐχόντων τῶν ἀναγκαίων διὰ τὴν τῶν ἐξωτερικῶν ἐξαπώλειαν."

73. Laiou, *Constantinople*, p. 197.

74. Talbot, 46, lines 13–17 esp. lines 18–19 (*Regestes*, 1693).

75. Muntaner, *Chronicle*, p. cciii; see Vryonis, *Decline*, p. 255.

76. See Zakythinos, *Crise*, pp. 8–9, on the effects of the monetary failure. Nicol, *Last Centuries*, p. 117, explains the debasement of the coinage as a change of from 14 to 10 karats of gold.

77. Nicol, *Last Centuries*, p. 117.

78. Talbot, 107, entire letter (*Regestes*, 1729).

79. V, 183[v] (*Regestes* 1757).

80. V, 184[v]–184[r] (*Regestes*, 1757).

81. V, 167[v]–168[r] (*Regestes*, 1753). It was probably no longer in use for cult purposes; see Janin, *Géographie*, pp. 354, 358.

82. Talbot, 66, lines 67–68 (*Regestes*, 1709).

83. Maximos Treu, *Matthaios, Metropolit von Ephesos: Über sein Leben und seine Schriften* (Potsdam: Hakkert, 1901), 56.

84. Talbot, 22, lines 6–10 (*Regestes*, 1684).

85. Talbot, 22, lines 11–15 (*Regestes*, 1684).

86. *V*, 226[r] (*Regestes*, 1777). Laurent maintains (402) as does Talbot in her commentary on letter 22, line 6 (329), that the text αἰχμάλωτος

refers to refugees and not to prisoners. It is not inconceivable in the context that αἰχμάλωτος has its traditional meaning of a "body of captives," prisoners of war, or those taken by the sword. This explanation is particularly convincing in light of the fact that αἰχμάλωτος is used in the Byzantine eucharistic liturgy as "captive."

Although it is difficult to imagine that the Byzantines would tolerate Turkish trade in Christian prisoners, it was in fact common for Genoese to do so, either in or through Constantinople. This may well have involved Christian captives whom the Genoese would transport for sale in the markets of the Middle East. I am indebted to John Meyendorff for suggesting this context for Athanasios' use of the term. See Meyendorff, *Byzantium*, pp. 49–50. See also V, 185ʳ (*Regestes*, 1757) where he suggests to the senate: "ἤ μερισώμεθα κατὰ δύναμιν ἕκαστος ἐκ τῶν αἰχμαλώτων τινάς, ἤ ἔρανον." Pachymeres, 324, notes that prisoners were brought to Constantinople and ransomed from ships: "ὑπὲρ τούτων δῶμεν εἰς δύναμιν."

87. Gregoras, I:238.

88. TVA, 44.

89. Talbot, 37, lines 13–17 (*Regestes*, Appendix 7); Bănescu, "Athanase" 43. On Athanasios' detestation for things and persons Western, see my "Athanasios of Constantinople," 27–48.

90. Talbot, 35, lines 17–22, 53–57 (*Regestes*, 1630). Pachymeres repeats the charge that Andronikos refused to heed Athanasios' warnings regarding the Catalans; see Pachymeres, 399–400.

91. Pachymeres, 288; on leaving the city, Michael bitterly ordered the inhabitants not to admit Roger.

92. Pachymeres, 349; Gregoras, II:220.

93. Pachymeres, 522–23.

94. Muntaner, *Chronicle*, p. ccx; Pachymeres, 493–94; Zakythinos, *Crise*, pp. 8–10, 18–19. On this new coin, which was apparently produced in full value and debased editions, see Vitalien Laurent, "Le Basilicon: Nouveau nom de monnaie sous Andronic II Paléologue," *BZ*, 45 (1952), 50–58. Laurent suggests that Andronikos had planned to rouse the Byzantine sentiment against the Catalans who would be passing this inferior coinage on to the general public.

95. John L. Teall, "The Grain Supply of the Byzantine Empire, 330–1025," *DOP*, 13 (1959), 91. G. I. Brătianu, "La Question de l'approvisionnement de Constantinople à l'époque byzantine et ottomane," *B*, 5 (1930), 95, 107.

96. Andre Andréadès, "Byzance, paradis du monopole et du privilège," *B*, 9 (1934), 171–76. Although there were more state monopolies, the controls themselves were not greater than those of the medieval or Renaissance West.

97. G. I. Brătianu. *Recherches sur le commerce gênois dans la Mer Noire au XIIIᵉ siècle* (Paris: Geuthner, 1929), p. 128.

98. The same treaty was renewed on November 11, 1310, March 25, 1342, and September 9, 1349. See Angeliki Laiou, "The Provisioning of Constantinople During the Winter of 1306–1307," *B*, 37 (1967), 92–94; and G. I. Brătianu, *Études byzantines d'histoire économique et sociale* (Paris: Geuthner, 1938), pp. 161–62.

99. G. I. Brătianu, *La Mere Noire* (Munich: Societas academica Dacoromana, 1969), p. 264.

100. Heyd, *Histoire*, p. 465.

101. Constantelos, "Life and Social Welfare," 611–25.

102. Talbot, 106, lines 9–13, 17–21 (*Regestes*, 1606); see also Brătianu, "La Question," 101.

103. Pachymeres, II:461. Pachymeres reports that this failure to keep the oath to excommunicate the dishonest food merchants cost much credibility among the people; his enemies, for instance, attacked him as an oath-breaker.

104. KVA, 498.

105. Talbot, 93, lines 15–26 (*Regestes*, 1652).

106. Pachymeres, 597, 605.

107. Pachymeres, 460–61; Brătianu, *Recherches*, pp. 147, 149.

108. Pachymeres, 461. Talbot, 59, lines 9–13 (*Regestes*, 1703); Talbot, 65, lines 1–5 (*Regestes*, 1708); Talbot, 72, lines 1–5 (*Regestes*, 1649).

109. See Talbot, 78, lines 1–7 (*Regestes*, 1638); Talbot, 59, lines 17–21 (*Regestes*, 1703); Talbot, 65, lines 1–5 (*Regestes*, 1708).

110. Talbot, 74, lines 10–14, 16–20 (*Regestes*, 1653); the same image is used by Maximos the Confessor in describing the results of original sin; see Maximos, "Epistola 2" *PG*, 90:397A.

111. Talbot, 94, lines 10–14 (*Regestes*, 1608); Guilland, "Correspondance," 138–39, and G. I. Brătianu, "L'Approvisionnement de Constantinople sous les Paléologues et les empereurs ottomans," *B*, 6 (1931), 645.

112. V, $161^{r}$ (*Regestes*, 1751): "ταύτης ἀντιβολῶ τῆς φωνῆς, εὐγενείᾳ τετιμημένους καὶ δυσγενεῖς, πλουσίους καὶ πένητας, ἄνδρας ὁμοῦ καὶ γυναῖκας." Matt. 25:31–46 is quoted again in the same letter, V, 163.

113. V, $162^{r}$ (*Regestes*, 1751).

114. V, $103^{r}$ (*Regestes*, 1737): "δῶμεν πεινῶσι τροφήν, ἐνδύσωμεν διὰ τῶν πενήτων Χριστόν."

115. V, 162 (*Regestes*, 1751).

116. V, 165v (*Regestes*, 1752).

117. V, $103^{r}$ (*Regestes*, 1737). See Prov. 11:26.

118. V, $163^{r}$ (*Regestes*, 1751).

119. V, $167^{r}$ (*Regestes*, 1632).

120. V, $167^{v}$–$168^{r}$ (*Regestes*, 1753).

121. V, $96^{r}$ (*Regestes*, 1651).

122. V. $259^{v}$ (*Regestes*, 1640). These footloose monks caused great scandal by frequenting the homes of wealthy men and even of women. See

Henry Chadwick, "Pachomias and the Idea of Sanctity," in *The Byzantine Saint*, ed. Sergei Hackel (London: Fellowship of St. Alban and St. Sergius, 1982), p. 11. Chadwick, in discussing Gibbon's objections to Byzantine monasticism, notes; "When popular monks insinuate themselves into the noble households, . . . vast public and private wealth becomes absorbed in the maintenance of unproductive persons useless to society who enjoy a sacred indolence in the name of Holy Poverty." Athanasios would have been sensitive to such an analysis.

123. See Nicol, *Church and Society*, p. 25. Gregory Palamas, elected archbishop of Thessalonica in 1347, was unable to enter the city because of the zealot opposition to his support of Kantakouzenos; finally entered in early 1350. He sermonized, condemning the revolutionaries as "wild animals," but urging reconciliation and protection of the poor. See Gregory Palamas, "Homily I," in PG 151:12. See Meyendorff, *Gregory Palamas*, pp. 89–90, 92–93, 102, for an analysis of his description of the zealots.

124. John Kantakouzenos, *Historia* II, ed. L. Schopen (Bonn, 1832), pp. 570–71.

125. V, 161v–162r (*Regestes*, 1751): "ἵνα δανείσαντες ἐν τῇ γὴ καὶ ὀλόγα ἀπολάβωμεν ἐν τοῖς οὐρανοῖς καὶ πολλά. Τούτου γὰρ χάριν ἐδικαίωσε κύριος, πλουσίους εἶναὶ καὶ πένητας ἐν τῷ κόσμῳ, ἵνα τοὺς μὲν δι' ἐλεημοσύνης καὶ συμπαθείας, τοὺς δὲ δι' εὐχαρίστου ψυχῆς ἐν ὑπομονῇ, κληρονόμους ποιήσῃ τῆς βασιλείσς αὐτοῦ."

126. V, 164v (*Regestes*, 1752).

127. V, 103r (*Regestes*, 1737).

128. V, 162v (*Regestes*, 1751).

129. V, 165v (*Regestes*, 1752); he refers to Lazarus' rich counterpart as "being fried" (ἀποτηγανίζεται).

130. Avila, *Ownership*, p. 134. Avila writing as a social activist in a Filipino setting touches on the keypoints of the patristic teaching on property.

131. Basil of Caesarea, "Homily on Luke 12," PG 31:267–68, 278; also John Chrysostom, "Homily 12 on I Timothy," PG 62:501–662. Athanasios was certainly more practical and less naïve regarding property distribution and redistribution than either Basil or John Chrysostom.

132. V, 53r (*Regestes*, 1649); also Talbot, 72, lines 1–4 (*Regestes*, 1649).

133. Talbot, 73, lines 14–20 (*Regestes*, 1642).

134. Talbot, 93, lines 7–15 (*Regestes*, 1652).

135. Talbot, 100, lines 1–4 (*Regestes*, 1727).

136. Talbot, 93, lines 13–14 (*Regestes*, 1652).

137. Talbot, 73, lines 5–8 (*Regestes*, 1642); Athanasios later expands on this commission with the request for the addition of two demarchs, minor police officials, to that body; see Talbot, 100, lines 16–20 (*Regestes*, 1727).

138. Talbot, 100, lines 10–14 (*Regestes*, 1727). Since the time of Justinian, bishops were traditionally responsible for the assurance of weights

and measures. See Novel 128.15, in *Corpus Juris Civilis* III, edd. Schoell and Kroll, p. 641. Boojamra, "Christian *Philanthropia*," 354–56.

139. Novella 126.15, in *Corpus Iuris Civilis* III, edd. Schoell and Kroll, p. 641.

140. Peter Charanis, "Economic Factors in the Decline of the Byzantine Empire," *Journal of Economic History*, 13 (1953), 423.

141. See the *Book of the Prefect*, in Zepos and Zepos, p. 388.

142. Pachymeres, 525; Gregoras, 223; Muntaner, *Chronicle*, pp. ccxiii, ccviv, ccxv.

143. Pachymeres, 531–33; see also Laiou, *Constantinople*, pp. 164–65.

144. Pachymeres, 618–19, 621–23.

145. Pachymeres, 622–23; several imperial embassies were sent to de Rocafort offering him and his troops money and citizenship if they would resume Byzantine service. See Dölger, *Regesten*, No. 2302 (October 14, 1306).

146. Muntaner, *Chronicle*, p. ccxxv.

147. Muntaner, *Chronicle*, pp. ccxxi–ccxxiii.

148. Pachymeres, 552–53.

149. Angeliki Laiou, "Provisioning," 103.

150. Pachymeres, 628.

151. KVA, 495; translation taken from Laiou, *Constantinople*, p. 195.

152. Talbot, 67, lines 4–8 (*Regestes*, 1650).

153. Pachymeres, II:628; also see Laiou, "Provisioning," 100–101; Nicol, *Last Centuries*, p. 141.

154. Talbot, 67, lines 4–8, 23–25, 27–31 (*Regestes*, 1650).

155. Talbot, 67, lines 19–22 (*Regestes*, 1650).

156. Talbot, 67, lines 27–28 (*Regestes*, 1650).

157. Nicol, *Last Centuries*, p. 141.

158. Pachymeres, 628–29; Gregoras, 283.

159. Talbot, 78, lines 28–32 (*Regestes*, 1638).

160. KVA, 494–95.

161. TVA, 43–44.

162. Constantelos, "Life and Social Welfare," 17. St. Basil performed a similar service during the famine of the winter of 368–369. Gregory of Nazianzus tells us that "he collected contributions of all kinds of food to help relieve the famine. . . . He ministered to the bodies and souls of the needy, combining marks of respect with the necessary refreshment, thus offering them relief in two ways." See "Oration 43" in PG, 36:544c. See also Fedwick, *Charisma*, p. 38.

163. Talbot, 78, lines 39–43 (*Regestes*, 1638).

164. *V*, 166*v* (*Regestes*, 1632): "ἐσκεψάμεθα λέβητας στῆσαι ἐξ ἑψήματος τοῦ τυχόντος, ἢ καὶ κολλύβων προνοήσασθαι τοῖς ἀθλίοις . . . ἔνθεν πένητας καὶ πλουσίους καὶ λαικοὺς καὶ μονάζοντας ἀξιῶ . . .

συγκροτεῖν καὶ ἡμῖν ἀφ' ὧν ἕκαστος εὐπορεῖ πρὸς λέβητας, ἔκ τε ἐλαίου καὶ σίτου καὶ οἴνου ἰχθύος τε καὶ τυροῦ, καὶ ὀσπρίων καὶ παντοίας τροφῆς, καὶ τοῦ τυχόντος ὑποδήματος καὶ ἐνδύματος."

165. V, 166ᵛ–167ʳ (*Regestes*, 1632).

166. KVA, 494.

167. Talbot, 78, lines 41–45 (*Regestes*, 1638).

168. Pachymeres, 647.

169. See *Notitiae* of Andronikos II where the structure of the church in Anatolia is maintained "on paper," although the rankings of the metropolitan sees were changed slightly. See Gelzer, "*Notitiae*," 599–601.

170. John L. Boojamra, "The Affair of Alexis and Roman: Two Documents of 1361," *Greek Orthodox Theological Review*, 28 (1983), 176.

171. Talbot, 83, lines 1–4 (*Regestes*, 1718).

172. Gelzer, "*Notitiae*," 597–601. The Byzantines were masters of political and ecclesiastical fiction.

173. Meyendorff, *Byzantium*, p. 80.

174. Gregoras I:199–200. According to Gregoras, the money was used by John VI to repay his debts to the Turkish Emir Orkhan. Meyendorff, *Byzantium*, p. 113, notes that episodes from later in the fourteenth century "alone would be sufficient to explain the consistent policies of the Byzantine patriarchate, aiming at preserving its control over a united metropolitanate of Russia." See ibid., p. 118.

# 6

# Athanasios as a Judicial Agent

ATHANASIOS' FIRST PATRIARCHATE terminated with great bitterness and episcopal hostility in 1293, with his resignation and retirement to his monastery at Xerolophos. From there, he apparently continued to exercise influence over Byzantine social and political life. For reasons that do not concern us here, Andronikos wished to restore him ten years later. It was during this second tenure, the "years of trouble" of the early fourteenth century,[1] that he blossomed as a social advocate.

Athanasios was petitioned to resume the patriarchate by the emperor and a small delegation of nonplussed ecclesiastics who came to the door of his cell. According to Pachymeres, Athanasios spoke to the gathered clergy and people about his concern for the protection of the weak and those oppressed by corrupt officials and the wealthy. The emperor responded by commissioning him to hear complaints of injustice. Andronikos not only respected Athanasios' holiness and recognized his popularity (even during retirement) as an advocate of justice in Constantinople, but also realized that the corrupt administration of justice had occasioned much popular discontent with his administration, with the outbreak of occasional riots.[2] Pachymeres even reports that it was the venality of the judges and popular discontent that had drive Andronikos in 1296 to create his twelve judge tribunal (καθολικοὶ κριταί),[3] composed of ecclesiastics, senators, and leading citizens. Inasmuch as the tribunal had apparently failed,[4] perhaps he thought that Athanasios might fill the judicial vacuum, at least temporarily. After he was re-established on the patriarchal throne, Athanasios continued to hear cases, sometimes with the help of the permanent synod. It is clear that during his patriarchate the *synodos endemousa*, the so-called permanent synod of Constantinople, became established as a tribunal to which citizens could bring complaints and alleged cases of injustice. Athanasios used it as an agency of reform. Nothing further is known about the tribunal or its operation.[5]

Lemerle, who has studied the "permanent synod" and its functions for the period from 1315 to 1402, points out its increasing competence in secular affairs. He reasons that the imperial government, in spite of the judicial reforms of Andronikos II, was unable to handle judicial questions because of the extent of corruption.[6] This movement of judicial responsibility into the ecclesiastical courts represented both an increase in the competence of the church and a corresponding decrease in that of the government. The turning point in this process of judicial transfer from the secular to ecclesiastical courts can be traced to Athanasios. Although Lemerle jumps from this to Andronikos III's reforms of 1326, it is apparent from Athanasios' letters that the *synodos endemousa* picked up the slack under Athanasios and that he served as prefect of the city.

This was not an unusual role for a bishop and especially a patriarch: the episcopal hierarch was often the most stable element in troubled periods. Every bishop in his diocese was competent to hold a court of justice and to hear complaints, especially those involving members of the clergy. In frontier or marsh regions, it can be assumed that as civil officials fled, the remaining bishops took over the administration of justice as well as other functions. After the Latin conquest of 1204, the bishops had remained in their dioceses and the civil officials fled. The bishops apparently assumed the role of the civil functionaries, *defensores civitatis*, just as had happened in the West during the "barbarian" invasions and occupation in the later Roman empire. Eventually, the Turks recognized the local bishops as the officials responsible for the Christian population under Ottoman domination. To this point Bréhier has written that in the fourteenth century many legal matters were left to the local bishop, "dont les tribunaux arrivent à supplanter la justice impériale, les institutions écclesiastiques demeurant intactes en face de l'Etat desorganisé."[7]

Although Athanasios' return was contingent on the resignation of Patriarch John XII Kosmas (1294–1303), his successor as patriarch, Athanasios lost no time in using the commission granted him by Andronikos to hear cases of injustice. According to Pachymeres, Athanasios often had to sit day and night to hear complaints of the poor, handing down decisions in some cases and in others interceding for them with the emperor.[8] He gained popularity, thereby improving his chances for regaining the patriarchate. In fact, some of his opponents cynically adverted that his concern for the oppressed was merely a sham designed to win him support for the throne.[9] Athanasios continued to play a quasi-judicial role throughout his second patriarchate, with several outstanding examples of involvement in secular affairs to his credit.[10]

Athanasios' personal intervention is well documented in his letters. He intervened on behalf of guards who permitted a certain prisoner, Paxes, to escape;[11] he pleaded on behalf of a certain Oinaiotes, who was suffering from poverty and in need of a subsidy;[12] he intervened in 1307 on behalf of the widowed Irene Choumnos, asking that her deceased husband's retinue be left with her and that the emperor set aside a certain support for them.[13]

In at least three instances Athanasios' synod considered and passed decisions on secular suits. In the first, which is reported in a letter of Athanasios to the Grand Dioikete, he answers the complaints of the official about his condemnation by the synod for dishonest financial transactions. Athanasios warned him to stop protesting the decision lest he be fined more severely and cast into the depths of poverty experienced by his unfortunate victims.[14] In a second instance, in January 1304, he called the bishops to meet in session to judge the despot Michael on suspicion of treason.[15] Finally, charges of treason were brought against the bishop of Panion, who was likewise subject to the judgment of the synod.[16]

Athanasios referred specifically to the bishops in the Choumnos and the Paxes cases: "the bishops found here [τοῖς εὑρισκομένοις ἀρχιερεῦσιν ἐνταῦθα] in their great compassion decided to meet with me regarding this matter and to present an ardent petition to your divine majesty on this subject."[17] Athanasios complained in one instance that it was impossible to get a righteous decision from the assembled bishops, who apparently had sold their votes to one of the parties in a dispute:

> I have often mentioned to your divine majesty that if every bishop does not return to his assigned see, the Church will not cease to be troubled by confusion and rebellion, for I want them to have some concern for legal proceedings; for none of the nobles comes to trial without first negotiating with these [bishops].[18]

It is apparent that the *synodos endemousa* was acting as a civil court. He even described the members' coming to blows over decisions, "but not for [the sake of] justice"[19]—another clear reference to the *synodos endemousa* as a civil court. It is apparent from such incidents that many normal and traditional urban services and bureaucratic channels had broken down, and the role Athanasios assumed was to some extent the role once played by the prefect of the city and chief justice. His opponents complained that Athanasios did not render judgment in accordance with the canons, but conformed to his own new ideas.[20]

Athanasios became a justly popular and revered figure in Constantinople, especially in early 1304, immediately after his second accession to the patriarchal throne. For instance, after a conflagration had reduced to ashes the Kynegos commercial quarter of Constantinople, Athanasios was appointed as mediator to handle the numerous problems and litigations caused by the fire, the resultant looting, and the loss of deeds and titles. Reluctant to use court or urban officials (perhaps because of corruption), the emperor specifically entrusted all cases to Athanasios for just settlement.[21]

Never missing an opportunity to moralize, Athanasios emphasized that abuse of the laws had provoked divine wrath and caused fire, foreign domination, famine, and sickness.[22] The only way to avoid further hardship was to turn away from evil ways, to be reconciled with one's neighbor, and to perform charitable deeds—especially to benefit the fire victims. Even those whose belongings had been spared by the fire were subject to the ravages of thieves. Looters were first required to return the property they had taken and then to set up a relief fund for those who had lost their homes and possessions in the conflagration. Athanasios ordered that no one was to receive stolen goods, under pain of ecclesiastical censure. These things were to be brought to the church along with some sort of proof that all had been returned; pardon would then be accorded. If someone had witnessed a theft and not reported it, that person would be considered an accomplice, subject to the same redoubtable censure (φρικῶδες ἐπιτίμιον).[23]

## The Neara

In 1303, Andronikos, in his so-called *Promissory Letter* to Athanasios, guaranteed the patriarch free reign and imperial support in his reform zeal. The publication of the Neara was one of the few actual concessions the emperor made to Athanasios in keeping with his oath.[24] One of the most significant results of Athanasios' reforming zeal, the Ζήτησις or Neara, was a series of disciplinary measures issued by the *synodos endemousa* in 1304. Even though the legislation came out of the synod and was signed by twenty-one bishops, including two bishops-elect (ὑποψήφιοι), it bears the unmistakable mark of Athanasios' reforming zeal and largely reflects the contents of his correspondence, a movement toward justice and mercy. At the request of the bishops and Athanasios, Andronikos confirmed the Ζήτησις as civil law in May 1306, after which it was properly referred to as the Neara, or New Law. The appeal to the emperor illustrates the intimate cooperation between *imperium* and *sacerdotium* in Byzantium. Although there was not a clear distinction between civil and ecclesiastical legislation, ecclesiastical regulations had to be confirmed by the emperor and often the emperor legislated in ecclesiastical matters.[25] This interpenetration of civil and ecclesiastical legislation and especially nomocanonical literature became especially important as judicial functions moved increasingly into the hands of the church.[26]

The very content of the Neara, dealing as it did with questions at once moral and civil, indicates that with the decay of civil administration, including the exercise of justice, Athanasios increasingly cast himself in the role of civil arbiter, in effect the urban prefect. As we saw earlier, on the basis of his popularity among the people, he was already functioning in a quasi-judicial capacity even before his second patriarchate.

The fact that ecclesiastical legislation, largely ethical in tone, became civil law is not as significant as the patriarch's effort to initiate legislation in civil questions, the opposite of what was then accepted by canonists, who held that the emperor could initiate ecclesiastical legislation. On the other hand, ecclesiastical canons promulgated as civil law were quite common in Byzantine tradition, and, as a result of the intimate association between ecclesiastical and imperial authority, the church almost invariably sought imperial support for its theological and disciplinary measures.[27] Ecclesiastical canons and church teaching were, in fact, confirmed by imperial legislation, becoming the law of the state. Justinian in his sixth Novel affirmed the equality of both civil and ecclesiastical law; the canons of the first four ecumenical councils, for instance, were backed by the coercive power of the state.[28] The problem inherent in such a relationship is self-evident. Not only is Christian morality of necessity a voluntary commitment, rooted in self-perception, but it is often concerned with things private; actions that are not in the public domain are only with great difficulty prosecuted publicly.

The *Neara* has been preserved in both a long and a short recension in several manuscripts. The longer recension, a result of additions made by the patriarchal and the imperial chancelleries, appears to have been a re-editing of the shorter version issued by the synod in 1304. There is some debate as to which of the recensions was produced by the fathers of the *synodos endemousa* and which was published officially, but the fact that the longer version was included in the Vaticanus Graecus 2219 supports the belief that it received the official approbation of both the government and the church. Laurent suggests that the lengthy period of time between the appearance of the short and the long editions was the result of opposition on a part of a significant number of ecclesiastical and lay officials.[29]

The *Neara*, which opens with a hortatory supplication (ζήτησις) to the emperor to "seek" righteousness and govern correctly, urges him to use his divinely originated authority to consecrate as the law of the empire the series of disciplinary measures which had been approved by the patriarch and the bishops and which would be beneficial to the empire.

Like many of Athanasios' letters, the *Neara*, covers a variety of civil and moral issues, including testation, marriage, rape, adultery, prostitution, murder, monastic discipline, the functioning of taverns and bathhouses, and the observance of fasts. Its regulations have a twofold aim: to eliminate social injustices and to correct moral infractions. Much of it deals with sexual offenses. As is obvious from the time of the Council of Elvira (fourth century) moral issues were in particular the concern of the bishop. It is not uncommon, as indeed was the case with Elvira, that the turmoil of social and political decay forced the church to redefine itself in disciplinary categories as a community with rules.[30]

The Neara contains one of the few new laws originating in the last centuries of the Byzantine empire concerning inheritance, a clearly civil concern with social implications. Although many of Athanasios' reforms are quite traditional, his so-called *trimoiria*, or tripartite division of an inheritance, is exceptional.[31] When a husband or wife died leaving no children, the surviving spouse was not to be deprived of some share of the deceased's estate. The reason was simple *philanthropia*: the survivor would not have to suffer the double calamity (διπλῆν συμφοράν) of losing both home and wealth (ἀβίωτος).[32] Instead of being appropriated by the local church, monastic community, or landlord to whom the deceased may have belonged as *paroikos* (dependent peasant),[33] the estate was to be divided into three parts: one-third to the government, town, or master of the deceased (ὁ ἀπελθών); one-third to the local church for the so-called "service" of the soul of the deceased; and one-third to the surviving spouse. But if there were no surviving spouse, this final third would go to the deceased's father, mother, sibling, or other person recognized as heir by law. If there were no other legal heir, then this final third was divided, with one-sixth of the total estate going to the government and one-sixth to the church.[34] Before Emperor Leo VI, who extended the right of inheritance to the wife by Novel 106,[35] the wife often inherited nothing when her husband died.[36]

Section four of the Neara takes up a similar theme and calls for the repeal of the law (νόμος ἀκυρωθῇ) according to which when a husband or a wife died leaving a child and the child in turn died the surviving spouse inherited all of the child's inheritance from the deceased parent. For Athanasios this was an unjust law inasmuch as the parents of the deceased spouse were left without anything from their son or daughter's wealth. For Athanasios the grandparents were subject to a double loss of their child and their wealth, which the child might have received from them as a gift or dowry. According to Neara, the law was to be changed so that on the death of the child, one-third of what the child had inherited from the deceased parent should go to the church for "remembrance" (μνημόσυνα), one-third to the parents of the deceased, and one-third to the spouse of the deceased.[37] Nothing is designated in this instance for the master of the deceased parent. The social emphasis of Athanasios' legislation is evident: the part of the inheritance which was set aside for μνημόσυνα was understood to be for the general welfare and the relief of the poor of the community[38] rather than for clergy in payment for having performed a funeral service or memorials. The church was to oversee the family's distribution of this money, the so-called soul-part, to the poor.[39]

The sense of social mutuality evident in sections one and four is also evident in section five, which requires murderers to be punished according to the law, though not to be deprived of their property or wealth, for this would not punish murderers but their family and spouse. Accordingly, the malefactor's property should be divided among his children, with a part assigned to the survivors of the victim and yet another part assigned to the government.[40]

Section two of the Neara takes up the theme, common in Athanasios' correspondence, of punishment of a variety of sexual offenses and perversions—prostitution, adultery, sodomy, incest, magic—and injustices that both excite the anger of God and incite the loss of souls.[41] He did not, however, suggest the means by which these prohibitions should be enforced or offenders punished. Well aware of corrupt judicial administration, he did warn judges to be honest in applying these laws without regard to gift or station; leaders, he reminded Andronikos, are not for mere decoration, but for action. Athanasios was well aware of the corrupt judicial administration in the capital.

Section three, on prostitution, orders that no woman shall "be forced sexually in any way, especially if she is a virgin." If she relinquished her honor willingly, however, her hair should be cut and she should be paraded in public. In the latter case, no theft was involved; inasmuch as she entered the liaison willingly nothing was taken from her.[42] In the first case, the seducer had to pay a fine to the government, but if he possessed no wealth, he was subject to normal punishment.[43] In the longer recension, a section calls for the confiscation of the goods of the proprietor of a brothel. In one letter, Athanasios placed under the ban of excommunication the owners of brothels and those who lure women into prostitution either by force or on the pretext of marriage.[44] Similarly those "who give or take abortions to destroy children" were subject to the same penance as murderers.[45]

In general, sexual morality was a prime concern for Athanasios. His didactic letters and his letters to the bishops urge the excommunication of men or women who indulged in sexual intercourse prior to the nuptial blessing.[46] In a letter to priests, Athanasios ordered that couples continuing illicit liaisons be forbidden the sacraments and turned over to the public officials (τῷ δημοσίῳ παράπεμπε), presumably for punishment.[47] Concerned also for the purity of marriage, he ordered that any person contracting a second or a third, unless there were no children, "must be given a penance."[48] In another letter, he prohibited a priest from celebrating the festivities (μὴ ἑστιᾶσθαι) of a person marrying for a second or third time, although canon law permitted such marriages.[49]

Pachymeres records the meeting of a synod in which Andronikos and Athanasios led a discussion of the question of whether fornication dissolved the betrothal bond.[50] Inasmuch as opinion within the synod was divided and a conclusion never reached, the question seems to have been left in Athanasios' hands. The hesitation of the synod to publish a conclusion is remarkable, for a synodal decree under the patriarch John VIII Xiphilinos (1066) had gained the force of law by a chrysobull of Nicephoros III Botaniates. Engagement began to be accompanied by an ecclesiastical blessing and was assumed to be the first stage in the marriage itself, carrying with it the same consequences for violations as marriage.[51] In another letter, Athanasios forbade intercourse between affianced persons prior to marriage,[52] and he imposed a penance on the parents who permitted their daughter to sleep with her fiancé before the "crowning ceremony"—that is, after the engagement.[53] Athanasios also condemned consanguinous marriages, including relationships created by adoption (ἐξ υἱοθεσίας), within the degrees of prohibition, as well as marriages between individuals of radically differing ages and between strangers if there were no witness present to affirm that neither partner was already married.[54] The obvious problem remained: the need not only to detect "hidden crime" and prosecute it, but also to devise appropriate punishments.[55] Such laws were purely rhetorical, proclaiming what ought to be; legal enforcement was another matter.

Athanasios completed the centuries-long process of bringing marriage completely within the province of the church. The longer version of the Neara affirms that marriages must be performed by a priest of the couple's parish (ἐνορία) or with his knowledge.[56] For the first time in Byzantine canonical legislation, the priest is clearly defined as the agent of the rite. Despite the tenth-century legislation of Leo VI and the eleventh-century legislation of Alexios I Comnenos, marriage apparently continued to be concluded without the benefit of ecclesiastical blessing but with its tolerance. Previous legislation had confined itself to the ecclesiastical form of the ceremony; by the decree of 1306 marriage was defined unequivocally as the responsibility of the parish priest. Presumably Athanasios was affirming that the church, in the person of the priest of the community, was the only legitimate agency to ensure that the conditions necessary for a valid marriage were verified. Any persons contracting a marriage without this approval and ceremony were to be fined by the government a sum equivalent to the dowry. Finally, following Byzantine canonical tradition, Athanasios affirms in the Neara that, except in cases where there were prohibiting factors and in cases of avowed celibacy, marriage was to be encouraged for all persons.[57]

Expanding several points in Athanasios' letters, the longer recension of the Neara promulgates, for instance, feast days and Sundays as work-free days on which the faithful were to attend liturgical services and abstain from all festivities.[58] In addition, all the faithful were obliged to observe all fast periods and especially the fast of Holy and Great Friday.[59]

With the obvious intention of eliminating temptation, the Neara enumerates regular weekly regulations for bathhouses and taverns (βαλανείῳ ἢ καπηλείῳ), declaring that they be closed from the ninth hour (3P.M.) on Saturday to the ninth hour on Sunday. On all other nights, citizens could make purchases in the taverns but could not drink there in company after sundown; hence, they were to be closed.[60] In February 1306, just before the publication of the Neara, Athanasios in a letter to Andronikos made a similar point, perhaps with the intention of inspiring Andronikos' action: "Command therefore together with other good works that it be clearly proclaimed that at this time [Great Lent] no one should enter bathhouses or taverns, but every Orthodox Christian should spend his time in the churches in contrition of spirit."[61]

A year after the publication of the Neara, Athanasios sent another letter to Andronikos urging the same principles concerning the holy fasts. In it he wrote more explicitly concerning Holy Week: all bathhouses and taverns must be closed from Monday morning to Saturday morning; men, women, and children must be in church, and, rather than eat fish sold "by the old women at the seashore," they should instead eat boiled wheat, fruits, and vegetables.[62] Likewise, later in 1307 he asked Andronikos to close workshops in order to conform to the same hours on Saturday and Sunday, with the obvious intention that the faithful have nothing to divert them from vespers and liturgy.[63] He felt that keeping these fasts was serious enough an exercise to warrant the punishment of excommunication for those who did not abide by them.[64]

The ultimate goal of all of Athanasios' reforms, and of the Neara in particular, is summed up in the closing paragraph, which affirmed that all order is from God and must be maintained in God's earthly commonwealth. The Byzantine Christian empire, since at least the time of Eusebios of Caesarea, was understood as a terrestrial copy of the heavenly archetype. Athanasios' passion for right order in the Christian world possessed a particular Christian content, paralleling the divine command. The Neara was but one small expression of this effort to identify the terrestrial image of the heavenly archetype.

## Notes

1. Gregoras, I:246; Pachymeres, 364; TVA, 66–67.

2. Pachymeres, 235–37; for a discussion of this and its significance, see Paul Lemerle, "Le Juge général des Grecs et la réforme judiciaire d'Andronic III," in *Mêmorial Louis Petit*, Archives de l'orient chrétien I (Bucharest: Institut français d'Études byzantines, 1948), p. 294.

3. Pachymeres, 235–37.

4. Pachymeres, 237: "Little by little, like vibrations of a musical cord, [the tribunal] weakened and died." In 1329, Andronikos III attempted a similar judicial reform; see Lemerle, "Juge," pp. 295–316.

5. Lemerle, "Juge," p. 295. Andronikos III tried again to reform the system of justice in 1329 on the occasion of a serious military defeat in Asia Minor; see Gregoras, 437–38.

6. Paul Lemerle, "Recherches sur les institutions judiciaires à l'époque des Paléologues. II. Le Tribunal du patriarcat ou tribunal synodal," *Analecta Bollandiana*, 68 (1950), 320.

7. See Bréhier, *Institutions*, p. 193.

8. Pachymeres, 370.

9. Pachymeres, 372. See Louis Petit, "La Réforme judiciare d'Andronic Paléologue," *EO*, 9 (1906), 134.

10. Pachymeres, 369–70.

11. Talbot, 51, lines 9–13 (*Regestes*, 1644). Talbot notes that Παξῆ is most probably a Turkish title and not a proper name; see Talbot, "Commentary on Letter 51," 361.

12. Talbot, 63, lines 11–14 (*Regestes*, 1706).

13. Talbot, 96, entire letter (*Regestes*, 1664). The marriage had lasted for four years, ending with the despot John's death in Thessalonica in 1307. See Gregoras, I:241.

14. Talbot, 26, lines 7–11 (*Regestes*, 1685); on the *megas dioiketes*, see Kodinos (Pseudo), *Traitê*, pp. 185, 323.

15. Pachymeres, 408. Dölger, *Regesten*, Nos. 2260, 2262.

16. Pachymeres, 623.

17. Talbot, 96, lines 16–20 (*Regestes*, 1664). Pachymeres exaggerated when he wrote (II:647) that Athanasios expelled the bishops and held synods with archimandrites. About 1306 Athanasios wrote (Talbot, 51, line 9 [*Regestes*, 1644]) that he met "together with the bishops who are here" to reach a decision. As Lemerle has noted, it is difficult to give the patriarchal tribunal "une definition juridique précise." See Lemerle, "Tribunal," 322–32. The number of cases heard by the patriarchal tribunal continued to grow after Athanasios' tenure because of the continued inadequacy of the imperial judicial system.

18. Talbot, 37, lines 25–29 (*Regestes*, Appendix 7).

19. Talbot, 48, lines 12–16 (*Regestes*, 1694). See also Talbot 16, entire letter (*Regestes*, 1678); Talbot, 25, lines 1–4 (*Regestes*, 1613).

20. Pachymeres, 583–617.

21. Pachymeres, 582.

22. V, 168$^{r}$–169$^{r}$ (*Regestes*, 1631).

23. V, 168$^{r}$–168$^{v}$ (*Regestes*, 1631).

24. For a discussion of the Γράμμα Ὑποσχετικὸν, see Laurent, "Serment," 138–39, where the text of the oath appears.

25. Chomatianos, "Πρὸς τὸν Κωνσταντῖνον Καβάσιλαν," Response 2, holds, with Balsamon, that the emperor could legislate in ecclesiastical affairs.

26. On the fourteenth-century nomocanonical works of Constantine Harmenopoulos and Matthew Blastares, see Bréhier, *Institutions*, pp. 356–57.

27. Much has been written on the relationship of the imperial power to the Church, and the term caesaropapism is all too familiar. Although justified in certain specific cases, it cannot be applied here. What is here described is an instance of Justinian's *symphonia*, with the balance in favor of ecclesiastical initiative. The best available discussion of this relationship is Dvornik, *Political Philosophy*, pp. 718–23; see also Joan Hussey, *The Byzantine World* (New York: Harper & Row, 1961), p. 92, and Geanakopolos, *Byzantine East*, pp. 55–83. The term "nomocanon" properly applies to ecclesiastical laws that had, in addition, the force of civil law.

28. A classic example of this is the first chapter of the famous Novel 131 of Justinian; see *Corpus Juris Civilis* III, edd. Schoell and Kroll, p. 38. In this location the canons of the first four ecumenical councils are declared to be on a par with Holy Scripture and are proclaimed to have universal authority and the force of law. For a discussion of the equally famous Novel 6, see Dvornik, *Political Philosophy*, pp. 815–18.

29. See *Regestes*, 393–95, for a discussion of the two recensions and the dating of the various manuscripts. The long recension appears in V, $50^{v}$–$52^{r}$ and is published in Zepos and Zepos, pp. 533–36. For the short recension, see text in Rhalles and Potles, V:121–26. In general, there is very little literature on the Neara and almost nothing in English. See Zachariae von Lingenthal, *Geschichte*, pp. 141–43; J. A. Morteuil, *Histoire du droit byzantin ou du droit romain dans l'empire d'Orient depuis la mort de Justinien jusqu'à la prise de Constantinople en 1453* III (Paris: Guilbert and Thorel, 1846), p. 393; Dölger, *Regesten*, No. 2295.

30. Samuel Laeuchli, *Power and Sexuality: The Emergence of Canon Law at the Synod of Elvira* (Philadelphia: Temple University Press, 1972), p. 88.

31. K. Triantaphyllopoulos, "Die *Novelle* des Patriarchen Athanasios über die τριμοιοία," *Byzantinisch-neugriechische Jahrbücher*, 8 (1931), 136. This work is the most extensive piece of literature relating to any particular aspect of the Neara. See also J. Zhishman, *Das Eherecht der orientalischen Kirche* (Vienna: Braumuller, 1864), pp. 177, 675; and Zachariae von Lingenthal, *Geschichte*, p. 141. Triantaphyllopoulos, "*Novelle*," 146, notes that the legislation is unique in Byzantium and may have had its origin in Syrian law sources from which both the Byzantine and the Nestorian churches drew. He is careful, however, to point out that he does not believe that Athanasios had before him Syrian sources, but rather that the trimoiria has its source in the "law pool" of the Hellenized East. Both churches, standing as theological antagonists, apparently shared a common legal background.

32. Rhalles and Potles, V:122, and Zepos and Zepos, p. 534. The shorter recension makes use of the word ἀβιωτικίον to describe the state of the widow or widower. It is most likely making a reference to the ἀβιωτικίον, which is described as "the ancient custom by which the legacy of the deceased *paroikos* is divided between the master and μνημόσυνα without taking account of the spouse or the nearest surviving relative." Paul Lemerle as quoted in *Regestes*, 394.

33. Rhalles and Potles, V:123: "τῶν εἰς παροικίαν ἐχόντων αὐτούς, ἢ καὶ Ἐκκλησιῶν, ἢ καὶ μονῶν." Laiou writes that in the fourteenth century the landlord inherited the property of a paroikos who died childless. See Angeliki Laiou-Thomadakis, *Peasant Society in the Late Byzantine Empire* (Princeton: Princeton University Press, 1977), pp. 55, 92. According to this section of the Neara the landlord would inherit, at most, one-third of the estate. Like many of Athanasios' reforms, these testamentary regulations probably fell into desuetude almost immediately after his patriarchate.

34. Rhalles and Potles, V:123: "τῇ δεσποτείᾳ τὸ ἥμισυ καὶ μνημοσύνοις χάριν ἐκείνου τὸ ἥμισυ." The use of τῇ δεσποτείᾳ in the short recension

implies the master of the paroikos. But the use in the same section of the long recension (Zepos and Zepos, p. 534) implies "a public authority." The short version is clearer as to who inherits, but the more generalized reference to ὁ δημόσιος in the long recension was promulgated by law.

35. *Les Novelles de Léon VI le Sage* edd. P. Noailles and A. Dain (Paris: "Les Belles Lettres," 1944), p. 347.

36. Justinian's Novels 53 and 118 modified this slightly.

37. Rhalles and Potles, V:124; Zepos and Zepos, p. 535. The law repealed is Novel 118 of Justinian, which held that an immediate heir closes out all other heirs. The synod held it to be unjust that the paternal grandfather's fortune should go to his son's wife and hence pass out of the family from which it originated.

38. Triantaphyllopoulos, "*Novelle,*" 137.

39. In a judgment of 1325, the Patriarch Isaiah of Constantinople ordered, based on Athanasios' Neara, that the "soul part" shall be divided half for the mother and half for the grandfather of the child, with the understanding that the money shall be issued in services to the poor; see Miklosich and Müller, I:134: also in Triantaphyllopoulos, "*Novelle,*" p. 138.

40. Rhalles and Potles, V:124–25; Zepos and Zepos, p. 535.

41. Zepos and Zepos, p. 535.

42. Zepos and Zepos, p. 535; Athanasios repeats the same point in V, 139ʳ (*Regestes*, 1747).

43. Dölger, *Regesten*, No. 2295, refers to the normal punishment as branding and flogging.

44. V, 139ᵛ (*Regestes*, 1747).

45. *V*, 235*r* (*Regestes*, 1779): "τὰς διδούσας καὶ λαμβανούσας τὰ ἀμβλωθρίδια πρὸς ἀναίρεσιν τῶγ βρεφῶν καὶ τὰς τὰ βρέφη ῥιπτούσας ἐπιτιμίῳ φονέων ὑποκεῖσθαι διδάσκοντες." See also Canon 21 of the Council of Ancyra (Rhalles and Potles, III:63), Canon 2 of St. Basil (Rhalles and Potles, IV:96), and Canon 91 of the Council in Trullo (Rhalles and Potles, II:518) for ecclesiastical legislation condemning abortions.

46. V, 226ʳ (*Regestes*, 1777): "μηδὲ πρὸ στεφάνου καὶ εὐλογίας γνωρίζειν."

47. V, 226ʳ (*Regestes*, 1777).

48. *V*, 140ʳ (*Regestes*, 1747): "οἱ γάμῳ δευτέρῳ ἁλόντες ἢ τρίτῳ ὁ καὶ πορνείαν κεκολασμένην φασίν, εἰ παῖδες μὴ προσεῖσι μηδὲ ὁρα πρὸς τὸ ἔξωρον, προσφόρῳ ἐπιτιμίῳ ἰατρευέσθωσαν." Byzantine nomocanonical legislation had been firmly established on the question of successive marriages from the time of the *Tomos Unionis* of 920, which settled the affair of the tetragamia, the conflict surrounding the fourth marriage of the Emperor Leo VI; for a general discussion of the centrality of this question in the Byzantine ecclesiastical tradition, see Boojamra, "Tetragamia," 113–

33. Although the Orthodox Church had traditionally condemned second and third marriages and subjected those who entered into them to ecclesiastical penances, no real issue developed until the tenth century, when civil law was brought into conformity with canon law (Novel 90 of Leo VI in *Novelles*, edd. Noailles and Dain, p. 299). The responsibility for marriage came formally into the province of the church; the church had to decide on the permissibility of a second or a third marriage. The *Tomos Unionis* explicitly forbade all fourth marriages. For third marriages a sliding scale of penances was established, which took into account the age of the persons and whether or not they had children by a previous marriage (Rhalles and Potles, V:6–7). For Byzantine ecclesiastical legislation prior to the tenth century, see Canon 3 of the Council of Neocaesarea (Rhalles and Potles, III:74), Canon I of the Council of Laodicia (Rhalles and Potles, III:171), and Canons 4, 50, and 80 of St. Basil (Rhalles and Potles, IV: 102, 203, 242).

49. V, 224r (*Regestes*, 1776): "γάμῳ διγάμου, πολλῷ δὲ τριγάμου, ἱερέα μὴ ἑστιᾶσθαι." A similar prohibition on the clergy, reflecting Byzantine ecclesiastical distaste for multiple successive marriages, is found in V, 229r (*Regestes*, 1778).

50. Pachymeres, 181.

51. *Regestes* 896 and 915; see Morteuil, *Droit byzantin*, p. 150.

52. V, 226r (*Regestes*, 1777).

53. V, 229r (*Regestes*, 1778).

54. V, 224r (*Regestes*, 1776): "ἀγνώστους λαμβάνειν γυναῖκας. εἰ μὴ μαρτυρηθῶσι μὴ ἔχειν." A similar prohibition is contained in V, 226v (*Regestes*, 1777). The canonical age for marriage in Byzantium was usually twelve years for a girl and fourteen for a boy; Beck, *Kirche*, p. 88; also Novel 109 of Leo VI in *Novelles*, edd. Noailles and Dain, pp. 355, 357.

55. On the difficulty of prosecuting moral offenses as civil crimes and the Byzantine legislation related to this problem, see Zhishman, *Das Eherecht*, pp. 16–17. Zhishman points out that later Byzantine legislation not surprisingly avoided the prosecution of private moral offenses.

56. Zepos and Zepos, p. 536. The same injunction is repeated, without the authority of the Neara, in V, 226r (*Regestes*, 1777): "ἱερέων γνώμης χωρὶς μὴ γίνεσθαι συνοικέσια." From the sixth to the ninth centuries imperial legislation continued to place more and more responsibilities for traditionally civil matters under the purview of the Church. In terms of marriage practices, the most significant changes occurred in the late ninth and early tenth centuries when Leo VI determined that all marriages between free citizens be accompanied by an ecclesiastical blessing. Alexius I expanded this to include slaves. See Novel 89 in *Novelles*, edd. Noailles and Daine, p. 297: "τὰ συνοικέσια τῇ μαρτυρίᾳ τῆς ἱερᾶς εὐλογίας ἐρρῶσθαι κελεύομεν." The same Novel also determined that adoption

was too serious a matter to be excluded from the purview of the Church and like marriage it had to be accomplished by an ecclesiastical blessing. For a discussion of marriage in the Byzantine Christian tradition, see John Meyendorff, *Marriage: An Orthodox Perspective* (Crestwood, N.Y.: St. Vladimir's Seminary Press, 1970), pp. 91–99; and Demetrios J. Constantelos, *Marriage, Sexuality, and Celibacy* (Minneapolis: Light & Life, 1935), pp. 44–53.

57. V, 228v (*Regestes*, 1778): Leo VI made the same point when he decreed in novel 89 that "between marriage and celibacy there is no intermediate state which is irreproachable." *Novelles*, edd. Noailles and Dain, p. 297.

58. Zepos and Zepos, p. 535.

59. Zepos and Zepos, p. 536; also V, 224v (*Regestes*, 1776).

60. Zepos and Zepos, p. 535; Athanasios' regulations are more rigorous than the tenth century *Book of the Prefect*, which determined that taverns must not open before 7 A.M. on Sunday (the second morning hour) and must close before 7 P.M. (the second evening hour); *Book of the Prefect* 19.2 in Zepos and Zepos, p. 389.

61. Talbot, 42, lines 18–22 (*Regestes*, 1646; dated February 1306).

62. Talbot, 43, lines 36–40 (*Regestes*, 1663; dated Lent 1307). Eating fish during Lent was prohibited in Byzantine custom; see Balsamon's commentary on Canon 50 of the council of Laodicea (Rhalles and Potles, III:217). I assume this regulation applied to Holy Week rather than all of Lent: the letter refers to the biblical image of the "bridegroom," (Matt. 25:5–10) commemorated during the first three nights of Holy Week in the Byzantine Church.

63. Talbot, 44, lines 22–25 (*Regestes*, 1665; dated Christmas 1307). Novel 54 of Leo VI ordered that everyone refrain from work on Sunday; *Novelles*, edd. Noailles and Dain, pp. 205–207. In addition to these three services Athanasios exhorted the faithful also to attend services for the dead (μνημόσυνα); V, 225v (*Regestes*, 1777); and V, 224v (*Regestes*, 1776).

64. *V*, 224v (*Regestes*, 1776).

# 7

# Conclusion

ATHANASIOS WAS A MAN OF HIS AGE and his world, operating within the presuppositions of the Byzantine imperial system. Hence, we may not judge his social and political reforms, his thinking, or his personality by reference to the twentieth century or to the values of an age that perceives no "fixed" reality. He was haunted, as were many noted churchmen before him, by the chasm he perceived between the everyday life of the Byzantine Christian and the ruling principles of Orthodox Christianity. In several specific instances he succeeded in narrowing the gap. Social and political corruption were especially focused when events were refracted through the prisms of baptismal theology, the Old Testament prophetic tradition, and the life of the monastic *cenobium.* These three working categories enabled Athanasios to make sense out of the political and social realities confronting him during a particularly painful "time of troubles," and they enable us to understand Athanasios and his place in the history of the late Byzantine empire and church.

If these were the three categories by which Athanasios organized his thinking meaningfully, the objectives for which he struggled were the freedom of the church and right order in Christian society, with all their implications for social and political life. Andronikos' first duty was to protect the integrity of the church as a political reality, and the emperor's piety certainly predisposed him in that direction.[1] Freedom was one of the ongoing struggles in Byzantine Church life, having been taken up by Theodore the Studite in the ninth century, Nicholas Mystikos in the tenth century, and Patriarch Polyeuktos in the late tenth century. Athanasios, working under the general theme of right order in Christian society, sought to reconstruct Byzantine life. It would be a distortion of history to separate his ecclesiastical from his social and political reforms, for they were rooted in the same series of imperatives and had the same objectives. For Athanasios not only were the price of wheat, the feeding of the poor, the bribery of officials, and unjust taxes spiritual issues, but they also had direct bearing on the establishment of right order in Christian society. With numbing repetition, Athanasios called upon Andronikos, the "pious ruler," to impose a return to Christian morality and repentance (ἐπιστροφὴ καὶ μετάνοια) as the only virtues that could save both the empire and the church.[2]

Twice during his life, Athanasios as patriarch of Constantinople faced situations of domestic and international decline and social injustice, especially apparent in the urban centers of the Byzantine empire. Athanasios' is a pessimistic picture of a "time of troubles." Emphasis on the negative, it could be argued, is built into the very nature of recorded history: the normal does not make headlines; efficient and just bureaucrats and bishops are insignificant in comparison with those who misbehave. Such is, no doubt, the explanation for Athanasios' failure to list all those who made contributions to refugees in the city.[3] It is, however, the very quantity of Athanasios' letters and the support of the contemporary historical sources that lead one to believe that Athanasios was certainly more than a literary pessimist.

This time of troubles[4] was also a period of ecclesiastical and monastic ascendancy, with Athanasios filling the leadership vacuum created by the weak, albeit pious, personality of Emperor Andronikos II. Athanasios was a vigorous leader, the fountainhead of a reform movement, at once spiritual and social, commonly referred to as Palamism. In spite of corruption in the church,[5] Athanasios garnered respect and prestige for his office by his moral integrity, care for the people of the empire, and expansion of patriarchal jurisdiction beyond imperial territory.[6] In fact, Athanasios so expanded the authority of the church into areas of civil life that it largely paralleled the role formerly played by the emperor in ecclesiastical life.

Did Athanasios' reform policy fail and, if so, why did it fail? Why did reform thinking find no echo during the fourteenth century? First, Athanasios easily alienated large numbers of powerful persons both in the church and in the civil bureaucracy. As any politician quickly learns, nothing effective can be done without the backing of a bureaucracy or a stable civil service, the single most significant factor in marking Byzantium as a modern political reality. In fact, in one of his letters Athanasios complained bitterly that he had no help in guiding the patrimony of Christ. In the case of his first patriarchate, he had hoped for the speedy return of the emperor from Anatolia so that things would change for the better through "examination and renewal" of divine ordinances (ἀνανεώσεως).[7] He apparently did not have the support of the civil hierarchy; it was precisely its members he attacked by name in several letters.

Second, his strongly ascetic nature and harsh personality also alienated many; he threatened not only their lifestyle but also their incomes and investments. Pachymeres notes that Athanasios' monastic training did not well suit him to govern others,[8] and personality often became the issue. The prophetic saint is not always the best person to initiate change. Had Athanasios been more amenable, more flexible, and more politically astute, he might have been less saintly but more successful.

Third, Athanasios was succeeded in the patriarchate by relatively weak men. Gregoras notes that "it would have been worthwhile if such a rule and a model [as that of Athanasios] had been maintained by his successors."[9] The patriarchate was one of the few agencies, if not the only, able to lead a genuine reform movement in the Byzantine empire. The church, without the leadership of a committed patriarch, could do little to effect change and ameliorate hardships. Eventually, under the leadership of Gregory Palamas, the hesychasts again took up his policies; for this reason Palamas refers to Athanasios as a forerunner of hesychasm.[10]

Fourth, Athanasios did not succeed in building a party of followers or give birth to a movement. For whatever reason, the Byzantine Church tended to produce no monastic orders devoted to a particular purpose and a series of daughter houses to propagate that purpose. Athanasios' followers were limited, and he apparently failed to develop a "team" to institutionalize his programs after his death.

Even though Athanasios' reform measures were short-lived, it can be shown that the very elements that gave birth to a renewal of hesychasm in Palamism gave rise to Athanasios' demand for social and political purity: the trend toward Christian maximalism and the drive toward Christian purity. Talbot misses this point: "Nor is there any hint in his writings that he was a forerunner of

hesychasm, or a master of the 'psycho-technical' method of prayer, as he is described by Gregory Palamas."[11]

She has failed to distinguish between hesychasm as a particular spiritual psychosomatic technique and its historical expression in Palamism. Palamism must, I believe, be seen as an aspect of a broader social, ecclesiastical, and moral reform, as a tendency toward Christian maximalism during a period of social, political, and military decline. It is in this sense that Athanasios was recognized as one of the forerunners of hesychast renewal in the mid-fourteenth century, a period of social and ecclesiastical troubles. In this regard, Gregory Palamas, metropolitan of Thessalonica, was well respected for his sense of social justice and his effort to deal with the issues raised by the zealots, whose revolution had collapsed just before he took over the diocese.[12] Similarly, it is neither accident nor coincidence that both of Athanasios' biographers, Theoktistos and Kalothetos, were noted hesychasts.[13]

Athanasios' motivating principles were foundational not only to his reforms and his thinking, but also to Byzantine Christianity. I have shown that his social and political reforms were consistent and often congruent with his ecclesiastical reforms, and a future study will indicate that his efforts to reform the moral life of the people of the empire were rooted in the same principles and followed the same pattern.

Athanasios was fundamentally successful, achieving great popularity among the common people of the city—a popularity that may have been lessened by his stern moral controls on the public life of the city, much as the heavy hand of Calvin's Company of Pastors in Geneva. The matrix for implementing the three foundational categories of reform was fourteenth-century Constantinople. If Athanasios had dealings that were more than ecclesiastical outside the city, they are not clear from his letters. His popularity and his veneration as a saint were in fact largely, if not completely, limited to Constantinople, which would indicate that this was his exclusive area of operation. If he was popular among the people of the city, it was for his social measures, not for his moral exhortations, which continually pointed out the weaknesses of a people in rebellion against the laws of God and the chastisement they would suffer. This interpretation was his inheritance from the rule based on the morality of the Hebrew prophets. His following was limited numerically. It was this, no doubt, unlike comparable Western movements, which kept his policies from becoming a "movement" of reform in the period immediately after his death.

That Athanasios' influence was deep-seated can be seen in the mid-fourteenth-century success of Palamism. The history of the church is filled with new beginnings, and although Athanasios' specific measures may have failed to become established, their general intention fed a new movement, Palamite hesychasm. His influence transcended the immediate issues of his patriarchates and properly belong to Byzantine Christian spiritual and moral development. His reforms were the culmination of the spiritual, moral, and political life of the Orthodox Church of Byzantium and the foundation for the development of a reform movement that prepared a purified Orthodoxy to face the threat of an Islamic overlordship and for the genuinely new role of leadership in secular matters by the church.

Recent research by Alice-Mary Talbot[14] and Ruth Macrides[15] had placed Athanasios in the context of Palamism through his canonization, which took place sometime in the middle of the fourteenth century.[16] Their research indicates clearly that he was canonized or was perceived to have been canonized in relation to the official endorsement of Palamism as orthodox. Both writers indicate that the traditional distinction between "official" and "popular" canonization more properly corresponds to "general" (or synodal, ἀνακήρυξις) as opposed to "particular" (or local, ἀναγνώρισις).[17] Athanasios was initially venerated by the monks of his own monastery at Xerolophos, with October 28 commemorating the date of his death.[18] Although it took the church of Constantinople several decades to include Athanasios' commemoration in the liturgical calendar, his popular veneration, according to the *Logos*, began immediately; according to his *vitae*, it began even before his death.[19]

In this context the whole process of canonization is taken out of the realm of the "Western influence," in which it was supposed to have been rooted, beginning in the eleventh century and especially in the fourteenth.[20] In the mind of Palamite supporters it was clear that the form of Athanasios' canonization as well as its timing was related to the political necessity to underwrite Palamism as the official doctrine of the Church of Constantinople. In fact, general or universal canonization meant the inclusion of the name of the saint in the calendar of the Great Church of Constantinople and, hence, in the calendar of all churches following the Constantinopolitan tradition.[21] To canonize Athanasios officially was to endorse Palamism officially.

Athanasios finally retired from the patriarchal office in September 1309, in a combination resignation and deposition. At least formally, his leaving was not a deposition; he did, however, resign in melancholic despair and with a sense of isolation.[22] He described his departure as a virtue in that he sought to prevent more lies from being spread and believed. Even monastic supporters had counseled him to leave and avoid more trouble. In the Byzantine Orthodox tradition it was always difficult for an emperor to depose a patriarch, especially a moderately popular patriarch. The risk was always present of fomenting a schism and thereby creating a greater problem than existed before, as was the case when Michael VIII deposed Arsenios in 1265 and Joseph in 1275. Athanasios left the patriarchate and apparently retired to his monastery at Xerolophos, where he no doubt continued informal contacts with the people of the city.[23] He lived quietly, we are told, performing miracles, seeing visions (which he communicated to the emperor), and teaching his disciples "spiritual disciplines" (ἀσκήσεως).[24] In fact, the last official reference to Athanasios' name in historical sources excludes him from any role whatsoever. In 1310 the Arsenites were restored to the official church by an agreement requiring that Athanasios never be considered as a candidate for the patriarchate again.[25]

The overriding goal of Athanasios' patriarchates—the social and ecclesiastical reform of the empire and its institutions—aroused the opposition of both ecclesiastical and political officials, which eventually forced his two resignations. But in spite of the hostility, Athanasios' continuing popularity among the lower classes and many monks led to a cult surrounding his relics. Talbot fixes the *terminus ante quem* for Athanasios' death at 1323;[26] Laurent at about 1315, but he offers no explanation.[27] Whatever the date of his death, his body was exhumed and transferred three years later to the monastic church of Christ the Savior.

Athanasios as a reformer was rooted in the Byzantine spiritual and political tradition. In fact, without the intimate association between the *hierosyne* and the *basileia* it would be impossible to approach reform without approaching revolution. Revolution was never a Byzantine option, precisely because the empire was an eternal entity. (This belief remained common until the early fifteenth century, when such men as George Gemistos Plethon could conceive of the end of Christian Byzantium and the rise of a nation based in Greece and rooted in Greek philosophical principles.) It was a period of transition, and like most periods of transition, whether personal or political, what had seemed permanent was now questioned. The myth of Byzantium as the *typos* of the divine archteype was crumbling in the face of political and military reality. The church especially, committed as it was to the myth of fixed conditions, did not readily embrace change. Revolution was an impossibility, and even the so-called zealot revolutionaries of Thessalonica in the fourteenth century claimed they were appropriating ecclesiastical properties in the name and for the sake of the lower clergy who had been disenfranchised by an unequal distribution of wealth.

In addition to the *symphonia* between the *hierosyne* and the *basileia*, Christianity, as Gerhard Ladner has shown, has *reform* built into it in the sense of rebuilding humanity, creating new persons. The image/likeness tension had been the root of Christian reform since the second century. Each of these categories, which can find resonance in the fathers of the Greek church, finds a healthy treatment in the letters and programs of Athanasios. Although he was neither a systematic nor a sophisticated thinker, he was thorough. He played his prophetic role with dogged repetition. We have seen that reform for Athanasios was reform in the traditional patristic sense of restoration as well as growth toward deification.

Neither *symphonia* nor the application of image-and-likeness theology to morality is conducive to revolution. The Byzantines intuited an inherent danger in the use of violence in social, moral, or even international situations. Furthermore, revolution can find no leader when all leaders insist on interpreting the failure of secular leadership in terms of divine chastisement for sins committed and on prescribing repentance as the remedy. For Athanasios, the solution to the social and political dilemmas of the empire was a return to Christian morality, the abandonment of which had led to injustice, exploitation, ecclesiastical corruption, and the evils that God had visited on the Byzantines as chastisement. For if we did not sow these troubles, we would not reap their fruits.[28] Such was the prophetic imperative.

Athanasios knew what solutions to apply, solutions both practical and spiritual: social justice had to be restored and the people had to offer repentance. Without this the empire would be lost. He also knew that such solutions as a crusade from the West or the employment of the Catalan mercenaries were deceptive.[29] What he perceived the long-term future of the empire to be is not clear; it is clear, however, that the sense was growing that the empire was not in principle eternal and that the church was not inextricably tied to that empire. Athanasios was no fool and understood well that the empire could never be restored to its position prior to the Latin occupation of 1204.

These various elements of social and political reform initiated by Athanasios belie the often repeated charges that Byzantine ecclesiastical, theological, and monastic thinking was preoccupied with a *theoria* devoid of any real contact with the world of the Byzantines. Athanasios was radical neither in what he did nor in what he wrote, but only in the extent to which he was willing to apply to social and ecclesiastical life, traditional monastic, spiritual, and scriptural imperatives in the area of social, moral, and ecclesiastical reform. He was radical inasmuch as he reversed the traditional Byzantine ecclesiastical pattern of permitting the government to correct social injustice and to punish wrongdoing. Certainly, he tried to involve Andronikos in this traditional role, but either the emperor ignored his pleas or the pleas were for action over which he could neither effect control nor formulate policy.

Had Athanasios been merely a canonical rigorist and writer of prophecy, he would have been content with only his letters and his teaching. Such was not the case; Athanasios fully involved himself in the affairs of the empire and the social order. In fact, canons were obvious by their absence.[30] Athanasios' writings and career so brilliantly represented Byzantine ethical and social thinking that he must be seen as one of the sources of the hesychast movement, which came to fruition in the mid-fourteenth century with Gregory Palamas and the Athonite monks. Athanasios' strong, ethical leadership and his sense of independence from the basileia prepared the Orthodox Church for life as a disenfranchised minority under the Turkokratia. Athanasios was indeed, as Theoktistos calls him in the "Oration on the Translation" of his relics, "the mighty trumpet of the church."[31]

## NOTES

1. On the centrality of "the freedom of the church" and its implications for ecclesiastical life, see Boojamra, *Church Reform*, 60–62, 66–69.

2. Talbot, 15, lines 7–11 (*Regestes*, 1611).

3. See text above, p. 107.

4. Laiou, *Constantinople*, pp. 243–83, refers to the decade after Athanasios' patriarchate as "After the Storm." Andronikos did manage to improve imperial finances, even through the political and military situation continued to degenerate. See Gregoras, I:317–18.

5. Boojamra, *Church Reform*, pp. 91–134.

6. The growth of patriarchal authority is reflected in Andronikos' decision in November 1312, to transfer the control of all Athonite monasteries directly to the patriarch. See Meyer, *Haupturkunden*, 190–94.

7. Talbot, 115, lines 56–59 (*Regestes*, 1309).

8. Pachymeres, 140.

9. Gregoras, I:182, 184. Niphon, Athanasios' successor, tolerated many of the abuses that Athanasios fought.

10. See John Meyendorff, *Les Triades pur la défense des saints hésychastes* (Louvain: Spicelegium Sacrum Louvainiense, 1959), Triad 1.2, 12, 99. It is known that the monastery of Christ near the Xerolophos quarter, where Athanasios twice retired, was a center of the hesychast movement; see Meyendorff, "Spiritual Trends," p. 62.

11. Talbot, xxix. Talbot does not repeat this claim in her later *Faith Healing in Late Byzantium.* This work is largely composed of an edited version of the text of the "Oration on the Translation of the Relics of Our Holy Father Athanasios," from codex Const. Chalc. mon 64, 157ʳ–199ʳ, by Theoktistos the Studite. See *Healing*, pp. 44–123.

12. See Meyendorff, *Gregory Palamas*, pp. 90–91. In his sermons Gregory Palamas violently attacked usury and social injustice; "Encomium" in *PG*, 101:618; and political turmoil resulting from the mistreatment of the poor, see also "Homily 1," PG, 101:12, 16, and "Homily 22," 192.

13. Talbot, *Healing*, p. 28.

14. See ibid., p. 27, where she writes: "The most tempting hypothesis is that he was revered as a precursor of Palamite hesychasm and was canonized to bolster the official recognition of Palamism as Orthodox doctrine." This seems to be a conclusion well founded in both Macrides' research on canonization (see note 13), and my conclusions about the nature of Athanasios' influence on Palamas.

15. Macrides, "Saints," 82–87.

16. No firm date is offered for the canonization, but it occurred before 1368, when Palamas was canonized. See Talbot, *Healing*, 27.

17. Ibid., pp. 22–23; Macrides, "Saints," pp. 84–85.

18. See A. Papadopoulos-Kerameus, "Zitija dvuh Vselenskih patriarhov XIVv., svv. Afanasija I i Isidora I," TVA iii*n*1. See K. Doukakes, Μέγας Συναξαριστὴς πάντων τῶν ἁγίων τῶν καθ' ἅπαντα τὸν μῆνα Ὀκτώβριον ἑορταζομένων (Athens, 1895), p. 455. On the history of Athanasios' relics

after 1453, see D. Stiernon, "Le Quartier du Xérolophos à Constantinople et les réliques Vénitiennes du Saint Athanase," *REB*, 19 (1961), 165–88. His relics became confused with those of the fourth-century St. Athanasios of Alexandria. The account of their fate was further complicated in 1973 when, in a gesture of ecumenical good will, the relics were transferred to Pope Shenouda III of the Coptic Orthodox Church, which celebrated their "rightful restoration," to an Alexandria our Athanasios had never seen. See *Al Montada*, 7 (May–June 1973), 5.

19. See the "Oration," in Talbot, *Healing*, pp. 57–59. Gregoras, I:180–81, reports that Athanasios would have been more popular had he kept to himself.

20. Macrides, "Saints," p. 83.

21. Talbot, *Healing*, p. 27.

22. Talbot, 115, especially lines 135–39 (*Regestes*, 1309). See also Theoktistos' description of Athanasios' last days, filled with peril and struggle, in "Oration," in Talbot, *Healing*, pp. 52–54.

23. Gregoras, I:258. See TVA, 41, and KVA, 500.

24. Gregoras, I:258–59.

25. Laurent, "Les Grandes Crises," 291.

26. Talbot, *Healing*, p. 13.

27. Vitalien Laurent, "La Direction spirituelle à Byzance: La Correspondance d'Irène-Eulogie Choumnaina Paléologine avec son second directeur," *REB*, 14 (1956), 48–86.

28. Talbot, 14, lines 33–37 (*Regestes*, 1677).

29. Talbot, 37, lines 13–16 (*Regestes*, Appendix 7).

30. *V*, 105*r*–121*r* (*Regestes*, 1738), where he details the canonical charges against the Arsenites.

31. "Oration," in Talbot, *Healing*, p. 46, line 31: "ἡ μεγάλη σάλπιγξ τῆς ἐκκλησίας."

# BIBLIOGRAPHY

## SOURCES

*Acta et diplomata graeca medii aevi sacra et profana* I–II. Edd. Franz Miklosich and J. Müller. Vienna: Gerold, 1860, 1890.

*Acta patriarchatus Constantinopolitani* II. Edd. Franz Miklosich and J. Müller. Vienna: Gerold, 1865.

"Actes d'Esphigmenou." Edd. L. Petit and W. Regel. *Vizantiiskii Vremennik*, 12 (1906), 1–118.

*Actes de Xéropotamou.* Ed. Jacques Bompaire. Archives de l'Athos 3. Paris: Lethielleux, 1964.

Andronikos II. "Γράμμα Ὑποσχετικον." Vitalien Laurent. "Le Serment de l'empereur Ancronic IIème Paléologue au patriarche Athanase Ier, lors de sa seconde accession au trône oecuménique." *REB*, 23 (1965), 138–39.

——. "Λόγος χρυσόβουλλος, ἐπὶ τῇ ἑνώσει. . . ." In *Anecdota Graeca* II. Ed. J. F. Boissonade. Hildesheim: Olms, 1962. Pp. 70–76.

——. "Novel 39." In *Anecdota Graeca* II. Ed. J. F. Boissonade. Hildesheim: Olms, 1962. Pp. 107–37.

Athanasius I. "Correspondence." In Codex Vat. Gr. 2219, fols. 1r–247r.

——. "Correspondence." PG 142:513–28.

——. "Correspondence with Andronicus." In Alice-Mary Talbot. *The Correspondence of Athanasius I, Patriarch of Constantinople.* Washington, D.C.: Dumbarton Oaks Press, 1975.

——. "Neara." In Σύνταγμα τῶν Θείων καὶ Ἱερῶν Κανόνων. Edd. G. Rhalles and M. Potles. Athens, 1855. Pp. 121–26.

——. "Neara." In *Jus Graecoromanum* I. Edd. J. Zepos and P. Zepos. Athens: Scientia Aalen, 1962. Pp. 533–56.

Attaliates, Michael. *Historia.* Ed. Immanuel Bekker. Bonn: Corpus Scriptorum Historiae Byzantinae, 1853.

*Basilicorum libri LX.* Series A. Edd. H. I. Schritema and N. Van Der Wal. Groningen, 1955.

Balsamon, Theodore. *Meditata.* PG 38:1017.

Basil of Caesarea. *Ascetica* II. PG 31:620–99.

——. *Regulae brevius tractatae.* PG 31:1079–1306.

——. *Regulae fusius tractatae.* PG 31:905–1052.

*The Book of Ser. Marco Polo the Venetian Concerning the Kingdoms and Marvels of the East* I. London: Murray, 1903.

Chomatianos, Demetrios. "Πρὸς τὸν Κωνσταντῖνον Καβάσιλαν." In *Analecta sacra et classica spicilegio Solesmensi parata* VI. Ed. J. B. Pitra. Rome, 1891. Cols. 631–32.

——. "Πρὸς τὸν Κωνσταντῖνον Καβάσιλαν." PG 119:948–49.

Choumnos, Nikephoros. "῎Ελεγχος κατὰ τοῦ κακῶς τὰ πάντα πατριαρχεύσαντος." In *Anecdota Graeca* V. Ed. J. F. Boissonade. Hildesheim: Olms, 1962. Pp. 255–88.

——. "Epitaphios to the Metropolitan of Philadelphia, Theoleptos." In *Anecdota Graeca* V. Ed. J. F. Boissonade. Hildesheim: Olms, 1962. Pp. 138–239.

——. "Θεσσαλονικεῦσι συμβουλευτικὸς περὶ δικαιοσύνης." In *Anecdota Graeca* II. Ed. J. F. Boissonade. Hildesheim: Olms, 1962. Pp. 137–187.

Comnena, Anna. *The Alexiad* II. Trans. Elizabeth Dawes. London: Routledge & Kegan Paul. 1928. Repr. 1967.

Constantine Porphyrogenetos. *De administrando imperio.* Edd. G. Moravesik and R. J. Jenkins. Washington, D.C.: Dumbarton Oaks Press, 1967.

*Corpus iuris civilis.* III. *Novellae.* Edd. Rudolph Schoell and Wilhelm Kroll. Berlin: Verlagsbuchhandlung, 1963.

Darrouzès, J. *Documents inédits d'ecclésiologie byzantine (X^e–XIII^e siècle).* Archives de l'Orient chrétien 9. Paris: Institut français des Etudes byzantines. 1966.

Eusebios of Caesarea. "Ecclesiastical History." In *Nicene and Post-Nicene Fathers* I. Ed. E. C. Richardson. Grand Rapids, Mich.: Eerdmans, 1952. Pp. 81–403.

——. "Oration on the Tricennalia." In *Nicene and Post-Nicene Fathers* I. Ed. E. C. Richardson. Grand Rapids, Mich.: Eerdmans, 1952. Pp. 405–79.

——. "Vita Constantini." In *Nicene and Post-Nicene Fathers* I. Ed. E. C. Richardson. Grand Rapids, Mich.: Eerdmans, 1952. Pp. 481–540.

Gelzer, Heinrich. "Ungedruckte und ungenügend veröffentlichte Texte der *Notitiae episcopatum.*" *Bayerliche Akademie der Wissenschaften, Abhandlungen der philosophisch-philologischen Klasse,* 21 (1901), 595–606.

Gregoras, Nikephoros. *Byzantina Historia* I. Ed. L. Schopen. Bonn: Corpus Scriptorum Historiae Byzantinae, 1829.

Hermas. *The Shepherd.* Trans. C. Taylor. 2 vols. London: SPCK, 1903, 1909.

*Jus graeco-romanum* III. Ed. K. E. Zachariae von Lingenthal. Leipzig: Weigel, 1856.

*Jus graeco-romanum.* Edd. J. Zepos and P. Zepos. 8 vols. Athens, Fexis, 1931.

Kalothetos, Joseph. "Βίος καὶ πολιτεία Ἀθανασίου Α' οἰκουμενικοῦ πατριάρχου." Ed. Athanasios Pantokratorinos. *Thrakika*, 13 (1940), 56–107.

——. "Βίος καὶ πολιτεία τοῦ ἐν ἁγίοις πατρὸς ἡμῶν ἀρχιεπισκόπου Κωνσταντινουπόλεως Ἀθαναοίου." Ed. Demetrios G. Tsames. In Ἰωσὴφ Καλοθέτου Συγγράμματα. Thessalonica: Center for Byzantine Studies, 1908. Pp. 453–502.

Kantakouzenos, John. *Historia* II. Ed. L. Schopen. Bonn: Corpus Scriptorum Historiae Byzantinae, 1832.

Kodinos, George (Pseudo). *Traitê des offices.* Ed. and trans. Jean Verpeaux. Paris: Centre National de la Recherche Scientifique, 1966.

Metochites, Theodore. "Ὑπομνηματισμοὶ καὶ Σημειώσεις Γνωμαικαί." *Miscellanea philosophica et historica.* Ed. C. Muller. Leipzig, 1823. Pp. 538–94.

Muntaner, Ramon. *The Chronicle of Muntaner* II. Trans. Lady Goodenough. London: Hayluyt Society, 1921.

*Les Novelles de Léon VI le Sage.* Edd. P. Noailles and A. Dain. Paris: Les Belles Lettres, 1944.

Pachymeres, George. *De Andronico Palaeologo.* Ed. I. Bekker. Bonn: Corpus Scriptorum Historiae Byzantinae, 1835.

Palamas, Gregory. *Homilies.* PG 151:9–551.

——. *Triades pour la défense des saintes hésychastes.* Ed. John Meyendorff. Louvain: Spicilegium sacrum Louvaniense, 1959.

Planudes, Maximus. *Planudis epistolae.* Ed. M. Treu. Breslau, 1890. Repr. Amsterdam: Hakkert, 1960.

Raynaldus, Oforicus. *Annales ecclesiastici.* Ed. A. Theiner. Bari: Ducus, 1870.

*Sacrorum Conciliorum nova et amplissima collectio* XI. Ed. Joannes D. Mansi. Florence and Venice, 1758–1798.

*The Septuagint Version of the Old Testament and Apocrypha.* London: Bagster, n.d.

*Service Book of the Holy Orthodox-Catholic Apostolic Church.* Trans. Florence Hapgood. Englewood, N.J.: Antiochian Archdiocese of North America, 1965.

Σύνταγμα τῶν Θείων καὶ Ἱερῶν Κανόνων. Edd. G. A. Rhalles and M. Potles. 6 vols. Athens, 1855.

Theoktistos the Studite. "Λόγος εἰς τὴν ἀνακομιδὴν τοῦ λειψάνου τοῦ ἐν ἁγίοις πατρὸς ἡμῶν Ἀθανασίου πατριάρχου Κωνσταντινουπόλεως" (= Logos). In Alice-Mary Talbot. *Faith Healing in Late Byzantium.* Brookline, Mass.: Hellenic College Press, 1983. Pp. 43–123.

——. "La Vie d'Athanase, patriarche de Constantinople." Ed. Hippolyte Delahaye. *Mélanges d'archéologie et d'histoire de l'École française de Rome*, 17 (1897), 39–75.

——. "Vita Athanasii." Ed. A. Papadopulos-Kerameus. *Zapiski istoriko-filogiceskago fakul'teta Imperatorskaga S. Peterburgskago Universiteta*, 76 (1905), 1–51.

*Voyages d'Ibn Batoutah II*. Edd. C. Defrémery and G. R. Sanguinetti. Paris: L'Imprimerie Nationale, 1914.

## Literature

Ahrweiler, Hélène. "L'Histoire et la géographie de la région de Smyrne entre les deux occupations turques (1081–1327), particulièrement au XIIIe siècle." *Travaux et mémoires* I. Paris: De Boccard, 1965. Pp. 1–204.

——. (ed.). *L'Idéologie politique de l'empire byzantin*. Paris: Presses Universitaires de France, 1975.

*Al Montada*. 7 (May–June 1973), 5.

Andréadès, André. "Byzance, paradis du monopole et du privilège." *B*, 9 (1934), 171–81.

——. "Les Juifs et le fisc dans l'empire byzantin." In *Mélanges Charles Diehl* I. Paris: Leroux, 1930. Pp. 7–29.

——. "De la Monnaie et de la puissance d'achat des métaux précieux dans l'Empire byzantin." *B*, 1 (1924), 75–115.

——. "De la Population de Constantinople sous les empereurs byzantins." *Metron*, 1 (1920), 68–119.

——. "La Population de l'empire byzantin." *Actes du IVe Congrès international d'Études byzantines*. Sophia: Institut archéologique bulgare, 1935. Pp. 117–26.

Arnakis, George. "'Οθμανοί. Συμβολὴ εἰς τὸ πρόβλημα τῆς Πτώσεως τοῦ ἑλληνισμοῦ τῆς μικρᾶς 'Ασίας: (1282–1337)." *Texte und Forschungen zur byzantinisch-neugriechischen Philologie*, 41 (1947), 71–130.

Atiya, Asiz. *The Crusade in the Later Middle Ages*. New York: Kraus, 1965.

Avila, Charles. *Ownership: Early Christian Teaching*. Maryknoll, N.Y.: Orbis, 1983.

Bănescu, Nicholas. "Le Patriarche Athanase I et Andronic II Paléologue: État religieux, politique, et social de l'empire," *Académie Roumaine, Bulletin de la Section Historique*, 23 (1942), 28–56.

Barker, Ernest. *Social and Political Thought in Byzantium*. Oxford: Clarendon, 1961.

Barraclough, Geoffrey. *The Medieval Papacy*. London: Thames & Hudson, 1968.

Baynes, Norman H. "The Byzantine State." *Byzantine Studies and Other Essays*. London: Athlone, 1955.

——. "Eusebius and the Christian Empire." *Mélanges Bidez* II. Brussels: Institut de Philologie et d'Histoire orientales, 1934. Pp. 13–18.

Beck, Hans-Georg. *Kirche und theologische Literatur im byzantinischen Reich.* Munich: Beck, 1959.

——. *Theodoros Metochites, die Krise des byzantinischen Weltbildes im 14. Jahrhundert.* Munich: Beck, 1952.

Bees, Nikos A. "Ἰωσὴφ Καλοθέτης καὶ ἀναγραφὴ ἔργων αὐτοῦ." *Byzantinische Zeitschrift*, 17 (1908), 86–91.

Benson, Robert L., and Constable, Giles. *Renaissance and Renewal in the Twelfth Century.* Cambridge: Harvard University Press, 1982.

Binon, S. "L'Histoire et la legende de deux chrysobulles d'Andronic II en faveur de Monembasie." *EO*, 37 (1938), 274–311.

——. *Les Origines lêgendaires et l'histoire de Xeropotamou et de Saint-Paul de l'Athos.* Louvain: Bureau du Museon, 1942.

Blum, John M., et al. *The National Experience.* New York: Harcourt, Brace & World, 1963.

Bompaire, J. "Sur trois Terms de fiscalité byzantine." *Bulletin de Correspondence hêllênique*, 80 (1956), 625–31.

Boojamra, John. "The Affair of Alexis and Roman: Two Documents of 1361." *Greek Orthodox Theological Review*, 28 (1983), 173–94.

——. "Athanasios of Constantinople: A Study of Byzantine Reaction to Latin Religious Infiltration." *Church History*, 48 (March 1979), 27–48.

——. "Christian *Philanthropia:* Justinian's Welfare Policy and the Church," *Byzantina*, 7 (1975), 345–74.

——. *Church Reform in the Late Byzantine Empire.* Thessalonica: Patristic Institute, 1982.

——. "Constantine and Justinian: A Study in Heteronomous Development." In *Orthodox Synthesis.* Ed. J. Allen. Crestwood, N.Y.: St. Vladimir's Seminary Press, 1981. Pp. 189–212.

——. "The Eastern Schism of 907 and the Affair of the Tetragamia." *Journal of Ecclesiastical History*, 25 (April 1974), 113–33.

Bowman, Steven. "Two Late Byzantine Dialogues with the Jews." *Greek Orthodox Theological Review*, 25 (Spring 1980), 83–93.

Brătianu, G. I. "L'Approvisionnement de Constantinople sous les Paléologues et les empereurs ottomans." *B*, 6 (1931), 641–56.

——. *Études byzantines d'histoire économique et sociale.* Paris: Geuthner, 1938.

——. *La Mer noire.* Monachii: Societas academica Daco-romana, 1969.

——. "Notes sur le projet de mariage entre l'empereur Michel IX Paléologue et Catherine de Courtenay, 1288–1295," *Revue historique du Sud-Est européen*, 1 (1924), 59–63.

——. "La Question de l'approvisionnement de Constantinople à l'époque byzantine et ottomane," *B*, 5 (1930), 83–107.

——. *Recherches sur le commerce gênois dans la Mer Noire au XIIIe siècle.* Paris: Geuthner, 1929.

Bréhier, Louis. "Andronic II." *Dictionnaire d'histoire et de géographie ecclésiastique* I. Paris: Letouzey et Ané, 1914. Cols. 1782–92.

——. "*L'Eglise et l'orient au moyen-âge: Les croisades.* Paris: Lecoffre, Gabalda, 1928.

——. *Études byzantines d'histoire economique et sociale.* Paris: 1938.

——. "Hiereus et Basileus." In *Memorial Louis Petit.* Archives de l'Orient chrétien 1. Bucharest: Institut français des Études byzantines, 1948. Pp. 41–45.

——. *Le Monde byzantin.* II. *Les Institutions de l'empire byzantin.* Paris: Michel, 1970.

——. "Le Recrutement des patriarches de Constantinople." *Actes du VIe Congrès international d'Etudes byzantines.* Paris: Editions Universitaires, 1948. Pp. 221–28.

Bridston, Keith. "The Future of Mission as Ecumenical Activity." *Greek Orthodox Theological Review,* 26 (Winter 1981), 325–32.

Brown, Peter. "A Dark-Age Crisis: Aspects of the Iconoclastic Controversy." *The English Historical Review,* 346 (1973), 1–34.

Buchon, J. A. C. *Nouvelles Recherches historiques sur la principauté française de Morée et ses hautes baronnies.* I. Paris: Renouard, 1838.

Camelot, T. *Foi et gnose: Introduction à l'étude de la connaissance mystique chez Clément d'Aléxandrie.* Paris: Vrin, 1945.

Caro, George. "Zur Chronologie der drei letzten Bücher des Pachymeres." *BZ,* 6 (1897), 114–25.

"Catalogus Codicum hagiographicorum Graecorum Bibliothecase Barberinianae de Urbe." *Analecta Bollandiana,* 19 (1900), 81–118.

Chadwick, Henry. "Pachomius and the Idea of Sanctity," in *The Byzantine Saint.* Ed. Sergei Hackel. London: Fellowship of St. Alban and St. Sergius, 1982. Pp. 11–25.

Chalandon, F. *Essai sur la règne d'Alexis Commène.* Paris: Picard, 1900.

Chapman, Conrad. *Michel Paléologue: Restaurateur de l'empire byzantin,* Paris: Figuière, 1926.

Charanis, Peter. "The Aristocracy of Byzantium in the Thirteenth Century." In *Studies in Roman Economic and Social History in Honor of Allan Chester Johnson.* Ed. P. R. Coleman-Norton. Princeton: Princeton University Press, 1951. Pp. 336–55.

——. "Economic Factors in the Decline of the Byzantine Empire." *Journal of Economic History,* 13 (1953), 413–34.

——. "Internal Strife in Byzantium During the Fourteenth Century." *B,* 15 (1940–1941), 208–30.

——. "Monastic Properties and the State in the Byzantine Empire." *DOP,* 4 (1948), 51–117.

——. "A Note on the Population and Cities of the Byzantine Empire in the Thirteenth Century." In *The Joshua Starr Memorial Volume.* Jewish

Social Studies 5. New York: Conference on Jewish Relations, 1953. Pp. 135–48.

——. "Observations on the Demography of the Byzantine Empire." In *Acts of the XIIIth International Congress of Byzantine Studies.* London: Oxford University Press, 1967.

——. "On the Social Structure and Economic Organization of the Byzantine Empire in the Thirteenth Century and Later." *Byzantinoslavica,* 12 (1951), 94–153.

Constable, Giles. "Renewal and Reform in Religious Life." In *Renaissance and Renewal in the Twelfth Century.* Edd. Robert L. Benson and Giles Constable. Cambridge: Harvard University Press, 1982.

Constantelos, Demetrios J. *Byzantine Philanthropy and Social Welfare.* New Brunswick, N.J.: Rutgers University Press, 1968.

——. "Emperor John Vatatzes' Social Concern: Basis for Canonization." *Kleronomia,* 4 (1972), 92–104.

——. "Life and Social Welfare Activity of Patriarch Athanasios I of Constantinople." *Theologia,* 41 (July–September 1975), 611–25.

——. *Marriage, Sexuality, and Celibacy.* Minneapolis: Light & Life, 1935.

——. "Mysticism and Social Involvement in the Later Byzantine Church: Theoleptos of Philadelphia, A Case Study." *Byzantine Studies/Études byzantines,* 6 (1979), 49–60.

Constantinidi-Bibikou, Hélène. "Documents concernant l'histoire byzantine, deposés aux Archives Nationales de France." In *Mélanges offerts à Octave et Melpo Merlier* I. Athens: Institut français d'Athens, 1956. Pp. 119–32.

Cranz, F. E. "Kingdom and Polity in Eusebius of Caesarea." *Harvard Theological Review* 45 (1952), 47–66.

Dade, Erwin. *Versuche zur Wiederrichtung der lateinischen Herrschaft in Konstantinopel im Rahmen der abendländischen Politik.* Jena: Biedermann, 1938.

Dalleggio D'Alessio, E. "Les Établissements dominicains de Pera (Galata)." *EO,* 39 (1936), 83–86.

——. "Recherches sur l'histoire de la latinité de Constantinople: Nomenclature des églises latines de Constantinople sous les empereurs byzantins." *EO,* 27 (1924), 448–60.

Darrouzès, Jean. "Listes synodales et notitiae." *Revue des Études Byzantines,* 28 (1970), 57–96.

——. *Recherches sur les* Ὀφφίκια *de l'Eglise byzantine.* Archives de l'Orient chrétien 11. Paris: Institut français d'Études byzantines, 1970.

De Muralt, Edouard. *Essai de chronographie byzantine* (1057–1453). Paris: Librairie "Orient" Editions. 1965.

Diehl, Charles. *History of the Byzantine Empire.* Trans. George Ives. Princeton: Princeton University Press, 1925.

——. "De quelques croyances byzantines sur la fin de Constantinople." *BZ*, 30 (1930), 192–96.

Dölger, Franz. *Regesten der Kaiserurkunden des oströmischen Reichs.* 4 vols. Berlin: Beck, 1960.

——, and Karayanopoulos, J. *Byzantinische Urkundenlehr.* I. *Die Kaiserurkunden.* Munich: Beck, 1968.

Dondaine, Antoine. " 'Contra Graecos' premiers écrits polémiques des Dominicains d'orient." *Archivum Fratrum Praedicatorum*, 21 (1951), 320–446.

Doukakes, K. Μέγας Συναξαριστὴς πάντων τῶν ἁγίων τῶν καθ' ἅπαντα τὸν μῆνα Ὀκτώβριον ἑορταζομένων. Athens, 1895.

Du Cange, C. du Fresne. *Glossarium ad scriptores mediae et infimae graecitatis* I–II. Graz: Akademische Druck- und Verlagsanstalt, 1892.

Dvornik, Francis. *Early Christian and Byzantine Political Philosophy.* 2 vols. Washington, D.C.: Dumbarton Oaks Press, 1966.

——. *Le Schisme de Photius.* Paris: du Cerf, 1950.

Ehrhard, Albert. *Lexikon für Theologie und Kirche.* Freiburg: Herder, 1930–1938.

——. *Uberlieferung und Bestand der hagiographischen Kirche* XXX. Berlin: Akademie, 1952.

Eliade, Mircea. *Images and Symbols: Studies in Religious Symbolism.* New York: Sheed & Ward, 1961.

Erickson, John. "The Orthodox Canonical Tradition." *St. Vladimir's Theological Quarterly*, 27 (1983), 155–68.

Every, George. *The Byzantine Patriarchate, 451–1204.* London: S.P.C.K., 1962.

Fedwick, Paul J. *The Church and the Charisma of Leadership in Basil of Caesarea.* Toronto: Pontifical Institute of Mediaeval Studies, 1979.

Finlay, George. *A History of Greece* III. Oxford: Clarendon, 1877.

Fisher, Elizabeth. "A Note on Pachymeres' 'De Andronico Palaeologo." *B*, 40 (1971), 230–35.

Florovsky, Georges. "Antinomies of Christian History: Empire and Desert." *Christianity and Culture.* Belmont, Mass.: Nordland, 1974. Pp. 67–100.

——. "Faith and Culture." *Christianity and Culture.* Belmont, Mass.: Nordland, 1974. Pp. 9–30.

——. "The Social Problem in the Eastern Orthodox Church." *Christianity and Culture.* Belmont, Mass.: Nordland, 1974. Pp. 131–43.

Francès, E. "La Feodalité byzantine et la conquête turque," *Studia et Acta Orientalia*, 4 (1962), 69–90.

——. "La Feodalité et les villes byzantines aux XIII^e et au XIV^e siècles." *Byzantinoslavica*, 16 (1955), 76–96.

Frazee, Charles. "The Christian Church in Cilician Armenia: Its Relations with Rome and Constantinople to 1198." *Church History*, 45 (1976), 166–84.

Galanté, G. *Les Juifs de Constantinople sous Byzance.* Istanbul: Babok, 1940.

Gasquet, A. *De l'Authorité impériale en matière religieuse à Byzance.* Paris: Thorin, 1879.

Geanakopolos, Deno J. *Byzantine East and Latin West: The Two Worlds of Christendom in the Middle Ages and Renaissance.* Oxford: Blackwell, 1966.

——. *Emperor Michael Palaeologos and the West.* Cambridge: Harvard University Press, 1959.

——. *Interaction of the "Sibling" Byzantine and Western Cultures in the Middle Ages and Italian Renaissance.* New Haven: Yale University Press, 1976.

Gelzer, Heinrich. "Ungedrückte und ungenügend veröffentlichte Texte der *Notitiae episcopatum.*" *Bayerische Akademie der Wissenschaften. Abhandlungen der philosophisch-philologischen Klasse*, 21 (1901), 529–641.

Gennadios (Arambatzoglou), Metropolitan of Heliopolis. "Ἡ πτώτη ἀπὸ τοῦ θρόνου ἀποχώρησις τοῦ πατριάρχου Ἀθανασίου Α'." *Orthodoxia*, 27 (1953), 145–50.

Gibbons, Henry A. *The Foundations of the Ottoman Empire.* London: Cass, 1968.

Gill, Joseph. "Emperor Andronicus II and the Patriarch Athanasius I." *Byzantina*, 2 (1970), 11–20.

Gouillard, J. "Quatre procès de mystiques à Byzance (960–1143)." *REB*, 36 (1978), 5–81.

Grabar, André. "Pseudo-Codinus et les cérémonies de la cour byzantine au XIVe siècle." In *Art et société à Byzance sous les Paléologues.* Venice: Institut hellénique d'Etudes byzantines et post-byzantines, 1971. Pp. 193–221.

Gribomont, Jean. "Le Monachisme au IVe siècle en Asie Mineure de Gangres au Messalianisme." *Studia Patristica* II. Berlin: Akademie, 1955. Pp. 400–16.

——. "Les Règles morales de saint Basile et le Nouveau Testament." *Studia Patristica* II. Berlin: Akademie, 1957. Pp 416–26.

Grumel, V. "La Date de l'avènement du patriarche de Constantinople Niphon Ier." *REB*, 13 (1955), 138–39.

——. "Le Mois de Marie des Byzantins." *EO*, 31 (1932), 257–69.

——. *Traité d'études byzantines.* I. *La Chronologie.* Paris: Presses Universitaires de France, 1958.

Guilland, Rodolphe. "La Correspondance inédite d'Athanase, patriarche de Constantinople (1289–1293, 1304–1310)." In *Mélanges Charles Diehl* I. Paris: Presses Universitaires de France, 1930. Pp. 121–40.

——. *Essai sur Nicéphore Grégoras.* Paris: Geuthner, 1926.

——. "Les Poesies inédites de Théodore Métochite." *B*, 3 (1926), 264–302.

Hajjar, Joseph. *Le Synode permanent dans l'église byzantine des origines au XIe siècle.* Orientalia Christiana Analecta 164. Rome: Pont. Institutum Orientium Studiorum, 1926.

Halecki, Oscar. *Un Empereur de Byzance à Rome.* London: Variorum, 1972.

Halkin, François. *Bibliotheca hagiographica graeca* I. Brussels: Société des Bollandistes, 1957.

——. "L'Hagiographie byzantine au service de l'histoire." In *Acts of the XIIIth International Congress of Byzantine Studies.* London: Oxford University Press, 1967. Pp. 345–54.

Hausherr, I. "Direction spirituelle en Orient autrefois," *Orientalia Christiana Periodica,* 31 (1955), 144.

——. "La Méthode d'oraison hésychaste." *Orientalia Christiana Periodica,* 9 (1927), 77–94.

Heisenberg, A. *Aus der Geschichte und Literatur der Palaiologenzeit.* Munich: Bayerische Akademic der Wissenschaften, 1920.

Herbut, J. *De ieiunio et abstinentia in Ecclesia byzantina ab initiis usque ad saec. XI.* Rome: Corona Laterannensis, 1968.

Hermann, Emilio. "Charisticaires." *Dictionnaire de droit canonique* III. Paris: Letouzey et Ané, 1939. Cols. 611–17.

——. "The Secular Church." In *The Cambridge Medieval History* IV.2. Ed. Joan Hussey. Cambridge: Cambridge University Press, 1967. Pp. 105–34.

——. "Recerche sulle istituzioni monastische byzantine: Typica ktetorika, caristicari e monasteri 'liberi.'" *Orientalia Christiana Periodica,* 6 (1940), 204–75.

Heyd, W. *Histoire du commerce du Levant au moyen-âge* I. Leipzig: Harrassowitz, 1959.

Huart, Clement. "Les Origines de l'empire ottoman." *Journal des Savants,* 15 (1917), 155–66.

Hussey, Joan. *The Byzantine World.* New York: Harper & Row, 1961.

——. "The Later Macedonians, the Comneni, and the Angeli." In *The Cambridge Medieval History* IV.1. Ed. Joan Hussey. Cambridge: Cambridge University Press, 1966. Pp. 193–250.

Iorga, N. "Ramon Muntaner et l'empire byzantine." In *Contributions catalans à l'histoire byzantine.* Paris: Gamber, 1927. Pp. 9–39.

Izeddin, M. "Un Texte arabe sur Constantinople byzantine." *Journal Asiatique,* 246 (1958), 453–57.

Jacoby, David. "La Population de Constantinople à l'époque byzantine." *B*, 30 (1961), 81–90.

——. "Les Quarters juifs de Constantinople à l'époque byzantine." *B*, 36 (1967), 167–227.

Janin, Raymond. "Athanase Ier." *Dictionnaire d'histoire et de géographie ecclésiastique* IV. Paris: Letouzey et Ané, 1925. Cols. 1379–81.

——. "La Bithynie sous l'empire byzantine (1071–1337)." *EO*, 20 (1921), 301–19.

——. *Constantinople byzantine: Développement urbain et repertoire topographique.* Paris: Institut français d'Études byzantines, 1964.

——. "L'Empereur dans l'église byzantine." *Nouvelle Revue de Théologie*, 77 (1955), 44–51.

——. "Formation du Patriarcat oecuménique de Constantinople." *EO*, 13 (1910), 135–40, 213–19.

——. *La Géographie ecclésiastique de l'empire byzantin.* III. *Les Églises et les monastères.* Paris: Institut français d'Études byzantines, 1964.

——. "Le Palais patriarcal de Constantinople." *REB*, 20 (1962), 131–55.

Jenkins, Romily. "A Cross of the Patriarch Michael Cerularius," *DOP*, 21 (1967), 235–40.

Jombart, E. "Cohabitation." *Dictionnaire de Droit canonique* III. Paris: Letouzey et Ané, 1942. Cols. 970–82.

Jugie, Martin. "Les Origines de la méthode des hesychastes." *EO*, 30 (1931), 179–85.

Kellner, K. A. Heinrich. *Heortology.* London: Paul, Trench, Trubner, 1908.

Klimakos, John. *The Ladder of Divine Ascent.* Trans. L. Moore. London: Harper, 1959.

Kurmbacher, Karl. *Handbuch der byzantinischen Literatur.* Berlin, 1897.

Ladner, Gerhart. *The Idea of Reform.* Cambridge: Harvard University Press, 1959.

——. "Terms and Ideas of Renewal." In *Renaissance and Renewal in the Twelfth Century.* Edd. Robert L. Benson and Giles Constable. Cambridge: Harvard University Press, 1982. Pp. 1–33.

Laeuchli, Samuel. *Power and Sexuality: The Emergence of Canon Law at the Synod of Elvira.* Philadelphia: Temple University Press, 1972.

Laiou, Angeliki. "A Byzantine Prince Latinized: Theodore Palaeologus, Marquis of Montferrat." *B*, 38 (1968), 386–410.

——. *Constantinople and the Latins: The Foreign Policy of Andronicus II.* Cambridge: Harvard University Press, 1972.

——. "The Provisioning of Constantinople During the Winter of 1306–1307," *B*, 37 (1967), 91–113.

Laiou-Thomadakis, Angeliki. *Peasant Society in the Late Byzantine Empire.* Princeton: Princeton University Press, 1977.

Langer, William, and Blake, Robert. "The Rise of the Ottoman Turks." *American Historical Review*, 37 (1983), 468–505.

Laurent, Vitalien. "Le Basilicon: Nouveau nom de monnaie sous Andronic II Paléoloque," *BZ*, 45 (1952), 50–58.

——. "La Chronologie des higoumènes de Lavra de 1283 à 1309." *REB*, 28 (1970), 97–110.

——. "La Chronologie des patriarches de Constantinople au XIIIe siècle (1208–1309)." *REB*, 37 (1950), 145–55.

——. "La Date de la mort de Jean Beccos." *EO*, 25 (1926), 316–19.

——. "Deux Nouveaux manuscrits de 'l'Histoire Byzantine' de Georges Pachymères." *B*, 11 (1936), 43–57.

——. "La Direction spirituelle à Byzance: La Correspondance d'Irène-Eulogie Choumnaina Paléologine avec son second directeur." *REB*, 14 (1956), 48–86.

——. "La Direction spirituelle des grande dames de Byzance," *REB*, 8 (1950), 64–84.

——. "Les Droits d l'empereur en matière ecclésiastique: L'accord de 1380–1382." *REB*, 13 (1955), 5–20.

——. "Les Grandes Crises religieuses à Byzance: La Fin du schisme arsenite." *Académie Roumaine, Bulletin de la Section Historique*, 26.2 (1945), 225–313.

——. "Grégoire X et le projet d'une ligue antiturque." *EO*, 37 (1938), 257–73.

——. "L'Idée de guerre sainte et la tradition byzantine." *Revue Historique du Sud-Est européen*, 23 (1946), 71–98.

——. "La Liste épiscopale du synodikon de la metropole de Lacédémone." *REB*, 19 (1961), 208–26.

——. "Notes de chronologie et d'histoire byzantine de la fin du XIIIe siècle." *REB*, 27 (1969), 209–34.

——. "La Patriarche d'Antioche Cyrille II (1287–1308)." *Analecta Bollandiana*, 48 (1950), 310–17.

——. "Une Princesse byzantine au cloître." *EO*, 29 (1930), 29–60.

——. "Le Serment de l'empereur Andronic IIème Paléologue au Patriarche Athanase Ier, lors de sa seconde accession au trône oecuménique (September 1303)." *REB*, 23 (1965), 124–39.

——. "Les Signataires du second synode des Blachernes." *EO*, 26 (1927), 129–49.

——. "Un Théologien unioniste de la fin du XIIIe siècle: Le Metropolite d'Adrianople Théoctiste." *REB*, 11 (1953), 187–96.

Lawther Clarke, William K. *The Ascetical Works of St. Basil.* London: SPCK, 1925.

——. *Basil the Great: A Study in Monasticism.* Cambridge: Cambridge University Press, 1913.

Lemerle, Paul. "Un Chrysobulle d'Andronic II Paléologue pour le monastère de Karakala." *Bulletin de Correspondance hellénique*, 60 (1935), 428–46.

——. *L'Émirat d'Aydin: Byzance et l'Occident.* Paris: Presses Universitaires de France, 1957.

——. "Esquisse pour une histoire agraire de Byzance: Les Sources et les problèmes." *Revue Historique*, 219 (1935), 32–74, 254–84.

——. "Le Juge général des grecs et la réforme judiciaire d'Andronic III." In *Mêmorial Louis Petit.* Archives de l'orient chrétien 1. Bucharest: Institut français d'Études byzantines, 1948. Pp. 292–316.

——. "Recherches sur les institutions judiciaires à l'époque des Paléologues. II. Le Tribunal du patriarcat ou tribunal synodal." *Analecta Bollandiana*, 68 (1950), 318–33.

Loenertz, Raymond. "La Chancelier impérial à Byzance au XIII<sup>e</sup> et au XIV<sup>e</sup> siècle." *Orientalia Christian Periodica*, 26 (1960), 275–300.

——. "Notes d'histoire et de chronologie byzantine." *REB*, 20 (1962), 171–80.

McGiffert, Michael. "God's Controversy with Jacobean England." *The American Historical Review*, 88 (1983), 1151–74.

Macrides, Ruth. "Saints and Sainthood in the Early Palaiologan Period." In *The Byzantine Saint.* Ed. Sergei Hackel. London: Fellowship of St. Alban and St. Sergius, 1982. Pp. 67–87.

Magdalino, Paul. "The Byzantine Holy Man in the Twelfth Century." In *The Byzantine Saint.* Ed. Sergei Hackel. London: Fellowship of St. Alban and St. Sergius, 1982. Pp. 51–87.

Marinescu, C. "Tentatives de mariage de deux fils d'Andronic II Paléologue avec des princesses latines." *Revue historique du Sud-Est européen*, 1 (1924), 139–43.

Matschke, Klaus-Peter. "Politik und Kirche im spätbyzantinischen Reich: Athanasios I, Patriarch von Konstantinopel (1289–1293, 1303–1309)." *Wissenschaftliche Zeitschrift der Karl-Marx-Universität Leipzig, Gesellschafts- und Sprachwissenschaftliche Reiche*, 15 (1966), 479–86.

Meyendorff, John. *The Byzantine Legacy in the Orthodox Church.* Crestwood, N.Y.: St. Vladimir's Seminary Press, 1982.

——. *Byzantine Theology.* New York: Fordham University Press, 1974.

——. *Byzantium and the Rise of Russia.* Cambridge: Cambridge University Press, 1981.

——. "The Council of 381 and the Primacy of Constantinople." *Catholicity and the Church.* Crestwood, N.Y.: St. Vladimir's Seminary Press, 1983.

——. "Les Débuts de la controverse hésychaste." *B*, 23 (1953), 87–120.

——. "Grecs, Turcs, et Juifs en Asie Mineure au XIV<sup>e</sup> siècle." *Byzantinische Forschungen.* 1 (1966), 211–17.

——. "L'Hésychasme, Problèmes de semantique." In *Mélanges d'histoire des religions offerts à Henri-Charles Puech.* Paris: Presses Universitaires de France, 1974. Pp. 543–47.

——. *Introduction à l'étude de Grégoire Palamas.* Paris: du Seuil, 1959.

——. *Marriage: An Orthodox Perspective.* Crestwood: N.Y.: St. Vladimir's Seminary Press, 1970.

——. "Society and Culture in the Fourteenth Century Religious Problems." In *Actes du XIVe Congrès International des Études byzantines.* Bucharest: Académie de la République Socialiste Roumaine, 1971. Pp. 41–65.

——. "Spiritual Trends in Byzantium in the Late Thirteenth and Early Fourteenth Centuries." In *Art et société à Byzance sous les Paléologues.* Venice: L'Institut hellénique d'Études byzantines et post-byzantines de Venise, 1971. Pp. 53–71.

——. *A Study of Gregory Palamas.* London: Faith, 1964.

——. *Les Triades pour la défense des saints hésychastes.* Louvain: Spicilegium Sacrum Louvainiense, 1959.

Meyer, L. *Saint Jean Chrysostome, maître de perfection chrétienne.* Paris: Beauchesne, 1933.

Meyer, P. *Die Haupturkunden für die Geschichte der Athoskloster.* Amsterdam: Hakkert, 1965.

Michel, Anton. *Die Kaisermacht in der Ostkirche (843–1204).* Darmstadt: Gentner, 1959.

Miller, William. *The Latins in the Levant.* New York: Barnes & Noble, 1964.

Moranville, H. "Les Projets de Charles de Valois sur l'empire de Constantinople." *Bibliothèque de l'École des Chartes,* 2 (1890), 63–86.

Morison, Ernest F. *St. Basil and His Rule.* Oxford: Clarendon, 1912.

Morris, Rosemary. "The Political Saint of the Eleventh Century." In *The Byzantine Saint.* Ed. Sergei Hackel. London: Fellowship of St. Alban and St. Sergius, 1982. Pp. 43–50.

Morrison, Karl. *The Mimetic Tradition of Reform in the West.* Princeton: Princeton University Press, 1982.

Morteuil, J. A. *Histoire du droit byzantin ou du droit romain dans l'empire d'Orient depuis la mort de Justinien jusqu'à la prise de Constantinople en 1453* III. Paris: Guilbert and Thorel, 1846.

Mouly, George. *Psychology for Effective Teaching.* New York: Holt, Rinehart & Winston, 1962.

Murphy, Margaret. *St. Basil and Monasticism.* New York: AMS, 1971.

Nicol, Donald M. *Church and Society in the Last Centuries of Byzantium.* Cambridge: Cambridge University Press, 1979.

——. "Kaisersalbung: The Unction of Emperors in Late Byzantine Coronation Ritual." *Byzantine and Modern Greek Studies,* 2 (1976), 37–52.

——. *The Last Centuries of Byzantium, 1261–1453.* New York: St. Martin's, 1972.

Omont, H. "Projet de réunion des Eglises grecque et latine sous Charles le Bel en 1327." *Bibliothèque de l'École des Chartes,* 53 (1892), 254–57.

Onatibia, I. "Torres." *New Catholic Encyclopedia,* XIV. Cols. 206–207.

Osborn, Eric. *Ethical Patterns in Early Christian Thought.* Cambridge: Cambridge University Press, 1978.

Ostrogorsky, George. *History of the Byzantine State.* Trans. Joan Hussey. New Brunswick, N.J.: Rutgers University Press, 1969.

——. "The Palaeologi." In *The Cambridge Medieval History* IV.1. Ed. Joan Hussey. Cambridge: Cambridge University Press, 1966.

——. "Pour l'Histoire de l'immunité à Byzance." *B*, 28 (1958), 165–254.

Papadakis, Aristeides. *Crisis in Byzantium.* New York: Fordham University Press, 1983.

——. "Ecumenism in the Thirteenth Century: The Byzantine Case." *St. Vladimir's Theological Quarterly*, 27 (1983), 155–68.

——. "Late Thirteenth-Century Byzantine Theology and Gregory II of Cyprus." In *Byzantine Ecclesiastical Personalities.* Ed. Nomikos Vaporis. Brookline, Mass.: Holy Cross Press, 1975. Pp. 57–72.

Papadopulos, Averkios T. *Versuch einer Genealogie der Palaiologen (1259–1453).* Amsterdam: Hakkert, 1962.

Papadopulos-Kerameus, A. "Νικηφορος Μοσχόπουλος." *BZ*, 12 (1903), 215–23.

Pargoire, J. "Constantinople: Le Couvent de l'Evergétès." *EO*, 9 (1906), 228–32.

——. "Les Monastères doubles chez les Byzantins." *EO*, 9, (1906), 21–25.

Parisot, V. *Cantacuzène, homme d'état et historien.* Paris, 1845.

Petit, Louis. "La Réforme judiciaire d'Andronic Paléologue." *EO*, 9 (1906), 134–38.

Pierre, Hieromoine. "Notes d'ecclésiologie orthodoxe." *Irénikon*, 10 (1933), 111–39.

Possione, Peter. "Chronologia." In George Pachymeres. *De Andronico Paleologo.* Ed. I. Bekker. Bonn: Corpus Scriptorum Historiae Byzantinae, 1835. Pp. 835–70.

Raybaud, Leon-Pierre. *Le Gouvernement et l'administration central de l'empire byzantin sous les premiers Paléologues.* Paris: Sirey, 1968.

*Les Regestes des actes du patriarcat de Constantinople* I.4. Ed. Vitalien Laurent. Paris: Institut français d'Études byzantines, 1971.

Rouillard, Germaine. "Le Politique de Michel VIII Paléologue à l'égard des monastères." *REB*, 1 (1943), 73–84.

——. "Recensements de terres sous les premiers Paléologues." *B*, 12 (1937), 105–18.

——. *La Vie rurale dans l'empire byzantin.* Paris: Librairie d'Amérique et d'Orient, 1953.

Rubio y Lluch, A. *Diplomatari de l'Orient Català (1309–1409).* Barcelona: Institut d'Estudis Catalans, 1947.

——. *Paquimères y Muntaner.* Memóries de la secció historico-arquelologica del Institut d'Estudes Catalans 1. Barcelona, 1927.

Runciman, Steven. *The Byzantine Theocracy.* New York: Cambridge University Press, 1977.

Salaville, S. "Après le Schism arsénite: La Correspondance inédite du Pseudo Jean Chilas." *Académie Roumaine, Bulletin de la Section Historique* 25 (1944), 174–93.

——. "Deux Documents inédits sur les dissensions religieuses byzantines entre 1275 et 1310." *REB*, 5 (1947), 111–30.

——. "Un Directeur spirituel à Byzance au début du XIVe siècle: Théolepte de Philadelphie." In *Mélange Joseph de Ghellinck* II. Gembloux: Duculot, 1951. Pp. 866–87.

——. "Formes ou méthodes de prière d'après un Byzantin de XIVe siècle, Théolepte de Philadelphie." *EO*, 39 (1940), 1–25.

——. "Une Lettre et un discours inédits de Théolepte de Philadelphie." *REB*, 5 (1947), 101–15.

——. "Le Titre ecclésiastique de 'proedros' dans les documents byzantins." *EO*, 29 (1930), 417–34.

——. "La Vie monastique greque au début du XIVe siècle." *REB*, 2 (1944), 119–25.

Sathas, C. N. Μνημεῖα ἑλληνικῆς ἱστορίας. In *Documents inédits relatifs à l'histoire de la Grèce* IV. Paris, 1882.

Schumberger, G. *Expeditions des "almugavares" ou routiers Catalans en Orient.* Paris: 1902.

Schmid, Pai. "Zur Chronologie von Pachymeres, Andronikos L. II–III." *BZ*, 51 (1950), 82–86.

Ševčenko, Ihor. "Alexios Makrembolites and his 'Dialogue Between the Rich and the Poor.' " *Zbornik Radova Vizantološkog Instituta*, 6 (1960), 187–228.

——. "The Decline of Byzantium as Seen Through the Eyes of its Intellectuals." *DOP*, 15 (1961), 167–86.

——. *Études sur la polémique entre Théodore Métochite et Nicéphore Choumnos.* Brussels: Byzantion, 1962.

——. "Léon Bardales et les juges généraux, ou la corruption des incorruptibles." *B*, 19 (1949), 247–49.

——. "Nicolas Cabasilas' 'Anti-Zealot' Discourse: A Reinterpretation." *DOP*, 11 (1957), 79–171.

——. "Society and Intellectual Life in the Fourteenth Century." In *Actes du XIVe Congrès International d'Études byzantines.* Bucharest: Académie de la Republique socialiste Roumaine, 1971. Pp. 7–30.

Sharf, Andrew. *Byzantine Jewry from Justinian to the Fourth Crusade.* London: Routledge & Kegan Paul, 1971.

Smith, Mahlon H. *And Taking Bread. . . .* Paris: Beauchesne, 1978.

Stein, Ernest. "Introduction à l'histoire et aux institutions byzantines." *Traditio*, 7 (1949–1951), 95–168.

Stiernon, D. "Le Quartier du Xérolophos à Constantinople et les reliques vénitiennes du Saint Athanase." *REB*, 19 (1961), 165–88.

Svoronos, N. G. "Le Serment de fidélité à l'empereur byzantin et sa signification constitutionnelle." *REB*, 11 (1951), 106–42.

Sykoutres, John. "Περὶ το σχίσμα τῶν 'Αρσενιατῶ." *Hellenika*, 2 (1929), 267–322; 3 (1930), 15–44.

Tafrali, O. *Thessalonique au quatorzième siècle.* Paris: Geuthner, 1913.

Talbot, Alice-Mary. *Faith Healing in Late Byzantium.* Brookline, Mass.: Hellenic College Press, 1983.

——. "The Patriarch Athanasius and the Church." *DOP*, 27 (1973), 7–33.

Tatakis, Basil. *La Philosophie byzantine.* Paris: Presses Universitaires de France, 1959.

Teall, John. "The Grain Supply of the Byzantine Empire (330–1025)." *DOP*, 13 (1959), 87–139.

Tellenbach, G. *Church, State, and Christian Society.* Trans. R. F. Bennett. Oxford: Blackwell, 1966.

Thomas, John Philip. "A Byzantine Ecclesiastical Reform Movement." *Medievalia et Humanistica*, 12 (1984), 1–16.

——. *Private Religious Foundations in the Byzantine Empire.* Washington, D.C.: Dumbarton Oaks Press, 1987.

Thompson, E. M. *Handbook of Greek and Latin Palaeography.* New York: Appleton, 1893.

Treadgold, Warren. "The Revival of Byzantine Learning and the Revival of the Byzantine State." *The American Historical Review*, 84 (December 1979), 1245–66.

Treu, Maximos. *Matthaios, Metropolit von Ephesus: Über sein Leben und seine Schriften.* Potsdam: Hakkert, 1901.

Triantaphyllopoulos, K. "Die *Novelle* des Patriarchen Athanasios über die τριμοιοία." *Byzantinisch-neugriechische Jahrbücher*, 8 (1931).

Troeltsch, Ernst. *The Social Teaching of the Christian Churches* I. Trans. O. Wyon. London: Stewart, 1931.

Underwood, Paul A. *The Kariye Djami* I. New York: Pantheon, 1966.

Vasiliev, A. A. *History of the Byzantine Empire* II. Madison: University of Wisconsin Press, 1958.

Verpeaux, Jean. "Contribution à l'étude de l'administration byzantine." *Byzantinoslavica*, 16 (1956), 276–91.

——. *Nicéphore Choumnos.* Paris: Picard, 1959.

Vryonis, Speros. *The Decline of Hellenism in Asia Minor and the Process of Islamization from the Eleventh through the Fifteenth Century.* Berkeley: University of California Press, 1971.

Webster, Alexander. "Antinomial Typologies for an Orthodox Christian Social Ethic for the World, State, and Nation." *Greek Orthodox Theological Review*, 28 (Fall, 1983), 221–54.

Zachariae von Lingenthal, Karl. *Geschichte des griechisch-römanischen Rechts* IV. Berlin: Weidmann, 1892.

Zakythinos, D. A. *Crise monétaire et crise économique à Byzance du XIIIe au XVe siècles.* Athens: L'Hellénisme contemporain, 1948.

Zhishman, J. *Das Eherecht der orientalischen Kirche.* Vienna: Braumuller, 1864.

# INDEX

CPSIA information can be obtained at www.ICGtesting.com
Printed in the USA
BVOW070917160812

297932BV00002B/1/A